FOOD TECHNOLOGY AND RESEARCH ADVANCEMENT

ENV BOOKS SERIES

FOOD TECHNOLOGY AND RESEARCH ADVANCEMENT

Editors

Dr. Avnish Chauhan
Associate Professor
Phonics Group of Institutions
Roorkee (Uttarakhand)
(India)

&

Dr. Pawan Kumar 'Bharti'
Society for Environment, Health Awareness of
Nutrition & Toxicology (SEHAT)
B-225/5D, Top Floor, Subhash Gali
Road No. 7, Block B, Ashok Nagar
Shahdara, Delhi -110 093
(India)

Associate Editor

Dr. Alka Chauhan
Society for Environment, Health Awareness of
Nutrition & Toxicology (SEHAT)
B-225/5D, Top Floor, Subhash Gali
Road No. 7, Block B, Ashok Nagar
Shahdara, Delhi -110 093
(India)

DPH

DISCOVERY PUBLISHING HOUSE PVT. LTD.
INDIA

Published by:
Namit Wasan
DISCOVERY PUBLISHING HOUSE PVT. LTD.
4383/4B, Ansari Road, Darya Ganj
New Delhi-110 002 (India)
Phone : +91-11-23279245, 43596064-65
Fax : +91-11-23253475
E-mail : discoverypublishinghouse@gmail.com
namitwasan9@gmail.com
sales@discoverypublishinggroup.com
web : www.discoverypublishinggroup.com

First Edition: **2018**

ISBN: 978-93-86841-49-0

Food Technology and Research Advancement

Printed at:
Infinity Imaging Systems
Delhi

ENV Books Series, India

Calls descriptive and error free chapters for upcoming volumes of books on various environmental issues. Send your manuscripts to envbooks@gmail.com

Founding Editor (Editor-in-Chief)

Dr. Pawan Kumar 'Bharti'
Society for Environment, Health, Awareness of Nutrition & Toxicology (SEHAT-India)
1775, Sohanganj, Near Clock Tower, Delhi-7, (India)
E-mail:*gurupawanbharti@rediffmail.com*

Other Important Titles by Editor-in-Chief:

1. **Advances in Biotechnology and Ecological Sciences**
   Bharti, P.K., Chauhan, A. and Ray, J. (eds.)
   (ISBN: 978-93-5056-358-8).
2. **Advances in Agriculture and Ecology**
   Bharti, P.K.; Chauhan, A. and Ezeaku Peter Ikemefuna (eds.)
   (ISBN: 978-93-5056-362-5).
3. **Agriculture and Environmental Biotechnology**
   Bharti, P.K. and Chauhan, A. (eds.)
   (ISBN: 978-93-5056-479-0).
4. **Agriculture Crops and Food Security**
   Bharti, P.K., and Chauhan, A. (eds.)
   (ISBN: 978-93-5056-881-1)
5. **Agriculture Development and Sustainable Environment**
   Ray, J. and Bharti, P.K. (eds.)
   (ISBN: 978-93-5056-759-3).
6. **Agriculture Ecology and Environment**
   Bharti, P.K. and Olubukola O. Babalola (eds.)
   (ISBN: 978-93-5056-480-6).
7. **Agriculture Ecology, Sustainable Development and Agribusiness Management**
   Mehta Piyush; Sharma Pankaj; and 'Bharti' P.K. (eds.)
   (ISBN: 978-93-5056-851-4).
8. **Agriculture, Environment and Nano-science**
   Bharti, Pawan K. (ed.)
   (ISBN: 978-93-5056-760-5).

9. **Agricultural Practices and Crop Disease Control**
Chauhan Alka and Sharma Anubhuti (eds.)
(ISBN: 978-93-5056-859-0).

10. **Agro-biodiversity: *Conservation and Sustainable Development***
Sharma, Pankaj; Singh, Narayan; and Bharti, P.K. (eds.)
(ISBN: 978-93-505-782-1).

11. **Agro-forestry and Climate Change**
Bharti, Pawan K. and Singh, Narayan (eds.)
(ISBN: 978-93-5056-514-8).

12. **Agro-forestry and Sustainable Agriculture**
Sharma, Pankaj; Bharti, P.K. (eds.)
(ISBN: 978-93-5056-786-9).

13. **Air Pollution and Ecosystem Health**
Swami Abhishek and Bharti, P.K. (eds.)
(ISBN: 978-93-5056-877-4).

14. **Aquaculture and Fisheries Environment**
Gupta, S.K. and Pawan K. Bharti (eds.)
(ISBN: 978-93-5056-408-0).

15. **Aquatic Biodiversity and Pollution**
Bharti, P.K.; Chauhan, A. and Kaoud, H.A.H. (eds.)
(ISBN: 978-93-5056-359-5).

16. **Aquatic Ecology and Biotechnology**
Bharti, P.K. and Zaki, M.S.A. (eds.)
(ISBN: 978-93-5056-451-6).

17. **Aquatic Environment and Toxicology**
Bharti, Pawan K. (ed.)
(ISBN: 978-93-5056-236-9).

18. **Biodiversity, Biotechnology and Environmental Conservation**
Bharti, P.K. and Bhandari, G. (eds.)
(ISBN: 978-93-5056-750-0).

19. **Biodiversity, Biotechnology & Pollution Control**
Bharti, P.K., and Chauhan, A. (eds.)
(ISBN: 978-93-5056-887-3)

20. **Biodiversity of Aquatic Ecosystem: *Significance, Threat and Conservation***
Bharti, P.K. and Kaoud, H.A.H. (eds.)
(ISBN: 978-93-5056-297-0).

21. **Biological Diversity and Ecology**
Arya, M.K.; Bharti, P.K. and Ritesh Joshi (eds.)
(ISBN: 978-93-5056-785-2).

22. **Bioremediation and Microbial Biotechnology**
Gupta, Sandeep; and Bharti, P.K. (eds.)
(ISBN: 978-93-5056-783-8).

23. **Biotechnological Approaches and Water Ecosystem**
Zaki, M.S.A.; and Bharti, P.K. (eds.)
(ISBN: 978-93-5056-779-1).

24. **Biotechnology, Agro-ecology and Environment**
Chauhan, Avnish and Bharti, P.K. (eds.)
(ISBN: 978-93-5056-757-9).

25. **Biotechnology and Environmental Management**
Arya Arun; Maheswari Raaz K., & Bharti, P.K (eds.)
(ISBN: 978-93-5056-862-0).

26. **Clean Technologies and Environmental Protection**
Chauhan, A.; Sharma, S. and Bharti, P.K. (eds.)
(ISBN: 978-93-5056-731-9).

27. **Climate Change and Agriculture**
Bharti, P.K. and Chauhan, Avnish (eds.)
(ISBN: 978-93-5056-148-5).

28. **Climate Change and Biodiversity**
Bharti, P.K. and Chauhan, Avnish (eds.)
(ISBN: 978-93-5056-360-1).

29. **Climate Change, Disaster Management and Environment**
Chauhan, Alka; Bharti, P.K. (eds.)
(ISBN: 978-93-5056-784-5).

30. **Conservation and Cultivation of Medicinal Plants**
Bharti, P.K. and Singh Narayan (eds.)
(ISBN: 978-93-5056-740-1).

31. **Crop Irrigation and Farming System**
Chauhan, Alka and P.K. Bharti (eds.)
(ISBN: 978-93-86841-40-7).

32. **Crop Productivity and Plant Disease Management**
Chauhan, Alka; Bharti, P.K. and Sadana, Deepti (eds.)
(ISBN: 978-93-5056-791-3).

33. **Eco-toxicology and Eco-technology**
Bharti, P.K. and Zaki, M. (eds.)
(ISBN: 978-93-5056-313-7).

34. **Energy Technologies for Clean Environment**
Bharti, Chhavi Kumar and Bharti, P.K. (Eds.)
(ISBN: 978-93-86841-22-3).

35. **Environmental Biotechnology and Application**
Bharti, P.K. and Chauhan, Avnish (eds.)
(ISBN: 978-93-5056-262-8).

36. **Environmental Conservation and Biotechnology**
Chauhan, A. and P.K. Bharti (eds.)
(ISBN: 978-93-5056-512-4).

37. **Environmental Economics and Sustainability**
José G. Vargas-Hernández; Khalid Alam Monowar and Bharti, P.K. (eds.)
(ISBN: 978-93-86841-37-7).

38. **Environmental Health and Problems**
Bharti, P.K. and Gajananda, Kh. (eds.)
(ISBN: 978-93-5056-263-5).

39. **Environmental Pollution and Biodiversity**
Bharti, P.K.; Chauhan, Avnish and Kumar, P. (eds.)
(ISBN: 978-93-5056-149-2).

40. **E-waste and Environmental Issues**
Bhalla, R., and Bharti, P.K. (eds.)
(ISBN: 978-93-5056-886-6)

41. **Experiments on Enhancement of Agricultural Yield**
Chauhan, Alka and P.K. Bharti (eds.)
(ISBN: 978-93-86841-50-6).

42. **Farming Techniques and Crop Production**
Chauhan Alka; Sharma Anubhuti; Ray Jaswant and 'Bharti' P.K. (eds.)
(ISBN: 978-93-5056-855-2).

43. **Faunal Biodiversity and Biotechnology**
Sethi, V. Kumar; Bharti, P.K. (eds.)
(ISBN: 978-93-86841-44-5).

44. **Fisheries and Toxicology**
Zaki, M.S.A.; Bharti, P.K. and Chauhan, A. (eds.)
(ISBN: 978-93-5056-452-3).

45. **Fish Habitat and Aquaculture**
Bharti, P.K.; Gupta Kr. Sanjay (eds.)
(ISBN: 978-93-5056-744-9).

46. **Forest and Biodiversity Conservation**
Chauhan Alka; Bharti, P.K. (eds.)
(ISBN: 978-93-5056-873-6).

47. **Food Processing, Management and Nanotechnology**
Chauhan, Avnish; Bharti, P.K. (eds.)
(ISBN: 978-93-5056-796-8).

48. **Freshwater Ecosystem and Xenobiotics**
Bharti, P.K.; Zaki, M. and Chauhan, A. (eds.)
(ISBN: 978-93-5056-299-4).

49. **Geospatial Technology and Ecosystem Assessment**
'Bharti' Chhavi Kumar; Chauhan, Alka & Bharti, P.K. (eds.)
(ISBN: 978-93-86841-36-0).

50. **Geospatial Technology and Water Management**
Chauhan, Alka; Bharti, P.K. (eds.)
(ISBN: 978-93-5056-885-9).

51. **Heavy Metals and Metalloids in Biosphere:** ***Impacts & Assessment***
Chauhan, Avnish, Gupta, Sandeep; and Bharti, P.K. (eds.)
(ISBN: 978-93-5056-860-6).

52. **Land Reclamation, Soil Quality and Agriculture**
Bharti, P.K., and Chauhan, A. (ed.)
(ISBN: 978-93-5056-882-8).

53. **Limnology and Aquatic Science**
Sharma, S., and Bharti, P.K. (eds.)
(ISBN: 978-93-5056-735-7).

54. **Medicinal and Nutritional Values of Plants**
Chauhan, Alka; Bharti, P.K. (eds.)
(ISBN: 978-93-5056-883-5).

55. **Medicinal Plants:** ***Distribution, Utilization and Significance***
Sharma, P.; Bharti, P.K. and Narayan Singh (eds.)
(ISBN: 978-93-5056-734-0).

56. **Microbial Applications and Environment**
Bharti, Pawan K. (ed.)
(ISBN: 978-93-5056-515-5).

57. **Microbial Ecology and Habitat**
Bharti, Pawan K. (ed.)
(ISBN: 978-93-5056-514-8).

58. **Microbial Environment and Bioremediation**
Chauhan Alka; K. Rathoure Ashok; and K Maheshwari Raaz (eds.)
(ISBN: 978-93-5056-856-9).

59. **Microbiological and Pharmacological Aspects of Biodiversity**
Sharma, P., Sharma, N.G.; Sharma, P., and Bharti, P.K. (ed.)
(ISBN: 978-93-5056-878-1).

60. **Natural Ecosystem and Climate Change**
Bharti, P.K., and Kh. Gajananda (ed.)
(ISBN: 978-93-5056-745-6).

61. **Organic Farming and Bio-fertilizers**
Sethi, Vinaya Kumar; and Bharti, P.K. (eds.)
(ISBN: 978-93-86841-23-0).

62. **Pest Management and Agro-Techniques**
Biswas, Asim; Bharti, P.K., Chauhan, Avnish (eds.)
(ISBN: 978-93-5056-794-4).

63. **Plant Biotechnology and Industrial Applications**
Chauhan, A., and Bharti, P.K. (ed.)
(ISBN: 978-93-5056-884-2).

64. **Plant Disease Management:** ***Control & Elimination Strategies***
Chauhan, A., and Bharti, P.K. (ed.)
(ISBN: 978-93-86841-41-4).

65. **Prakriti me Aushadhi (*in Hindi*)**
Singh, J.R.; Bharti, P.K. and Bharti, B.
(ISBN: 978-93-5056-200-0).

66. **Production of Fruits and Vegetables:** *Technologies and Challenges*
Chauhan, Avnish; Bharti, P.K. and Chauhan, Alka (ed.)
(ISBN: 978-93-86841-25-4).

67. **Seed Technology, Plant Growth and Cropping System**
Tyagi, P.K. and Bharti, P.K. (eds.)
(ISBN: 978-93-5056-738-8).

68. **Seed Treatment, Plant Health and Agro-technology**
Chauhan, A. and Bharti, P.K. (eds.)
(ISBN: 978-93-5056-810-1).

69. **Soil Characteristics and Agro-ecology**
Avnish Chauhan and Bharti, P.K. (eds.)
(ISBN: 978-93-5056-758-6).

70. **Soil Contamination and Conservation**
Ezeaku, P.I. and Bharti, P.K. (eds.)
(ISBN: 978-93-5056-737-1).

71. **Soil Quality and Contamination**
Bharti, P.K. and Chauhan, Avnish (eds.)
(ISBN: 978-93-5056-361-8).

72. **Sustainable Aquaculture Management**
Gupta, S.K.; Bharti, P.K (eds.)
(ISBN: 978-93-5056-797-5).

73. **Waste Disposal and Management**
Bharti, P.K.; Tabassum, B. and Bajaj, P. (eds.)
(ISBN: 978-93-5056-729-6).

74. **Waste Generation and Utilization**
Bajaj Priya; Tabassum, B., and Bharti, P.K. (eds.)
(ISBN: 978-93-5056-792-0).

75. **Waste Management and Environmental Health**
Tabassum, B., Bajaj Priya, and Bharti, P.K. (eds.)
(ISBN: 978-93-5056-777-7).

76. **Water Resources:** *Mapping Monitoring and Management*
Tyagi, P.K., Chauhan, Avnish and Bharti, P.K. (eds.)
(ISBN: 978-93-5056-861-3).

77. **Water Resources and Agriculture**
Bharti, P.K. and Ezeaku Peter Ikemefuna (eds.)
(ISBN: 978-93-5056-481-3).

78. **Waste Resources Management:** *Monitoring and Assessment*
Gupta, Sandeep and Bharti, P.K. (eds.)
(ISBN: 978-93-5056-799-9).

Preface

Food is simply the stuff that need to make us alive. Food is the plant, animals, vegetable, milk, glucose and many things what we eat. Technology is the process of working with latest engineering methods and technique.

"Food technology is the science that compact with all technique and activities involved in preserving, processing and manufacturing the food stuff". Food technology is not only the branch of engineering but also the branch of food science, hotel management and home science.

A food technologist work for the new method development for the food manufacturing and preserving for keeping the food safe and hygienic and enhance the color, flavor and resistance from the natural harms like microorganism and toxins.

The food processing organizations are involved in the processing, preservation, packaging, labeling development, quality management and research and development of the dairy products, food grains, confectionery products, fish products, meat & poultry products and fruit & vegetable products.

Science like chemistry, biology, engineering, nutrition and microbiology is used by the food technology to make the food safer and make available throughout the year in case of seasonal food

In the past, the food technology was accepted and discovered for just preserving and adding the flavor and color into the food stuff, but later on, by the development of science and engineering this technology has been used for the drying, de-caffeination, self-cooking food and for various research areas in the food science.

As deep as we are going into the dimensions of food technology, we require the experts and professionals in this field. The subject comprises of both science and engineering. Many academies and colleges in India have started to offer variety of courses in the field of food technology too.

The present book updates the subject content of food technology, food quality, quality evaluation, food contamination and quality enhancement technology.

Thanks are due to publisher and contributors from various institutions and universities.

The book will be helpful for the researchers, academia working in the field of food technology, food quality, quality evaluation, food contamination and quality enhancement technology, food technology, food quality, quality evaluation, food contamination and quality enhancement technology.

–Editors

(envbooks@gmail.com)

Contents

Preface

1. **Introduction** 1-5
2. **Future Trend and Opportunities for Functional and Genetic Food in Indian Market** 6-19
   Priti Gupta; Anurag Vashney; Anubhuti Sharma
3. **Food Allergy:** ***A Serious Disorder*** 20-36
   Priyanka Shukla
4. **Insects:** ***The New Alternative Food and Medicine for 21st Century*** 37-49
   V.K. Mishra and Satyapriya Singh
5. **An Unique Approach to Commercial Fish Farming in West Bengal, Pond Farming of** ***Chitala chitala*** **and Variation in Morphology of Alimentary Tracts of Few Small Indigenous Fishes** 50-71
   Subrato Ghosh
6. **Quinoa -** ***The Super Food*** 72-88
   Priyanka Shukla
7. **Mitigation Strategies for Fodder Scarcity** 89-109
   S.S. Kadam; Mohd. Arif; R.R. Dhutmal and Ashok Kumar
8. **Developmental Biology of** ***Pseudodiaptomus serricaudatus*** **(crustacea: copepoda) Reared at Different Temperatures and Algal Diets in the Laboratory** 110-123
   G. Padmavati
9. **Microgreens:** ***A Noval Approach of Food and Nutritional Security*** 124-156
   M. Siva; G. Ranganna; M.M. Nagaraju; T. Thomson; G. Koteswararao; T. Kranthikumar and M. Surendrababu

10. **Case Studies on Achievement of Makhana Farmers and Two Fishermen Cooperative Societies on Prawn and Fish Production** 157-180
Subrato Ghosh and Himadri Chandra

11. **Incidence of Zoonotic Parasites in Egyptian Raw Vegetable Salads** 181-189
Sylvia O. Ahmad; El Fadaly H.A; Mona S.Zaki and Barakat A.M.A.

Index 191-195

Pages: 1-5
Food Technology and Research Advancement
Edited by: **Dr. Avnish Chauhan and Dr. Pawan Kumar 'Bharti'**
ISBN: 978-93-86841-49-0
Edition: **2018**
Published by: **Discovery Publishing House Pvt. Ltd., New Delhi (India)**

1 Introduction

Food technology is a branch of food science that deals with the production processes that make foods.

Early scientific research into food technology concentrated on food preservation. Nicolas Appert's development in 1810 of the canning process was a decisive event. The process wasn't called canning then and Appert did not really know the principle on which his process worked, but canning has had a major impact on food preservation techniques.

Louis Pasteur's research on the spoilage of wine and his description of how to avoid spoilage in 1864 was an early attempt to apply scientific knowledge to food handling. Besides research into wine spoilage, Pasteur researched the production of alcohol, vinegar, wines and beer, and the souring of milk. He developed pasteurization—the process of heating milk and milk products to destroy food spoilage and disease-producing organisms. In his research into food technology, Pasteur became the pioneer into bacteriology and of modern preventive medicine.

Food Technology is a science which deals with the techniques and principles involved in processing and preserving the food substances. The application of food science helps in manufacturing safe, wholesome and nutritious food products. The study of food technology is to develop new methods and systems for keeping food products safe and resistant from natural harms such as bacteria and other micro-organisms. Food processing helps in preservation enhances the flavor and reduces the toxins in the food product which results in better distributional efficiency and easy marketing of the food product.

The modern food processing techniques is the key to flourishing supermarkets we have today. Extra nutrients can be added while processing the food and processed food is less susceptible to spoilage. Some of the techniques used are spray drying, juice concentrates, freeze drying and the introduction of artificial sweeteners, colorants, and preservatives. Of late, many products such as dried instant soups, reconstituted fruits and juices, and self cooking meals were developed for the convenience of working people.

The food processing industries are involved in processes such as primary and secondary processing, preservation, quality management, packaging and labeling of a variety of products such as dairy products, fish products, fruit & vegetable products, meat & poultry products, confectionery products and food grains.

Few specializations in this field are:

- Dairy
- Sugar
- Alcohol
- Bakery and confectionery items
- Oil and oil seed processing
- Fruits and vegetables
- Meat- Fish
- Cereals

Food Technology involves a blend of physical, chemical or microbiological processes and techniques for transforming raw ingredients into food and also other forms in food processing industry. Food processing refers to converting the raw ingredients into edible components or transforming food into other edible forms. Food Technology deals with the various chemical processes that food products undergo to make them consumable and ready to market. Food processors typically take clean, harvested crops or butchered animal products and use them to produce attractive, marketable food products with long shelf-life. Similar processes apply to animal feed.

Scope of Food Technology

- As organic chemists, food technologist advises on the methods by which the raw materials have to be converted into processed food.
- As biochemists, they suggest improvements in flavor, texture, storage, and quality.
- As home economists, they become the expert in dietetics and nutrition and they test the food and recipes according to the directions on the containers.
- As engineers, they are required for planning, designing, improving and maintaining the processing systems.
- As research scientists, they carry out experiments regarding improvement in yield, flavor, nutritive value and general acceptability of the packaged food.

- As managers and accountants, they manage administration and the finances apart from supervising the processing work.

Research and Development

Developments in food technology have contributed greatly to the food supply and have changed our world. Some of these developments are:

Instantized Milk Powder

D.D. Peebles (U.S. patent 2,835,586) developed the first instant milk powder, which has become the basis for a variety of new products that are rehydratable. This process increases the surface area of the powdered product by partially rehydrating spray-dried milk powder.

Freeze-drying:

The first application of freeze drying was most likely in the pharmaceutical industry; however, a successful large-scale industrial application of the process was the development of continuous freeze drying of coffee.

High-Temperature Short Time Processing:

These processes for the most part are characterized by rapid heating and cooling, holding for a short time at a relatively high temperature and filling aseptically into sterile containers.

Decaffeination of Coffee and Tea:

Decaffeinated coffee and tea was first developed on a commercial basis in Europe around 1900. The process is described in U.S. patent 897,763. Green coffee beans are treated with water, heat and solvents to remove the caffeine from the beans.

Process optimization:

Food Technology now allows production of foods to be more efficient, Oil saving technologies are now available on different forms. Production methods and methodology have also become increasingly sophisticated.

Agriculture has made a tremendous contribution to the quality of life. It is not just an industry, it is the foundation of our civilization. Agriculture provides the basic essentials for living: the food we eat, the beverages we drink, the clothing we wear, and the materials for our homes. Without agriculture, we would have none of these.

Agriculture also provides us with many of our traditions and values. We celebrate agriculture by attending food festivals, visiting farms and wineries, planting gardens, and watching our favorite cooking shows on television. In the United States, consumers are fortunate to have a food supply that is affordable, safe, plentiful, flavorful, nutritious, and convenient. Thanks to agriculture, we can enjoy a bounty of food.

Agriculture plays a valuable role in our everyday lives by not only providing us with food, but also by maintaining a strong economy. On a worldwide basis, more people are in some way involved in agriculture than in all other occupations combined. Agriculture is largest industry—not computers or cars or entertainment—employing more than 500 million people in agriculture-related jobs.

In the past century, there have been tremendous changes in agriculture. Farmers have become extremely efficient and have taken advantage of newer technologies. As a result, they are producing a wider variety of crops and producing them more efficiently.

Developments in science and technology have contributed to better soil, nutrient, water, and pest management, and to more efficient methods of planting, harvesting, storing, processing, and transporting farm products. These developments have resulted in more and better quality food than ever before.

To keep agriculture on the cutting edge, many farmers now implement a variety of technologies, including precision agriculture, remote sensing, computers, the internet, specialized software, global positioning, drip irrigation, and biotechnology. The Global Positioning System (GPS) is a key technology utilized in precision agriculture. Linking to a system of satellites, a farmer uses a receiver to pinpoint his or her position to within inches. The information helps the farmer identify precisely where to plant, and when and where to apply pesticides and fertilizer.

Agricultural advancements also appear in much smaller forms, such as seeds. For farmers to optimize agricultural production, they must have competitively priced, high quality, high-yielding seed varieties with characteristics desired by consumers. Many of these varieties will result from advances in genetics and modern biotechnology.

Agricultural practices and advancements differ globally—since plants have their own differences and the location plays a role on their development as well. But through the exchange of knowledge from different agriculturally-involved individuals from all over the world, improvement of techniques can be experienced as well.

It has made an impact on how information is shared, and being able to use this information for the advancement of the agricultural sector gives a great positive impact that is beneficial for everyone. IT has become a bridge for people from all over the world.

Agriculture in India is the core sector for food security, nutritional security, and sustainable development & for poverty alleviation. It contributes approx. 18% of GDP.Milestones in agriculture development in India includes: Green revolution, Evergreen revolution, Blue revolution, White revolution, yellow revolution, Bio technology revolution and the most recent one is Information and communication technology revolution.

REFERENCES

https://www.sarvgyan.com/courses/engineering/food-technology

https://en.wikipedia.org/wiki/Food_technology

https://www.omicsonline.org/scholarly/food-technology-journals-articles-ppts-list.php

https://www.myklassroom.com/Engineering-branches/38/Food-Technology

https://www.careers360.com/food-technology-course

http://www.foodinsight.org/Background_on_Agricultural_Practices_and_Food_Technologies

http://www.thehansindia.com/posts/index/Young-Hans/2017-05-22/Transforming-agriculture-with-e-technology/301765

http://www.fao.org/docrep/W9474T/w9474t03.htm

Pages: 6-19

Food Technology and Research Advancement
Edited by: Dr. Avnish Chauhan and Dr. Pawan Kumar 'Bharti'
ISBN: 978-93-86841-49-0
Edition: 2018
Published by: Discovery Publishing House Pvt. Ltd., New Delhi (India)

2 Future Trend and Opportunities for Functional and Genetic Food in Indian Market

Priti Gupta; Anurag Vashney; Anubhuti Sharma[#]

ABSTRACT

Epidemiological and clinical studies have demonstrated the relationship between diet and health status. Now a days consumer is more concern about the healthy food which also cover-up of health deficiencies. It's very difficult to find a home which is healthy and free of illness Therefore, consumer aspect for packets of healthy supplements which is readily availablein the market. It has been started not onlyin U.S.A. & U.K.butin India also.Thus, this review gives an idea about the current status and challenges in field of future food in Indian market.

Key words: Nutraceutical/Functional Food, Genetically modified food, Food regulation.

Introduction

The global community faces a major challenge in providing enough food to feed a growing and more demanding world population. Climate change and life style makes this is an even greater challenge. Food borne illnesses are a burden on public health and contribute significantly to the cost of health care. Foodborne illness is caused by consuming contaminated foods or beverages. Therefore, Food safety has become one of the prime concern world -wide. People can be exposed to hazardous chemicals and microorganisms through the unsafe food. Both poor and rich countries are becoming more vulnerable when it comes to food security, says Birgit Kopainsky, a System Dynamics researcher at the University of Bergen's (UiB) Department of Geography[1]. Last few years were chaotic year for the food industry. Maggi, one of the country's most loved brands, was

Department of Food Science, FDDI, Sector - 24, NOIDA - 304 022 (India)
National Research Centre on Rapeseed-Mustard (NRCRM), Bharatpur (Rajasthan) (India)

banned by the Food Safety and Standards Authority of India. Food processing section highlights improvement in product quality and production safety. In collaboration with the Partnership for Food Safety Education, FDA's Center for Food Safety and Applied Nutrition released 'The Consumer Food Safety Educator Evaluation Toolbox and Guide.' The toolbox and guide were created to serve as a planning and evaluation tool to help consumer for food safety. To ensure that consumer food safety education programs are effective in achieving their goals and preventing foodborne illness, it is important that these programs incorporate a rigorous and thorough program evaluation, FDA said [2].

The food sector has emerged as a high-growth and high-profit sector due to its immense potential for value addition, particularly within the food processing industry. The Government of India has been instrumental in the growth and development of the food processing industry. The government of India through the Ministry of Food Processing Industries (MoFPI) is making all efforts to encourage investments in the food business and approved proposals for joint ventures (JV), foreign collaborations, export oriented unit etc.

Can we predict the future food production?

We can't predict the future at the best of times. Right now, with instability in the economy, geopolitics and the biosphere all looming large, this uncertainty seems particularly threatening Yet the need to plan for a sustainable, ethical food system has never been greater. Improving food security, tackling hunger, obesity and injustice, supporting animal welfare, and preserving the environment, all demand urgent action in pursuit of long-term aims. How can people striving for a better food system – civil society groups, public policymakers and businesses – begin to plan campaigns, policies or products for the future if it looks so uncertain? And how can we avoid the opposite trap, of assuming that the future will be like today, only more so? This is where scenarios can help our thinking. Businesses such as Shell, and the UK government through its Foresight programme, use scenarios to help them think creatively about future threats and opportunities and to avoid the danger of assuming that the future will be much like the present. We developed a set of four scenarios to help us think about how the UK's food system could develop over the next couple of decades. What might we be eating in 2022, and why? Where could it have come from? Where might we be eating it – and how might it get there? We want to share these scenarios because we found them useful and we believe others may too. We also know how much effort and time it takes to develop scenarios such as these – not just our own but also that of the people from across the food sector who contributed to a series of three workshops. We, in turn, have taken part in other organisations scenario processes and appreciate the commitment it entails. We believe that a toolkit such as this can make many of the benefits of scenarios accessible to other organisations at a minimal cost to themselves and to their stakeholders. Our scenarios are not predictions or projections. Instead they represent four plausible stories about how the future could turn out, based on current trends and factors likely to drive change, as well as on significant uncertainties about how they are likely to play out. None of the scenarios is likely to 'come true', but elements in each may well do. We can use these scenarios to ask 'what if…?' questions, to help us 'future-proof ' our strategies: 'if the world turns out like this, will our policy still work or be a priority?' Scenarios can also help us think about desirability of certain futures: 'if that happened, would our food system be better or worse for people, animals and the environment? And what do we need to do to encourage or avoid it from happening?'. These scenarios formed part of the evidence for our project on food distribution. The project report, 'Food distribution: an ethical agenda', examines the impact of food distribution networks on our environment, economy, culture and communities, and their contribution to climate change. It offers a sustainable vision for the future of food distribution, and provides a roadmap for government, business and civil society to get us there. It is available on our website at www.foodethicscouncil.org. The workshops which we used to develop these scenarios took place before the full impact of the current financial crisis was evident. The current recession may well throw up new trends that were unclear at the time, render others less significant or change the pace at which some of these trends unfold. Nonetheless, we believe that the scenarios described here still provide an extremely useful and thought-provoking tool for considering the future of our food system. Let food be the medicine and medicine be the food to predict the relationship between appropriate foods for health and there therapeutic benefits. New researches, technologies and life style enforced to the consumers to change their food habits. Now market is rich in food products and packet. The future food is now available in shape of packet food and acceptable easily everywhere. More numbers of articles will be available in ready to eat packets.

Creating scenarios is not an exact science – and the results are not supposed to be forecasts or projections, but plausible possibilities. Scenario-building relies on using a clear process to channel knowledge and expertise from a diverse range of sources. We created our scenarios through extensive desk research and interviews, and a series of three creative, facilitated workshops, with experts drawn from industry, government agencies and civil society. From desk research and interviews with experts we built a longlist of possible trends and drivers of change that might shape the future to 2022. In some cases these were already strong whereas, in others, only 'weak signals' of emerging trends were detectable. By grouping together similar trends and drivers we arrived at a shortlist, which we took to our first workshop. At this event, through deliberation and debate, participants further grouped trends and drivers into 'clusters' of trends that might combine to drive change in a particular direction. The clusters were then ranked in terms of their importance (how significantly they are likely to effect change into the future) and uncertainty (how sure we can be about the direction of travel that particular drivers will take). Through a process of consensus-building, two drivers of change, agreed to be both highly important and highly uncertain, were selected to act as the framework for our scenarios. By placing these drivers (the shift of global political, cultural and economic influence from West to East; the role of food in UK society) along perpendicular axes, we created four 'spaces' in which our scenarios could play out:

Future Food

Many types of dietis availablefor a particular purpose of in terms of health benefits. Specialized food for patients, food for kids, and food for households ladies. Food iscategories as per several target customers. Full food chain will be change and from the starting - crops stage food to final food packed. It has been identified & marked target customer on the crops period. Food revolution is accepted in 2020 to 2050.Some of future food we discussed here are.

Nutraceutical/Functional Food

Foreseeing the consequences, Nutraceutical started research for their remedies. Nutraceuticals has proven health benefits and their consumption will keep diseases at bay and allow humans to maintain an overall good health. The expanding neutraceuticals market indicates that end users are seeking minimally processed food with extra nutritional benefits and organoleptic value. This development, in turn is propelling expansion in the neutraceuticals markets globally. Functional food is an additional function related to health or prevention of disease[3,4]. It adds new ingredients or more of existing ingredients. Functional food makes it name for designed food which has physiological benefits and/or reduce many type of disease like chronic disease ahead to basic nutritional functions. It is being similar in appearance of conventional food which has more nutrients and healthy supplements. It will be consumed as diet food. Food processing industries will grow in this segment. Many industries will start processing conventional food into functional food by adding ingredients of nutrition, vitamin and energy supplements. Packet food trend will grow. These food processing industries will start processing many types of packet food as per their target customerand these packets always advertising their contents of health supplement and recommended by team of doctors. Food Market will stand and depend on food processing industries shoulder. This market makes nexus of packet food. Consumer will be attracted by healthy advertisement for dietary food and then they will be habitual of their ingredient and added flavors. Mostly consumer will not be able to recognized the actual taste of conventional food. Consumer health awareness continues to rise, the increasing availability of health information going hand in hand with the aging of populations and increased propensity for lifestyle diseases. The growing importance of the Senior (50+) demographic will influence functional food sales making it essential marketers cater for this audience's needs. Functional food consumption is growing fast The US market was worth US$21.3bn in 2006 whilst the European market reached US$8bn. The interest in functional foods and drinks has been fuelled by a desire for convenience, as well as health. Busier lifestyles are making it harder to meet nutritional requirements using traditional food and drinks. Consumers are wary about health related claims on food and drink products and skeptical of their efficacy. The breadth of functional claims and the lack of governance and independent validation have fuelled consumer concern. Success in the market is increasingly dependent on establishing a relationship of trust with the consumer.

Today's Multi-Minding Woman What is "multi-minding"? It is the perpetual state of mind for today's typical 25-54-year-old woman, who must constantly deal with the multiple dimensions of her life, whether she's sorting out a work project, helping with a child's school project or even relaxing in front of a TV show. At any one moment, she is thinking about choices related to career, household, spousal, motherhood and personal responsibilities. Consequently, these women have moved from "multi-tasking" to a new level of activity — "multi-minding." As a result, these women have little time for commercial messages. Ketchum has created the Women 25 to 54 offering to precisely address this challenge. Building on a history of capturing media attention for some of the world's foremost brands and branded products, Ketchum's marketing and communications specialists break through to multiminding 25-54-year-old women with a four-phase program that identifies, creates, disseminates and reinforces credible messaging for today's multi-minding women:

1. "What Really Matters" Credibility Index - The first phase concisely and accurately identifies the messages and messengers that will quickly and credibly resonate with multiminding women.
2. "Quick-Connect" Messaging - The second phase creates "bite-sized," repeatable messaging for women by employing Ketchum's Quick-Connect Message Map.
3. "E-Surround" Programming - The third phase determines the right mix of editors, experts, equals, and entertainment marketing outlets to target with communications containing messages that blend with women's lifestyles and surround women with credible information.

4. Consistent Confirmation - In the final phase, post-program activities reinforce purchasing decisions and drive word-of-mouth endorsements.

Furthermore, In India Obesity of children, Malnutrition population and nutritional deficiencies, heart disease occur on a large amount. Loosing food roots (Both in China and India rural traditional diets are considered to be natural and healthy, urbanization has brought problems to manage the daily diet. Citizens have lost their touch how to choose foods and how to compile their daily meal. This causes health problems: growing figures of diabetes, obesity and coronary heart diseases.) Rational and social marketing will still be of demand in 2030. After 25 years advertising will most probably be more appealing to emotions. Advertising/information does not reach millions of mostly illiterate Indians living in remote areas. However, the mobile network will soon cover the whole country. The number of users is increasing by 5 millions each month. In future mobile phones could be used for brand building, advertising and dissemination information. Indians are definitely not as brand-conscious as the Europeans. Price counts more. However, there are already signs of increased brand consciousness. In 2030 most food purchased will be branded and people will have their favorite brands they will get stuck to.

Dietary factors play an important role in premature chronic disease appearance, disease progression, morbidity, and mortality. Approximately 40-50% proportion in cardiovascular disorders, 35-50% proportion in cancers, and 20% proportion in osteoporosis is attributable to dietary factors[5,6]. Use of food as medicine for treatment and prevention of various disorders is not a recent development. Fortification of table salt with iodine and wheat flour with iron/folic acid has been used with specific aims of prevention of iodine deficiency goiter and anemia for long. Similarly, food fortified with vitamin A, which has found to be a feasible and cost effective approach to reduce vitamin A deficiency. A growing interest in relationship between diet and health has added impetus to the demand for information on nutraceuticals. This increased interest has been aided by advances in science and technology, increasing health care costs, changes in food laws affecting label, and product claims and aging population in various countries. Along with offering treatment, use of nutraceuticals favors a preventive treatment model as well.[7-10]

Genetically Modified Food

Genetically modified (GM) foods are foods derived from organisms whose genetic material (DNA) has been modified in a way that does not occur naturally, e.g. through the introduction of a gene from a different organism. Currently available GM foods stem mostly from plants, but in the future foods derived from GM microorganisms or GM animals are likely to be introduced on the market. Most existing genetically modified crops have been developed to improve yield, through the introduction of resistance to plant diseases or of increased tolerance of herbicides. In the future, genetic modification could be aimed at altering the nutrient content of food, reducing its allergenic potential, or improving the efficiency of food production systems. All GM foods should be assessed before being allowed on the market. FAO/WHO Codex guidelines exist for risk analysis of GM food[11-12]. Herbicide tolerance and insect resistance are the main GM traits that are currently under commercial cultivation, and the main crops are: soybean, maize, canola and cotton. GM crops are now commercially planted on about 100 million hectares in some 22 developed and developing countries. Argentina, Brazil, China and India are the largest developing-country producers of transgenic crops. The choice of GM crops varies among the developing countries, with insect resistant cottonbeing the most important commercially produced transgenic crop in Asian and African countries, while herbicide-resistant soybean followed by insect-resistant corn is predominant in the Latin American continent. GM crops are not universally accepted throughout the international market. Trading blocs such as the European Union (EU) have banned the import of crops with inserted genes, citing concerns about human health and the environment.

The World Health Organization (WHO) has generally given GM crops high marks."GM foods currently available on the international market have passed safety assessments and are not likely to present risks for human health," the WHO guidelines note. "In addition, no effects on human health have been shown as a result of the consumption of such foods by the general population in the countries where they have been approved," the guidelines say. According to WHO, there's no way to make a broad statement on the health effect of GM foods; each individual product needs to be tested for safety. Modi is well-known to have supported Bt cotton during his tenure as chief minister of the western Indian state of Gujarat. He also resumed field trials which were stuck in a limbo in India since 2010 due to an unofficial moratorium. The government currently is evaluating individual reports on certain crops (including the GM mustard seed), but there is no umbrella policy in place yet. However, in India, some environmentalists have called GM crops "toxic" and hazardous to health. Some have expressed concerns their consumption could "transfer antibiotic resistance, toxicity, and allergenicity.[13-15]" They argue that since genetic modification is a pretty recent technology, the effects of prolonged consumption of GM foods on human health aren't known. There may be a political hue to the debate in India: staunch Hindu nationalist organizations typically oppose the use of the technology, perceiving it as foreign. There is a need to make people aware of the ill effects, especially after pest attacks devastated GM cotton crops recently. Another issue is cost. "Farmers buy the Bt cotton seeds, and the costs of the pesticides which they buy from the same companies are probably tenfold of what they used to pay," Shivani Shah, a campaigner with Greenpeace, told the New York Times in 2012[16 17]. "So it's creating a system of dependency. It is a deliberate idea of increasing costs and increasing royalties—there is no intention of reducing those costs through economies of scale." (In response, the Indian government has capped the prices of these seeds.) So while there is high productivity, overall costs for farmers, too, have increased.

It's not certain that Bt cotton's pricing issues would necessarily apply to other GM crops. "A key thing to understand about GM crop technologies is that they really need to be assessed on a case-by-case basis," says Dominic Glover, a research fellow at the Institute of Development Studies at the University of Sussex in the UK. "It makes a difference if you are talking about a cash crop like cotton or a food crop such as *brinjal* [a kind of aubergine], or a trait such as insect resistance or one such as herbicide tolerance."

Food Regulation in India

Emerging people don't always know:

1. Awareness about food safety is increasing, but still rather low. Products containing e.g. pesticides, chemicals, heavy-metals and food contaminations are rather common.
2. Government has come up with new food safety-act and working towards increasing the quality standards. Food safety authority has recently been set up.
3. Huge investments are being made into the development of the supply chain.
4. Advertising of safety processed food is seen: packaged milk and its safety are being advertised. People still need to be educated about the food safety and the benefits processes can bring about.
5. People will increasingly look at symbols and standards telling about the quality and safety of the product.

Indian consumers tend to buy fresh. Fresh food is considered to be safe. Indian definition (as per Food Safety and Security Act passed in 2006, yet to implement). A traditional medicine is not a part of nutraceuticals. Foods for special dietary use are specifically processed or formulated to satisfy particular dietary requirements, which exist because of a physical or physiological condition or specific disease and disorder [10]. These are presented as such where in the compositions of these foodstuffs must differ significantly from the Indian Standard (IS) composition of ordinary foods of comparable nature. [11] A food stuff (as a fortified food or a dietary supplement) that provides health benefits, if indeed a claim was made that implied medicinal benefit regarding a nutraceutical product, the product would be required to comply with the regulatory requirements for medicinal products, in respect of safety, efficacy, and quality testing and marketing authorization procedures[12]. For decades, FDA regulated dietary supplements as foods to ensure that they were safe and that their labeling was truthful and not misleading. In 2006, the Indian government passed Food Safety and Standard Act to integrate and streamline the many regulations covering nutraceuticals, foods, and dietary supplements. The act calls for the creation of the Food Safety and Standards Authority (FSSA).

Food Safety and Standard Authority of India (FSSAI)

Food Safety and Security (FSS) Act was passed by the parliament in 2006. In 2008, FSSAI came into existence. It has prepared the draft rules and regulations for implementation of FSS Act 2006 which is going through process of prepublication consultation. The FSSA incorporates the salient provisions of the Prevention of Food Adulteration Act 1954, and is based on international legislations, instrumentalities, and the Codex Alimentarius Commission.[13] The aims to establish a single reference point for all matters relating to food safety and standards, by moving from multi level, multi departmental control to a single line of command. This unified Act, FSSA, will enable unidirectional compliance and address the need for a single regulatory body. In their endeavor to carry out the provisions of the FSSA, the FSSAI shall be assisted by a Central Advisory Committee (CAC), Scientific Panels (SPs), and a Scientific Committee (SC); each with specific responsibilities. On September 5, 2008, the GOI notified the establishment of the FSSAI consisting of a chairman and members, who in turn will initiate the rule making process. [14,16] The implementation of the Act is reportedly in progress, and the FSSAI has notified its intention to the implementation of FSSA in a phased manner started from January, 2010.[17-18]

Nutrition Labeling and Education Act (NLEA)

In 1990 (NLEA) defines how food is labeled, including nutrition labeling, in accordance with definitions established by FDA, and providing for the use of claims about the relationship between nutrients and diseases or health-related condition.

Benefits of Regulation

1. Allows greater legal security and more predicable environment.
2. Supports innovation (food and drink products).
3. Prevents unfair competition from manufactures using false or misleading claims.
4. If positive claims cannot be made, the regulation does not oblige anyone to make negative claims about the product.

The World in 2030, what might it be? One means to look ahead to the future is to think back to the past. Taking today's timeline of 2007, what changes have occurred in the past 23 years, back to the year 1984? Then we can look to the future, evaluating the depth and impact of the changes experiences from the period 1984 to 2007. In 1984, as example of the literature (Cambridge History of World Food) indicates the following: "Household food security has been defined as the access of all people at all times to sufficient food for an active and health life (World Bank 1986). Two of the biggest determinants of household food consumption are income and prices. Rising income and falling food prices increase a household's ability to obtain an adequate diet. However, an accumulating body of evidence shows that it is not simply the level of household income but who earns that income that is important in improving a household's food intake. Income controlled by women is more likely to be spent on food than is male-controlled income (Braun and Kennedy 1994). At similar levels of income, households with more women controlled income are more likely to be food secure. Evidence for the positive influence of female control of income on household food expenditure (Haddad and Hoddinott 1991), caloric intake (Garcia 1991), and anthropometric indicators (Thomas 1990) is increasing in both Africa and Asia. This influence may be explained by a number of factors: (1) societal gender roles that cast women in the role of gatekeepers; (2) different preferences – women may prefer to spend more on children's food because they spend more time with them. (3) different constraints. Whatever the reason, getting income into the hands of women seems to be one way of enhancing the household's food security." A number of different food trends have been playing themselves out over the past twenty years some of which are scientifically correlated and others coincidental. An interesting inverse relationship exists between the decrease in home food production over the past few decades and the astronomical rise in obesity. The exact nature of the relationship is more for scientists to ponder and unravel than kitchen gardeners, but it seems logical that the easier and cheaper food becomes, the more of it we tend to eat (Kitchen Gardeners International). In 1985 more people were concerned about salt than fat; and now that has flipped. To Bauer that's not the most significant conclusion. If you look at 1985 versus 2005 it indicates we're less concerned about everything: salt, additives, fat, cholesterol and sugar. Is that possible, considering how much more we know about them these days? The NPD Group Health Track did a questionnaire fielded each year to its National Eating Trends panel, which includes about 2000 respondents. The panel is balanced to the U.S. Census on key demographic variables (including household income, household size, age, education, employment). The chart really reflects is the huge increase in information that has been published in the last 20 years. In many cases, Americans have become saturated with too much conflicting information and people don't have a clear picture of what to avoid (Michael Bauer). In another example, there is currently great concern over fat intake, however, a study conducted from 1920 to 1984 indicates that: "Coronary heart disease mortality has declined in the United States since 1968. Because diet has been implicated, a search was conducted of published individual assessments of food intake since 1920. One hundred seventy-one studies, ranging from 8 to 20,000 subjects and covering all ages, all ethnic groups, and both sexes, were analyzed by regression, with valuesweighted by number of subjects in each study. Results show fat intakesrising from approximately 34% energy in the 1930s to 40-42% in the late 1950s to mid 1960s then falling steadily to approximately 36% energy in 1984. This trend was seen for all age and sex groups. Saturated andmonounsaturated fatty acid intakes fell from 18-20% energy in the early 1950s to 12-13% energy in 1984 whereas polyunsaturated fatty acid intakesrose from 2-4% energy to 7.5%. These results differ markedly from food supply trends and indicate a fall in US fat intake, which preceded the decline in heart disease mortality". (Trends in individual consumption of dietary fat in the United States, 1920-1984.Stephen and Wald.Division of Nutrition and Dietetics, College of Pharmacy, University of Saskatchewan Saskatoon, Canada.).

Future Challenges to Food Industry based on Trends in Life Science

Some prospective challenges to the future for the food industry are: (1) Advancing our understanding of challenges related to the aging population, including chronic diseases, Alzheimer's, cancer, heart disease and diabetes; (2) Innovations in early diagnosis (including imaging and non-imaging diagnostic equipment); predictive tests, maintaining wellness, and health-care delivery; (3) Genomics, proteomics, metabolomics, and other "omics" that have the potential to advance our ability to treat many medical challenges; (4) In the area of pharmaceuticals and biopharmaceuticals we can expect the development of more targeted drugs with higher efficacy, new drugs and vaccines (including technologies to expedite their development) to address infectious diseases, nano or molecular drug delivery structures, etc.; (5) To reduce costs of drug development, we will see "in silico" drug development (systems biology) as the basis for a new paradigm for drug discovery and development, new bioprocesses for the production and purification of biopharmaceuticals, and advances in novel drug production technologies using transgenic animals and plants; In the area of health services, we can expect advances in telehealth, remote surgery, devices and infrastructure that support the development of care services (e.g. home care).

1. We can expect greater use of ICT in terms of electronic health records, registries and databases, communications infrastructure, bioinformatics and high-performance computing, decision support software and interoperable measurement systems. Some characteristics that will begin to define the world in 2030 include.
2. Set in a social context: developed within the context of an understanding of the evolution of science and its interplay with society and humanity.
3. Reflexive: disciplined, open, tested by others and critically self-aware.
4. Varied in size and scope: includes many different scales, scopes, intentions, tools, techniques and locations from curiosity-driven to project-based science; from "big science" to smaller projects.
5. Focused on human development: focus on the potential to contribute to ongoing human development.
6. Integrated around big issues: cross-disciplinary approach to strategic issues.
7. Global: work with the best in the world and to serve the wider world.
8. Transparent: meeting demands for greater transparency and accountability.
9. Committed to knowledge-in-use: commitment to get information into routine use within our society and economy, and to do so as quickly as possible.
10. Foresighted: practice of strategic foresight is inherent.
11. Selectively focused: co-operate, learn from and build on the work of others, focused on what is of importance to Canadians. The next decade will see dramatic advances in biomonitoring, including early indicators for cancer, diabetes and other chronic diseases. In addition to advanced biomarkers, there will be new and simpler ways of testing (e.g. a "breathalyzer for cancer", wrist watch monitors, saliva tests, and "smart toilets"). The results from these will be integrated into the electronic health record accessible by individuals and their health care providers.

Conclusion

It is the wish of all people to live healthy. It is natural that people s focus is shifting from medical treatment for sickness to a positive approach for prevention of diseases to stay healthy. In order to prevent diseases and be healthy, new food products, which have been proven by the human trials to be effective to prevent diseases, should gradually penetrate into the society. This will improve QOL (quality of life) of all people. India is currently a nascent market for nutraceuticals and genetic food without a concrete business model in place. Both MNCs as well as domestic companies in the pharmaceutical and food and beverage space have tested the market with a variety of launches, with some success. This has resulted in increased product launches in the recent past. However, in terms of ingredients, especially in the case of plant extracts and phytochemicals, Indian companies have entrenched their place as suppliers, both locally as well as globally. Globalization of the nutraceutical/functional food and GM food industries present significant challenges to stakeholders, not the least of which is the regulatory variance between countries active in the marketplace. it is very important to comply with the regulatory framework, so that the business is run smoothly.

REFERENCES

1. http://www.qualityassurancemag.com/article/new-consumer-food-safety-educator-evaluation-tool-available/
2. http://timesofindia.indiatimes.com/business/india-business/Packaged-food-market-to-touch-50-billion-by-2017-Study/articleshow/50159133.cms
3. Bucher T, van der Horst K, Siegrist M (16 September 2011). "The Fake Food Buffet – A New method in Nutrition Behavior Research." British Journal of Nutrition. 107: 1-8.
4. Food and Agriculture Organization of the United Nations (FAO). Report on Functional Foods, Food Quality and Standards Service (AGNS), 2007.
5. "FOSHU, Ministry of Health, Labor and Welfare, Japan". Government of Japan.
6. Peterson and Qureshi. Genotype and Environment Effects on Tocols of Barley and Oats. Cereal Chemistry, 1993, 70: 157-162.
7. Peterson DM. Oat antioxidants. Journal of Cereal Science, 2001, 33: 115-129. 11.
8. Rakesh Sharma and Ram B. Singh, Department of Engineering and Technology, Tallahassee Community College, Tallahassee, Florida 32304, USA in Bioactive Foods and Nutraceutical Supplementation Criteria in Cardiovascular Protection. 2013; 154.
9. Kathleen Crandell and Stephen Duren, Kentucky Equine Research, Inc.,Versailles, KY In Nutraceuticals: What are they and do they Work, 2003,28.
10. Nelson NJ. Purple Carrots, Margarine Laced with Wood pulp, Nutraceuticals move into the Supermarket. Journal of National Cancer Institute. 1999; 91: 755-757.
11. Temple WJ and Gladwin KK. Fruits, Vegetables, and the Prevention of Cancer: Research Challenges. Nutrition. 2003; 19: 467-470.
12. Zeisel SH. Regulation of Nutraceuticals Science. 1999; 285: 185-186.
13. Regulation of Functional Food in Indian Subcontinent, Food and Beverages News. http://www.efenbeonline.com/view story.asp type=story and id=880
14. Pandey M, Verma RK, Saraf SA. Nutraceuticals: New Era of Medicine and Health. Asian Journal of Pharmaceutical and Clinical Research. 2010; 3: 11-5.
15. The Food Safety and Standard Authority of India New Delhi, India. Implementation of Food Safety and Standards Act in the States/UT to Start from January, 2010. http://www.fssai.gov.in/PressReleases/ViewPressReleases.aspx.
16. Madhavan M, Sanyal K. Legislative Brief: The Food Safety and Bill for Nutraceuticals, 2005. Parliamentary Research Service, Chanakyapuri, Authority of India New Delhi, 2006. http://www.prsindia.org/uploads/media/1167478283/legis1167478357 Legislative Brief Food Safety Standards Bill 2005.pdf.

17. B Chauhan, G Kumar, N Kalam, Current Concepts and Prospects of Herbal Nutraceutical: A Review, Journal of Advance Pharmaceutical Technology and Research. 2013 Jan-Mar; 4(1): 4-8.
18. TATA Strategic Management Group. The Health & Wellness Foods Industry in India. An Overview. 2009.

Pages: 20-36

Food Technology and Research Advancement
Edited by: Dr. Avnish Chauhan and Dr. Pawan Kumar 'Bharti'
ISBN: 978-93-86841-49-0
Edition: 2018
Published by: Discovery Publishing House Pvt. Ltd., New Delhi (India)

3

Food Allergy
A Serious Disorder

Priyanka Shukla

ABSTRACT

The first authentic report of food hypersensitivity, over 2300 years ago, is attributed to Hippocrates for his findings that there exist individual differences in reactions to milk ingestion. Food allergies are estimated to affect 4 to 6 percent of children and 4 percent of adults, according to the Centers for Disease Control and Prevention. Food allergy symptoms are most common in babies and children, but they can appear at any age. An allergic response is thought to be an aberrant, misguided, systemic immune response to an otherwise harmless antigen. Quantitatively, food proteins account for one of the largest antigenic challenges confronting the human immune system. Nonetheless, only a small number of foods instigate the majority of abnormal immune responses.

Key words: Food hypersensitivity, Food allergies, Allergic response, Abnormal immune response.

Introduction of Food Allergens

A food allergy occurs when the body's immune system detects a certain food as harmful and reacts by causing symptoms. This is an allergic reaction. Foods that cause allergic reactions are allergens. The signs and symptoms may range from mild to severe. They may include itchiness, swelling of the tongue, vomiting, diarrhoea, hives, trouble breathing, or low blood pressure. This typically occurs within minutes to several hours of exposure. When the symptoms are severe, it is known as anaphylaxis. Food intolerance and food poisoning are separate conditions.[7] Food intolerances affect nearly everyone at some point. People often have an unpleasant reaction to

National Institute of Food Technology, Entrepreneurship and Management, Kundli - 131 028 (Haryana) (India)

something they ate and wonder if they have a food allergy. One out of three people either say that they have a food allergy or that they modify the family diet because a family member is suspected of having a food allergy. But only about 5% of children have clinically proven allergic reactions to foods. Inteens and adults, food allergies occur in about 4% of the total population [26].

Countries are responsible for the safety of food consumed by their people. However, as food production and consumption patterns become more global, countries are working together through organizations such as the CODEX Alimentarius Commission and Organisation for Economic and Development (OECD) to provide food safety guidelines that should enable expanding trade, with some level of safety assured. Laws and mechanisms of regulation differ in each country and it is important to harmonize across countries to protect all at-risk consumers.

Food allergy and celiac disease (CD) are often hard to accurately diagnose. Relatively few consumers are affected, but a few are at risk of severe life-threatening reactions that are acute (IgE mediated allergy) or chronic (CD). There are complex genetic factors that increase the likelihood of sensitivity, but also many complex environmental factors have great influence in controlling sensitization or tolerance, but they are not proven or highly predictive. Diet, vitamin intake, exposure and development airway allergy (pollen, moulds and arthropods), intestinal microbiota, parasite exposure and various viral or bacterial infections are likely modulatory agents.[8]

Table 3.1: Symptoms of food allergy syndrome [21]

S.No.	Allergic Reactions	Symptoms
1.	Mild systemic reactions	Generalized urticaria, pruritus, rhinitis
2.	Moderate systemic reactions	Angioedema, dysphrecea, abdominal pain, diarrhoea, nausea, vomiting, vertigo
3.	Severe systemic reactions	Severe diarrhoea, dyspnea, with wheezing
4.	Life threatening systemic reactions	Anaphylactic shock, severe breathing difficulties, cyanosis, hypertension, and loss of consciousness

When symptoms are related to a drop in blood pressure, the person is said to be in anaphylactic shock. Anaphylaxis occurs when IgE antibodies are involved, and areas of the body that are not in direct contact with the food become affected and show symptoms.[11] This occurs because no nutrients are circulated throughout the body, causing the widening of blood vessels. This vasodilation causes blood pressure to decrease, which leads to the loss of consciousness. Those with asthma or an allergy to peanuts, tree nuts, or seafood are at greater risk for anaphylaxis.[10]

Major Reasons for Food Allergens

Eight foods are responsible for the majority of allergic reactions:

- Cow's milk including whey, casein, curds, lactalbumin, nougat, rennet caesin.
- Eggs including albumin, eggnog, meringue, surimi.
- Fish includes cod, bass, flounder.
- Peanuts include beernuts, goobers, peanut flour, nutmeat.
- Shellfish including crab, lobster,oysters, shrimp.
- Soy including TVP, textured soy protein, hydrolyzed soy protein, soy sauce, miso.
- Tree Nuts including cashew, almond, brazil nuts, pistachio, macadamia, walnuts, pecan, hazelnut, pine nut.
- Wheat includes bran, bulgur, couscous, durum, farina, gluten, matzoh, kamut.

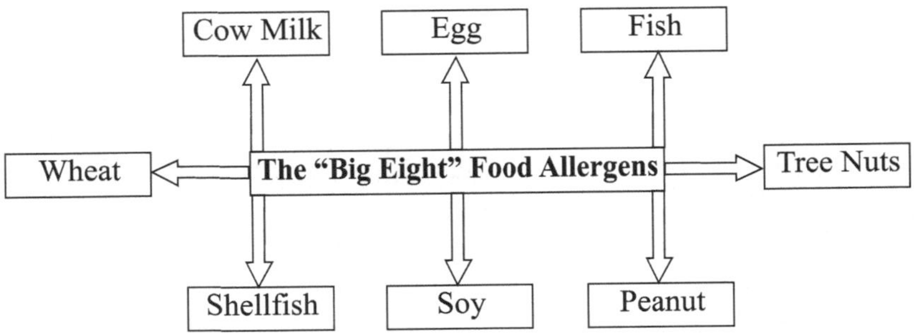

Table 3.2: Severe reactions in children and adults

Allergen	Children	Adults
All foods (IgE)	3 - 8%	1 - 4%
Cow's milk	2.5%	0.3%
Eggs	1.5%	0.2%
Ground nut	1%	0.6%
Nuts	0.5%	0.6%
Fish	0.1%	0.4%
Shellfish	0.1%	2%
Soybean	0.4%	0.3%
Wheat	0.3%	0.3%
Sesame seed	0.1%	0.1%
Celiac	0.5%-1.2%	0.5%

Source: http://www.allergycareindia.org/

Food Allergens in Non-food items

Non-food items, such as medications, cosmetics, vaccines, and craft supplies, may contain food ingredients. Labeling laws do not apply to these products. If there are questions about a product's ingredients, it is often helpful to call the manufacturer.

Vaccines – Gelatin, egg, and chicken products may be used in the production of certain vaccines.

- Gelatin – Gelatin is included in measles, mumps, rubella (MMR), varicella, diphtheria, tetanus, acellular pertussis (DTaP), and Japanese encephalitis vaccines.
- Egg – Egg protein is present in yellow fever vaccine and some influenza vaccines. People with egg allergies can be given the egg-based influenza vaccine safely; you should consult with your allergy specialist for guidance.
- Chicken – Chicken proteins may be present in the yellow fever vaccine.

Medications and asthma inhalers – Non-prescription and prescription medications (in tablet, capsule, and inhaler form) can contain food allergens.

- Lactose – Lactose is a sugar derived from milk. Although lactose used in medications is unlikely to contain milk proteins, some experts recommend that highly allergic patients avoid using products that contain lactose (eg, use metered dose inhalers rather than dry powder inhalers that contain lactose).
- Soy lecithin – Soy lecithin is the fatty derivative of soy, and it contains trace amounts of soy proteins. Certain asthma inhalers contain small amounts of soy lecithin, which could potentially cause an allergic reaction in a person who was highly allergic to soybeans or peanuts. You should discuss the risks and benefits of these inhalers with your healthcare provider.
- Casein – Casein is a cow's milk protein that has been used as an anti-stick agent on latex gloves.

Cosmetics and crafts – Cosmetics may contain a variety of food-derived ingredients, including milk, nut oils, wheat, and soy. Craft items, such as modeling dough, may contain wheat. Egg white is sometimes used to smooth finger-paints. If there is a question about a product's ingredients, call the manufacturer.

Types of Food Allergies

1. **Immunoglobulin E (IgE) mediated**: Symptoms result from the body's immune system making antibodies called Immunoglobulin E (IgE) antibodies. These IgE antibodies react with a certain food.
2. **Non-IgE mediated**: Other parts of the body's immune system react to a certain food. This reaction causes symptoms, but does not involve

an IgE antibody. Someone can have both IgE mediated and non-IgE mediated food allergies.

IgE Mediated Food Allergies

The IgE mediated food allergies most common in infants and children are eggs, milk, peanuts, tree nuts, soy and wheat. The allergic reaction can involve the skin, mouth, eyes, lungs, heart, gut and brain. Some of the symptoms can include:

- Skin rash, itching, hives
- Swelling of the lips, tongue or throat
- Shortness of breath, trouble breathing, wheezing
- Stomach pain, vomiting, diarrhoea
- Feeling like something awful is about to happen

(a) Cross-Reactivity and Oral Allergy Syndrome

Having an IgE mediated allergy to one food can mean child is allergic to similar foods. For example, if your child is allergic to shrimp, he or she may be allergic to other types of shellfish, such as crab or crayfish. Or if your child is allergic to cow's milk, he or she may also be allergic to goat's and sheep's milk. The reaction between different foods is called cross-reactivity. This happens when proteins in one food are similar to the proteins in another food. Cross-reactivity also can occur between latex and certain foods. For example, a child who has an allergy to latex may also have an allergy to bananas, avocados, kiwis or chestnuts.

Some people who have allergies to pollens, such as ragweed and grasses, may also be allergic to some foods. Proteins in the pollens are like the proteins in some fruits and vegetables. So, if your child is allergic to ragweed, he or she may have an allergic reaction to melons and bananas. That's because the protein in ragweed looks like the proteins in melons and bananas. This condition is oral allergy syndrome.

Symptoms of an oral allergy syndrome include an itchy mouth, throat or tongue. Symptoms can be more severe and may include hives, shortness of breath and vomiting. Reactions usually occur only when someone eats raw food. In rare cases, reactions can be life-threatening and need epinephrine.

Non-Ig E Mediated Food Allergy

Non-IgE mediated food allergies are caused by a reaction involving other components of the immune system apart from IgE antibodies. The reactions do not appear immediately after the ingestion of the food and usually relate to reactions in the gastrointestinal tract such as vomiting, bloating and diarrhoea.

The mechanism of non-IgE-mediated food allergy is not well understood. Although the immune system is presumed to be involved, IgE antibodies are not associated with this condition, hence the term "non-IgE-mediated" food allergy. This term is an umbrella term for a range of gastrointestinal food allergies that affect the full length of the gut.

(a) Eosinophilic esophagitis

Eosinophilic esophagitis is an inflamed oesophagus. The oesophagus is a tube from the throat to the stomach. An allergy to a food can cause this condition.With EoE, swallowing food can be hard and painful. Symptoms in infants and toddlers are irritability, problems with eating and poor weight gain. Older children may have reflux, vomiting, stomach pain, chest pain and a feeling like food is "stuck" in their throat. The symptoms can occur days or even weeks after eating a food allergen.EoE is treated by special diets that remove the foods that are causing the condition. Medication may also be used to reduce inflammation.

(b) Food Protein-Induced Enterocolitis Syndrome (FPIES)

FPIES is another type of food allergy. It most often affects young infants. Symptoms usually don't appear for two or more hours. Symptoms include vomiting, which starts about 2 hours or later after eating the food causing the condition. This condition can also cause diarrhoea and failure to gain weight or height. Once the infant stops eating the food causing the allergy, the symptoms go away. Rarely, severe vomiting and diarrhoea can occur which can lead to dehydration and even shock. Shock occurs when the body is not getting enough blood flow. Emergency treatment for severe symptoms must occur right away at a hospital. The foods most likely to cause a reaction are dairy, soy, rice, oat, barley, green beans, peas, sweet potatoes, squash and poultry.

(c) Allergic Proctocolitis

Allergic proctocolitis is an allergy to formula or breast milk. This condition inflames the lower part of the intestine. It affects infants in their first year of life and usually ends by age 1 year. The symptoms include blood-streaked, watery and mucus-filled stools. Infants may also develop green stools, diarrhoea, vomiting, anaemia (low blood count) and fussiness. When properly diagnosed, symptoms resolve once the offending food(s) are removed from the diet.

How to identify or diagnose food allergies

People with food allergies are typically told to completely avoid the offending food. However, it is often difficult to do this in real life. As a result, anyone with food allergies must be prepared to treat an unexpected allergic reaction at any time and in any setting. In general, people with food allergies must strictly avoid eating or drinking anything that contains even a minuscule amount of a food allergen. It is usually not possible to know what amount of the allergen will trigger an allergic reaction.

Eating, touching, and inhaling allergens – Most people with food allergies react after eating a food. Other types of exposure, such as touching or inhaling the food, may lead to localized reactions (eg, hives) in children. However, this type of exposure is unlikely to cause severe reactions in most people with food allergies.

Smelling foods is also unlikely to cause a severe reaction. As an example, the smell of peanut butter is related to volatile organic compounds (VOCs), substances that evaporate easily. The smell of peanut butter is not related to particles of peanut butter in the air, so it is not likely to trigger an allergic reaction.

However, inhaling tiny food particles (as a result of steaming, boiling, frying, grating, shedding, or grinding) can potentially trigger an allergic reaction in highly sensitive people. Thus, people who are very sensitive should avoid situations in which aerosolized food could be inhaled. Although peanut protein does not easily become airborne from peanut butter, it may from peanut flour or "dusty" roasted peanuts. Similarly, touching an allergenic food and then touching the eyes, nose, or mouth can cause an allergic reaction.

Personal Contact and Food Allergies

Saliva and other bodily fluids can potentially expose an allergic person to food allergens. Kissing or sharing straws, glasses, or utensils are the most likely ways that saliva may be spread from one person to another. Based upon a study of peanut butter, waiting several hours after eating an allergenic food and then eating a nonallergenic food(s) seems to reduce the level of allergen in the saliva and is suggested.

It is theoretically possible to have a food allergy reaction after other forms of contact, such as sexual intercourse or a blood transfusion. However, this type of reaction is uncommon. The partner of a person with a food allergy can consider not eating large amounts of the allergen before sex to further reduce this risk.

Diagnose

To confirm your diagnosis, an allergist may perform a food challenge. Food challenges are done by consuming the food in a medical setting to determine if that food causes a reaction. Anaphylaxis is a serious allergic reaction that happens very quickly. Without immediate treatment, it can be fatal.Diagnosis is usually based on a medical history, elimination diet, skin prick test, blood tests for food-specific IgE antibodies, or oral food challenge.[7][13]

Table 3.3: Methods used in diagnosis of food allergy [21]

S.No.	In Vitro	In vivo
1.	Skin prick test	Medical history
2.	Double blind placebo	Diet diary
3.	Controlled food challenge	Radioallergo sorbent test
4.	Elimination diet	Basophil histamine release assay (BHR)

- For skin-prick tests, a tiny board with protruding needles is used. The allergens are placed either on the board or directly on the skin. The board is then placed on the skin, to puncture the skin and for the allergens to enter the body. If a hive appears, the person is considered positive for the allergy. This test only works for IgE antibodies. Allergic reactions caused by other antibodies cannot be detected through skin-prick tests.[19]

  Skin-prick testing is easy to do and results are available in minutes. Different allergists may use different devices for testing. Some use a "bifurcated needle", which looks like a fork with two prongs. Others use a "multitest", which may look like a small board with several pins sticking out of it. In these tests, a tiny amount of the suspected allergen is put onto the skin or into a testing device, and the device is placed on the skin to prick, or break through, the top layer of skin. This puts a small amount of the allergen under the skin. A hive will form at any spot where the person is allergic. This test generally yields a positive or negative result. It is good for quickly learning if a person is allergic to a particular food or not, because it detects IgE. Skin tests cannot predict if a reaction would occur or what kind of reaction might occur if a person ingests that particular allergen. They can, however, confirm an allergy in light of a patient's history of reactions to a particular food. Non-IgE-mediated allergies cannot be detected by this method.
- Patch testing is used to determine if a specific substance causes allergic inflammation of the skin. It tests for delayed food reactions.[1][9][10]
- Blood testing is another way to test for allergies; however, it poses the same disadvantage and only detects IgE allergens and does not work for every possible allergen. Radio Allergo Sorbent Testing (RAST) is used to detect IgE antibodies present to a certain allergen. The score taken from the RAST is compared to predictive values, taken from a specific type of RAST. If the score is higher than the predictive values, a great chance the allergy is present in the person exists. One advantage of this test is that it can test many allergens at one time.[20]

ACAP-RAST has greater specificity than RAST; it can show the amount of IgE present to each allergen.[25] Researchers have been able to determine "predictive values" for certain foods, which can be compared to the RAST results. If a person's RAST score is higher than the predictive value for that food, over a 95% chance exists that patients will have an allergic reaction (limited to rash and anaphylaxis reactions) if they ingest that food. Currently, predictive values are available for milk, egg, peanut, fish, soy, and wheat.[11][12][4] Blood tests allow for hundreds of allergens to be screened from a single sample, and cover food allergies as well as inhalants. However, non-IgE-mediated allergies cannot be detected by this method. Other widely promoted tests such as the antigen leukocyte cellular antibody test and the food allergy profile are considered unproven methods, the use of which is not advised.[22]

Differential Diagnosis

Important differential diagnoses are:

- Lactose intolerance generally develops later in life, but can present in young patients in severe cases. It is due to an enzyme deficiency (lactase) and not allergy, and occurs in many non-Western people.
- Celiac disease is an autoimmune disorder triggered by gluten proteins such as gliadin (present in wheat, rye, and barley). It is a non-IgE-mediated food allergy by definition.
- Irritable bowel syndrome
- C1 Esterase inhibitor deficiency (hereditary angioedema), a rare disease, generally causes attacks of angioedema, but can present solely with abdominal pain and occasional diarrhoea.

Difference between Allergies and Asthma

Most people that have asthma also have allergies but you can tell the difference by the symptoms. If you feel any of the following symptoms then you may have asthma, not just allergies:

- Feeling out of breath
- Tightening of chest
- Wheeze and cough

If you find it very difficult to breathe or talk, your heart beats really fast, or if you feel that the skin around the ribs or neck is pulled tightly, then you may be having a very strong asthma attack. Call 911 to get help right away. Medicines used to treat allergies will not help relieve asthma symptoms. If you think you have asthma, you should see a doctor right away to get a diagnosis and the right treatment.

How to prevent food allergies

Breastfeeding for more than four months may prevent atopic dermatitis, cow's milk allergy, and wheezing in early childhood.[5] Early exposure to potential allergens may be protective.[13] Specifically, early exposure to eggs and peanuts reduces the risk of allergies to these.[6] To avoid an allergic reaction, a strict diet can be followed. It is difficult to determine the amount of allergenic food required to elicit a reaction, so complete avoidance should be attempted. In some cases, hypersensitive reactions can be triggered by exposures to allergens through skin contact, inhalation, kissing, participation in sports, blood transfusions, cosmetics, and alcohol.[18]

Treatment

The best treatment for food allergies is to avoid the food that causes the allergy. When that isn't possible, you can use medicines such asantihistamines for mild reactions and epinephrine for serious reactions.

Epinephrine

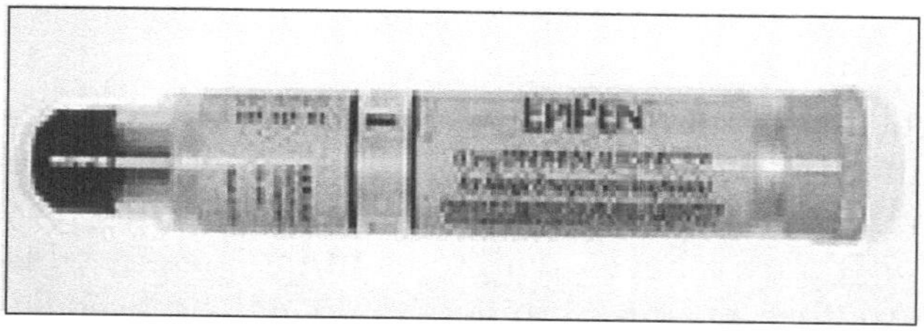

Epinephrine autoinjector

Epinephrine is another name for the hormone adrenaline, which is produced naturally in the body. An epinephrine injection is the first-line treatment for severe allergic reactions (anaphylaxis). If administered in a timely manner, epinephrine can reverse its effects.Epinephrine relieves airway swelling and obstruction, and improves blood circulation; blood vessels are tightened and heart rate is increased, improving circulation to body organs. Epinephrine is available by prescription in an autoinjector.[16]

Antihistamines

Consumer Reports Best Buy Drugs evaluated seven of the newest antihistamines by comparing how well they work, how safe they are, their side effects, and their cost. Consumer Reports recommends the following generic antihistamines as the best for most people:

- Cetirizine (tablets)
- Loratadine (tablets, dissolving tablets, or liquid)
- Alavert (dissolving tablets)

All of these medicines are available without a prescription. If you try an antihistamine and it does not work well for you, you should try another one until you find the right one. If you need to take an antihistamine every day, shop around to find the best price. There can be a big difference in price for these medicines from store to store, even in the generic form. Antihistamines can alleviate some of the milder symptoms of an allergic reaction, but do not treat all symptoms of anaphylaxis.[15] Antihistamines block the action of histamine, which causes blood vessels to dilate and become leaky to plasma proteins. Histamine also causes itchiness by acting on sensory nerve terminals. The most common antihistamine given for food allergies is diphenhydramine.

They do have side effects. You may:

- Feel sleepy or distracted
- Feel that your mouth, nose, or throat are dry
- Get a headache
- Feel dizzy
- Feel nausea
- Lose your voice (hoarseness)

Steroids

Glucocorticoid steroids are used to calm down the immune system cells that are attacked by the chemicals released during an allergic reaction. This treatment in the form of anasal spray should not be used to treat anaphylaxis, for it only relieves symptoms in the area in which the steroid is in contact. Another reason steroids should not be used is the delay in reducing inflammation. Steroids can also be taken orally or through injection, by which every part of the body can be reached and treated, but a long time is usually needed for these to take effect.[17]

How Food Regulation Safe Guard against Food Allergens

It is the primary responsibility of food manufacturers to provide safe foods, free from allergen cross-contamination. There must be a disciplined approach to allergen management. Depending upon the layout of the plant, ingredients handled and products made, each facility may have to incorporate different allergen management strategies. However, the following are basics that can be incorporated into any operation to provide an allergen-safe product:

- Adopt a "zero tolerance" philosophy for allergen cross-contamination.
- Conduct an allergen risk assessment as part of your Hazard Analysis and Critical Control Points (HACCP) program.
- Train all associates in allergen management strategy. Include Marketing, R&D, production, maintenance and sanitation.
- Make sure that incoming ingredients are clearly labeled and that the labels are reviewed periodically to assure suppliers have not changed ingredients without notice.
- Have a clear allergen storage policy including a procedure for spills cleanup.
- Design equipment to facilitate cleaning and prevent allergen harborage niches.

- Schedule production to prevent cross-contamination.
- Clean between runs of allergen ingredients. Use a visually clean standard or confirm with ezyme-linked immunosorbent assay (ELISA) test kits.
- Clearly identify work-in-process materials and rework. Have a clear rework policy.
- Reject in-process materials or finished product suspected of cross-contamination.
- Have a process for reviewing labels prior to use, and confirm that the correct labels are used in process.
- Conduct internal audits or use a third party auditor to assess the allergen management strategy.
- Evaluate and track consumer complaints involving allergen issues.
- Have a trained person on staff to respond to consumer calls regarding allergens.

Avoiding food allergens when dining out

- Consumers should clearly state that they have a food allergy to the person who is directly responsible for preparing the meal.
- Carry a supply of pre-printed cards with clear information about which foods cannot be taken. Remind the manager or cook that cooking containers and serving utensils cannot be contaminated with the allergenic food.
- Food that is fried in oil may be reused for frying allergenic foods and should be avoided. The oil becomes contaminated easily with protein from previously cooked foods.
- Buffets and solid bars should probably be avoided because of the high risk of cross contact.
- People with peanut or treenut allergies should be especially careful of ice-cream parlors, bakeries and Asian restaurants.
- Report allergic reactions to restaurant staff immediately. Do not wait to see if the reaction will get better on its own.

Adults and parents of children with food allergies must learn to carefully read food labels, prepare meals at home, and talk to others about their condition.

(a) **Food labeling** – Laws regarding food labeling vary by country. People with food allergies must consider not only a food's ingredients, but also any potential cross-contact (also called cross-contamination) that can occur as the food is prepared. It is also important to know that ingredients may change over time, and labels should be read each time you purchase a product.

In the United States, the Food Allergen Labeling and Consumer Protection Act mandates that nutritional labels on food packages clearly identify eight specified food allergy sources (milk, eggs, fish, crustacean shellfish, tree nuts, peanuts, wheat, and soy), although other foods may still appear under multiple names. Additionally, for tree nuts, crustacean shellfish, and fish, the specific type (eg, walnut or cashew, shrimp or lobster, tuna or salmon, etc.) must be labeled.

This law applies to all packaged foods manufactured in the United States and also to foods that are imported for sale in the US. However, the law does not apply to packaged fresh meat, poultry, or egg products. Updates to this law are available online from the Center for Food Safety and Applied Nutrition, a branch of the Food and Drug Administration[24].

Potential allergens other than the eight listed above may still be listed on food labels with unclear names (eg, garlic or sesame may be listed as a spice, natural flavor, or even an artificial flavor). If the label is unclear, call the manufacturer to clarify the ingredients.

In addition, it is important to understand that "substitute" foods, which are used to remove fats or other components of a food, may not remove the allergenic proteins. As an example, some egg substitutes (which are lower in cholesterol) still contain egg white proteins.

(b) **Advisory labeling** – A manufacturer may use certain phrases when a particular allergen is not an intended ingredient, but the ingredient may come in contact with the food during the manufacturing process. As an example, a blueberry muffin may not contain nuts, but may be made in a bakery where banana nut muffins are made. Manufacturers may use phrases such as: "may contain," "processed in a facility with," "manufactured on shared equipment with," and others. There are no laws regarding when this type of label should be used.

Although manufacturers use a variety of label terms in their voluntary advisory warnings, these do not necessarily reflect the level of risk. As an example, a muffin that says that it "may contain nuts" is no more or less likely to contain nuts than a muffin that says "processed in a facility with nuts."

Advisory labeling may help to reduce the risk of an allergic reaction, but may also significantly reduce the food choices available to people with food allergies. Most allergists recommend avoiding foods that have an advisory label because it is impossible to know the actual risk. Serious allergic reactions have occurred as a result of cross-contact.

Additives causing Allergic Reactions

Some food additives that may cause problems for some people include:

- **Flavour enhancers** – monosodium glutamate (MSG) 621
- **Food colourings** – tartrazine 102; yellow 2G107; sunset yellow FCF110; cochineal 120
- **Preservatives** – benzoates 210, 211, 212, 213; nitrates 249, 250, 251, 252; sulphites 220, 221, 222, 223, 224, 225 and 228
- **Artificial sweetener** – aspartame 951.

Eight different food additives are commonly known to cause adverse reactions. These are described briefly below.

(a) **Sulfites**: The term, sulfites encompasses a variety of very small chemicals that are commonly used as preservatives in foods. Sulfites prevent foods from turning brown when the food is exposed to air. Some of these are naturally occurring while most are added artificially to foods. Sulfites can cause mild to life- threatening symptoms in some people with asthma. Symptoms of adverse reactions to sulfites include: tightness in the chest, breathing difficulty, hives, stomach cramps, diarrhea, and sometimes, anaphylactic shock. Sulfites are most often found in wine, dried fruits, white grape juice, frozen potatoes, maraschino cherries, fresh shrimp, and certain jams and jellies. At one time, sulfites were used on fresh fruits and vegetables, such as in salad bars, to help retain color and freshness; however, the Food and Drug Administration (FDA) has banned use of sulfites for such use.

(b) **Aspartame (Nutrasweet)** is a calorie-free sweetener used in many foods and beverages. People who have a problem metabolizing the amino acid phenylalanine should not consume aspartame. Many other types of adverse reactions have been reported in relationship to aspartame but these reactions have not been adequately verified to conclude that they are truly caused by aspartame.

(c) **Parabens** are used to preserve foods and medications. They also are used in sunscreens and shampoos where they can cause reactions such as severe contact dermatitis. Examples of parabens are ethyl-, methyl, propyl-, and butyl-parabens.

(d) **Tartrazine** is a yellow dye most commonly used in beverages, candy, ice cream, desserts, cheese, canned vegetables, hot dogs, salad dressing, seasoning salts, and catsup. Adverse reactions can include hives or swelling, and possibly a trigger for asthma symptoms; however, studies have not documented this relationship Even though many studies have been done, it has been difficult to find children who consistently adversely react to tartrazine or other food dyes.

(e) **Monosodium glutamate, glutamic acid (MSG)**: Manufacturers and restaurants use MSG to enhance flavor in packaged meats and foods. Adverse reactions can cause headache, a burning sensation on the back of the neck, chest tightness, nausea, diarrhea, and sweating. There are rare reports that people with asthma who have consumed MSG have more severe asthma episodes. "Chinese Restaurant Syndrome"–sudden adverse reactions to eating food from Chinese restaurants–is often attributed to use of MSG in these prepared foods.

(f) **Nitrates and nitrites** are chemicals used to preserve foods, prevent deadly botulism infection, enhance flavors, and color foods. Symptoms are rare, but may include headache or hives in some people. Nitrates and nitrites are commonly used in hot dogs, bologna, salami, and other processed meats and fish.

(g) **Butylated hydroxytoluene (BHT) and butylated hydroxyanisole (BHA)** are preservative chemicals added to breakfast cereals and other grain products to prevent them from changing color, odor, and flavor. These substances have been linked to chronic hives and other skin reactions on rare occasions.

(h) **Benzoates** are preservatives used in some foods, including cakes, cereals, salad dressings, candy, margarine, oils, and dry yeast. Benzoate reactions are very rare.

Some food additives are more likely than others to cause reactions in sensitive people.

It is often the additives that are used to give a food a marketable quality, such as colour, that most commonly cause allergic reactions. Some of these hypersensitive reactions include:

- **Digestive disorders** – diarrhoea and colicky pains
- **Nervous disorders** – hyperactivity, insomnia and irritability
- **Respiratory problems** – asthma, rhinitis and sinusitis
- **Skin problems** – hives, itching, rashes and swelling.

It is important to realise that many of the symptoms experienced as a result of food sensitivities can be caused by other disorders. Medical diagnosis is important. If you try to diagnose yourself, you may restrict your diet unnecessarily and neglect an illness.

If you think you may have a food additive sensitivity, it's important to seek professional help since all of the symptoms you may be experiencing can also be caused by other disorders.

It may help to keep a food diary and note carefully any adverse reactions. In the case of a sensitivity being identified, the usual practice is to eliminate all suspect foods from the diet and then reintroduce them one by one to see which additive (or additives) causes the reaction. This should only be done under medical supervision, since some of the reactions – such as asthma – can be serious.

Summary

The time is ripe for a coordinated and well-resourced approach to accelerating progress in food allergy research. While there is currently no approved treatment for preventing food allergy reactions, a number of potential therapies show promise. However, these investigational therapies are not being advanced to the clinic as quickly as they could be due to a number of challenges – organizational, financial and scientific–that require a coordinated effort to overcome. Finding a way to expedite these trials would accelerate understanding and allow more families to have access to potentially beneficial therapies as soon as possible. At the same time, most experts believe the therapies currently under study will not be effective for all patients, and that a rational approach to the ultimate prevention and cure for food allergy will require a deep understanding of the root causes of food allergy. Fortunately, there has never been a better time to conduct research into the causes of human disease. There have been dramatic advances in the technologies and tools for studying human biology, and for developing highly relevant laboratory models, but these methods have not yet been broadly applied to food allergy.

Conclusion

Food allergy continues to grow as a public health issue–one in need of effective treatments that can prevent life threatening reactions, and ultimately a cure. It is critical to seize this moment in the timeline of food allergy research to greatly accelerate progress in the field. A number of promising treatments are already under investigation, and there is a tremendous opportunity to apply new scientific approaches to understand and address the root causes of food allergy. Realizing this promise will take a concerted, collaborative effort among individuals and families affected by food allergies, researchers, clinicians, research institutions, government agencies, industry and others.

REFERENCES

1. "Allergies and EGIDs | American Partnership for Eosinophilic Disorders". *Apfed.org*. Retrieved 2014-03-31.
2. Food Allergen and Anaphylaxis Network www.foodallergy.org/allergens.html
3. Food Allergies. Food Allergy Initiative. 2009. Accessed 27 March 2010.
4. Garcia-Ara, C; Boyano-Martinez T; Diaz-Pena JM; *et al*. (January 2001). "Specific IgE Levels in the Diagnosis of Immediate Hypersensitivity to Cows' Milk Protein in the Infant". Allergy Clin Immunol. 107 (1):185-90. doi:10.1067/mai.2001.111592.PMID 11150010.
5. Greer, FR.; Sicherer, SH.; Burks, AW. (Jan 2008). "Effects of Early Nutritional Interventions on the Development of Atopic Disease in Infants and Children: The Role of Maternal Dietary Restriction, Breastfeeding, Timing of introduction of Complementary Foods, and Hydrolyzed Formulas.". Pediatrics. 121 (1): 183-91. doi:10.1542/peds.2007-3022.PMID 18166574.

6. Ierodiakonou, D; Garcia-Larsen, V; Logan, A; Groome, A; Cunha, S; Chivinge, J; Robinson, Z; Geoghegan, N; Jarrold, K; Reeves, T; Tagiyeva-Milne, N; Nurmatov, U; Trivella, M; Leonardi-Bee, J; Boyle, RJ (20 September 2016). "Timing of Allergenic Food Introduction to the Infant Diet and Risk of Allergic or Autoimmune Disease: A Systematic Review and Meta-analysis.". *JAMA*. 316 (11): 1181-1192. doi:10.1001/jama.2016.12623.PMID 27654604.
7. National Institute of Allergy and Infectious Diseases (July 2012). "Food Allergy An Overview".
8. Nowak-Wegrzyn, A; Katz, Y; Mehr, SS; Koletzko, S (May 2015). "Non-IgE-mediated Gastrointestinal Food Allergy." The Journal of Allergy and Clinical Immunology. 135 (5): 1114-24. doi:10.1016/j.jaci.2015.03.025. PMID 25956013
9. Patch test in the diagnosis of food allergy". *2014-03-22*. Archived from the Original on 2014-03-10. Retrieved 2014-03-31.
10. Rokaite R, Labanauskas L, Vaideliene L (2014-01-24). "Role of the Skin Patch Test in Diagnosing Food Allergy in Children with Atopic Dermatitis". Medicina (Kaunas). 40: 1081-7. PMID 15547309.
11. Sampson, HA; Ho DG (October 1997). "Relationship between Food-specific IgE Concentrations and the Risk of Positive Food Challenges in Children and Adolescents". J Allergy ClinImmunol. 100 (4): 444-51. doi:10.1016/S0091-6749(97)70133-7.PMID 9338535.
12. Sampson, HA (May 2001). "Utility of Food-specific IgE Concentrations in Predicting Symptomatic Food Allergy". J Allergy ClinImmunol. 107 (5): 891-6. doi:10.1067/mai.2001.114708. PMID 11344358.
13. Sicherer, SH.; Sampson, HA. (Feb. 2014). "Food Allergy: Epidemiology, Pathogenesis, Diagnosis, and Treatment.". J Allergy ClinImmunol. 133 (2): 291-307; Quiz 308. doi:10.1016/j.jaci.2013.11.020. PMID 24388012.
14. Sicherer 2006, p. 12.
15. Sicherer 2006, p. 131.
16. Sicherer 2006, p. 133.
17. Sicherer 2006, p. 134.
18. Sicherer 2006, pp. 151-8.
19. Sicherer 2006, p. 185.
20. Sicherer 2006, pp. 187-8.
21. SV Gangal and B K Malik. (August 2003) "Food Allergy: How much of a Problem Really is this in India". Journal of Scientific and Industrial Research. 62: 755-765.
22. Wüthrich B (2005). "Unproven Techniques in Allergy Diagnosis". J Investig Allergol ClinImmunol. 15 (2): 86-90. PMID 16047707
23. www.aafa.org
24. www.fda.gov
25. www.kidswithfoodallergies.org.
26. WebMD

Pages: 37-49

Food Technology and Research Advancement

Edited by: Dr. Avnish Chauhan and Dr. Pawan Kumar 'Bharti'

ISBN: 978-93-86841-49-0

Edition: 2018

Published by: Discovery Publishing House Pvt. Ltd., New Delhi (India)

4 Insects

The New Alternative Food and Medicine for 21st Century

V.K. Mishra*[1] and Satyapriya Singh[2]

ABSTRACT

The practice of eating insect is known as Entomophagy. Many animals, such as spiders, lizards and birds, are entomophagous, as are many insects. People throughout the world have been eating insects as a regular part of their diets for millennia. Although this practice should be specified as human entomophagy, throughout this book entomophagy refers to human entomophagy. The earliest citing of entomophagy can be found in biblical literature; nevertheless, eating insects was, and still is, taboo in many westernized societies. The unconventional nature of entomophagy has meant that farming insects for food and feed has largely been absent from the great agricultural innovations in livestock farming that emerged in past centuries – with a few exceptions, such as bees, silkworms and scale insects (from which a red colorant is derived). Insects have also failed to feature on the agendas of agricultural research and development agencies worldwide, including at FAO (1973). Until recently, references to insects for food and feed have been largely anecdotal. It is therefore unsurprising that insects are still lacking from the diets of many rich nations and that their sale for human consumption remains part of a niche food sector of novelty snacks. Nevertheless, insect consumption is not a new concept in many parts of the world. From ants to beetle larvae – eaten by tribes in Africa and Australia as part of their subsistence diets – to the popular, crispy-fried locusts and beetles enjoyed in Thailand, it is estimated that insect-eating is practised regularly by at least 2 billion people worldwide.

[1] Department of Entomology and Agricultural Zoology, IAS, Banaras Hindu University, Varanasi - 221 005 (India)

[2] Division of Entomology, ICAR-Indian Agricultural Research Institute, New Delhi - 12 (India)

More than 1900 insect species have been documented in literature as edible, most of them in tropical countries. The most commonly eaten insect groups are beetles, caterpillars, bees, wasps, ants, grasshoppers, locusts, crickets, cicadas, leaf and plant hoppers, scale insects and true bugs, termites, dragonflies and flies.

Key words: Insects, New, Alternative food, Medicine, 21st century.

Introduction

Insects have played an important part in the history of human nutrition in Africa, Asia and Latin America (Bodenheimer, 1951). During the past few years there has been a new upsurge of interest in insects as food. One factor that may be responsible is an increasing awareness in the western world that insects are traditional and nutritionally important foods for many non-European cultures. Insects are a highly nutritious and healthy food source with low fat, high protein, vitamin, fibre and mineral content. Even within the same group of species, nutritional value may differ depending on the metamorphic stage of the insect, the habitat in which it lives, and its diet. Nevertheless, insects do provide valuable buffers against seasonal shortages of food (Dufour, 1987). Insects were an equally important resource for the Indians of western North America, which, like other indigenous groups, expended much organizational efforts in harvesting them. Hundreds of species have been used as human food. Some of the more important groups include grass- hoppers, caterpillars, beetle grubs and (sometimes) adults, winged termites (some of which are very large in the tropics), bee, wasp and ant brood (larvae and pupae) as well as winged ants, cicadas, and a variety of aquatic insects. Ordinarily, insects are not used as emergency food to ward off starvation, but are included as a planned part of the diet throughout the year or when seasonally available. Insects and the substances extracted from them have been used as medicinal resources by human cultures all over the world. Besides medicine, these organisms have also played mystical and magical roles in the treatment of several illnesses in a range of cultures. Science has already proven the existence of immunological, analgesic, antibacterial, diuretic, anesthetic, and antirheumatic properties in the bodies of insects. Several authors have surveyed the therapeutic potential of insects, either recording traditional medical practices or employing insects and their products at the laboratory and/or clinical level. Thus, insects seem to constitute an almost inexhaustible source for pharmacological research. Chemical studies are needed to discover which biologically active compounds are actually present within insect bodies. Other medical applications include maggot therapy and the use of bee products – such as honey, propolis, royal jelly and venom – in treating traumatic and infected wounds and burns (Van Huis, 2003). Insects being greatest in number as compared to other food and medicine source both for human beings and animals; can be adequately exploited for the betterment of mankind. The great potential these tiny creatures possess needs to be explored more.

Why Eat Insects?

Overall, entomophagy can be promoted for three reasons:

- **Health:**
  - Insects are healthy, nutritious alternatives to mainstream staples such as chicken, pork, beef and even fish (from ocean catch).
  - Many insects are rich in protein and good fats and high in calcium, iron and zinc.
  - Insects already form a traditional part of many regional and national diets.
- **Environmental:**
  - Insects promoted as food emit considerably fewer greenhouse gases (GHGs) than most livestock (methane, for instance, is produced by only a few insect groups, such as termites and cockroaches).
  - Insect rearing is not necessarily a land-based activity and does not require land clearing to expand production. Feed is the major requirement for land.
  - The ammonia emissions associated with insect rearing are also far lower than those linked to conventional livestock, such as pigs.
  - Because they are cold-blooded, insects are very efficient at converting feed into protein (crickets, for example, need 12 times less feed than cattle, four times less feed than sheep, and half as much feed as pigs and broiler chickens to produce the same amount of protein).
  - Insects can be fed on organic waste streams.
- **Livelihoods (Economic and Social Factors):**
  - Insect harvesting/rearing is a low-tech, low-capital investment option that offers entry even to the poorest sections of society, such as women and the landless.
  - Minilivestock offer livelihood opportunities for both urban and rural people.
  - Insect rearing can be low-tech or very sophisticated, depending on the level of investment.

Table 4.1: Nutritional value of various insects per 100 grams

Insect	Protein (g)	Fat (g)	Carbohydrate	Calcium (mg)	Iron (mg)
Giant Water Beetle	19.8	8.3	2.1	43.5	13.6
Red Ant	13.9	3.5	2.9	47.8	5.7
Silk Worm Pupae	9.6	5.6	2.3	41.7	1.8
Dung Beetle	17.2	4.3	.2	30.9	7.7
Cricket	12.9	5.5	5.1	75.8	9.5
Grasshopper	20.6	6.1	3.9	35.2	5.0
Grasshopper	14.3	3.3	2.2	27.5	3.0
June Beetle	13.4	1.4	2.9	22.6	6.0
Caterpillar	28.2	N/A	N/A	N/A	35.5
Caterpillar	9.7	N/A	N/A	N/A	1.9
Termite	14.2	N/A	N/A	N/A	35.5
Weevil	6.7	N/A	N/A	N/A	13.1
Beef (Lean Ground)	27.4	N/A	N/A	N/A	3.5
Fish (Broiled Cod)	28.5	N/A	N/A	N/A	1.0

Source: Data collected from *The Food Insects Newsletter*, July 1996 (Vol. 9, No. 2, ed. by Florence V. Dunkel, Montana State University) and *Bugs In the System* by May Berenbaum (Lowa state university, entomoology department febuary 25, 2000 by John Van Dyk)

Beneficial Role of Insects for Humans

Over the past 400 million years, evolution has produced a wide variety of arthropod species adapted to their environments. About 1 million of the 1.4 million described animal species on earth are insects, and millions more are believed to exist. Contrary to popular belief, of the 1 million described insect species, only 5000 can be considered harmful to crops, livestock or human beings (Van Lenteren, 2006). Insects play an equally vital role in waste biodegradation. Beetle larvae, flies, ants and termites clean up dead plant matter, breaking down organic matter until it is fit to be consumed by fungi and bacteria. In this way, the minerals and nutrients of dead organisms become readily available in the soil for uptake by plants. Animal carcasses, for example, are consumed by fly maggots and beetle larvae. Dung beetles – of which there are about 4000 known species – also play a significant role in decomposing manure. They can colonize a dung heap within 24 hours, preventing flies from developing on them. If the dung remains on the soil surface, about 80 percent of the nitrogen is lost to the atmosphere; the presence of dung beetles, however, means carbon and minerals are recycled back to the soil, where they further decompose as humus for plants. When cattle were introduced to Australia in 1788, waste biodegradation became an immediate problem, as endemic dung beetles were simply insufficient to decompose the increased amounts of manure.

Australian dung beetles had adapted to the dung of marsupials (e.g. kangaroos), which differs from bovine dung in various ways, including in size, texture and water content (Bornemissza. 1976). The Australian Dung Beetle Project was initiated to solve the problem, and dung beetles were introduced to the continent from South Africa, Europe and Hawaii (of 46 introduced species, 23 established).

Entomophagy around the World

Number of Edible Insect Species Identified

Providing definitive figures on the number of edible insect species worldwide is difficult for several reasons. First, a layperson is unlikely to describe an insect by its Linnaean nomenclature, making official estimates difficult. Matters are complicated by the use in many cultures of more than one vernacular name – also called ethnospecies – for the same insect species. By using only Latin names and correcting for synonyms, Yde Jongema of WUR conducted a worldwide inventory using the literature, including from Western countries and temperate regions, and listed 1900 edible insect species worldwide as of April 2012. Lower estimates do exist. (De Foliart, 1997) counted a "low" 1000 species, while (Ramos Elorduy, 2005) noted "at least" 1 681 species. Regional and national estimates have also been made: It is identified 250 edible species in Africa; (Ramos Elorduy, *et al.* 2008) listed 549 species in Mexico although (Cerritos, 2009) reported a mere 177 species in the country in China, documented 170 species; and it is reported 164 species in the Lao People's Democratic Republic, Myanmar, Thailand and Viet Nam; Researchers estimated that 428 species were consumed as food in the Amazon.

Major Groups of Edible Insects

Globally, the most common insects consumed4 are beetles (Coleoptera) (31 percent). This is not surprising given that the group contains about 40 percent of all known insect species.

The consumption of caterpillars (Lepidoptera), especially popular in sub-Saharan Africa, is estimated at 18 percent. Bees, wasps and ants (Hymenoptera) come in third at 14 percent (these insects are especially common in Latin America). Following these are grasshoppers, locusts and crickets (Orthoptera) (13 percent); cicadas, leafhoppers, planthoppers, scale insects and true bugs (Hemiptera) (10 percent); termites (Isoptera) (3 percent); dragonflies (Odonata) (3 percent); flies (Diptera) (2 percent); and other orders (5 percent). Lepidoptera are consumed almost entirely as caterpillars and Hymenoptera are consumed mostly in their larval or pupal stages. Both adults and larvae of the Coleoptera order are eaten, while the Orthoptera, Homoptera, Isoptera and Hemiptera orders are mostly eaten in the mature stage (Cerritos, 2009).

Nutritional Quality

1. Proximate composition

Based on a study of the nutritive value of insect species commonly eaten in Thailand, (Raksakantong, *et al.* 2010) concluded that insects represent the cheapest source of animal protein in Thailand and that their consumption should be encouraged because many people cannot afford fish or other meat. Their results help demonstrate the importance of edible insects for the intake of high quality protein in the population of this region. However, there is need for caution due to the caloric deficiency in the diet of these people as protein cannot be fully utilized if there is not enough energy in their meals. Insects have been shown to contain a large quantity of protein ranged from 38% in queen castes to 54% in dung beetles. These values are higher than those reported for edible insects in southwestern Nigeria (from 6% for *Brachytrypes* spp. to 30% for *Analeptes trifasciata*). Values are even higher for dung beetles at the larval and adult stages (50% to 53% for *Zonocerus variegatus*). However, the protein value for dung beetles was lower than the values reported in the wasp *Polybia sp.* (82%). The high protein content is an indication that the insects can be of value in human and animal rations, thus replacing more costly sources of animal protein that are usually absent in the diet of rural dwellers in developing countries. Besides the high amounts of protein that insects can provide, several investigations have demonstrated their high quality and high digestibility in a great variety of species. The quality of the protein, and thus its nutritional value, is determined by the amino acid composition and the digestibility of the protein. The essential amino acids from Thai edible insects, as well as the nutritional requirements for adults and preschoolers. Since children are in the growth phase, their need for amino acids is greater compared to adults. Most insects provide a sufficient range of amino acids to fulfill the nutritional requirements of children. The essential amino acid content score of edible Thai insects ranges from 34 to 100%. The limiting essential amino acid found in Thai edible insects is either threonine or lysine, while that of other insects from the State of Oaxaca, Mexico, is either tryptophan or lysine. The amino acids of different protein sources may have a complementary function. Therefore, Thai edible insects can effectively supply protein by complementing other animal protein sources. The carbohydrate content of Thai edible insects is relatively low, ranging from 7% in Longan stink bugs to 16% in cicadas. Similar results were observed in other insects from Nigeria, whose carbohydrate contents ranged from 7 to 20%. Recent research has revealed that insects have considerable amounts of polysaccharides that can enhance the immunity function of the human body. Low carbohydrate–high protein (LC-HP) diets, introduced originally for weight-loss regimens, also have significantly beneficial effects in reducing the risk of cardiovascular disease. Furthermore, such diets lower the intake of calories, resulting in expected weight loss. The lipid content of some Thai edible insects varies widely. (Raksakantong *et al.* 2010) found that the percentage of lipid ranged from 5% in June beetles to 37% in queen castes. Similar results were observed in other Thai edible insects, with lipid contents ranging from 3 to 20%. This finding is in agreement with previous studies in which lipid contents varied significantly between species. The giant water bug, which lives in freshwater, had the highest lipid content (20%), followed by the mole cricket (13%), which lives on grass, while water scavenger beetles had the lowest (3%). These results suggest that habitat, diet and insect species may contribute to lipid content. Lipids are essential in diets as they increase the palatability of foods by absorbing and retaining their flavours. Lipids are also vital in the structural and biological functioning of cells, helping in the transport of nutritionally essential fat-soluble vitamins.

2. Fatty Acid Composition and Concentration

Polyunsaturated fatty acid (PUFA) is the predominant fatty acid found in Thai terricolous edible insects, followed by saturated fatty acid (SFA) and monounsaturated fatty acid (MUFA). The concentration of total PUFAs in Thai terricolous insects ranged from 213 mg/100g in cicada to 1515 mg/100g in dung beetles, while Thai aquicolous insects ranged from 726 mg/100g in water scavenger beetles to 2544 mg/100g in giant water bugs. However, other studies reported that MUFA was the major fatty acid in other Thai edible insects. This indicates that habitat, diet and insect species may contribute to their fatty acid contents. The total concentration of PUFAs can be compared to red meat and some fish such as sand whiting and black bream and much more than that found in fresh vegetables. Consumption of PUFAs is of increasing interest as evidenced in the literature, especially n-3 PUFA, which have beneficial effects on reducing the risk of diabetes by reduction of glucose intolerance, prevention of insulin resistance, reducing blood pressure, lowering LDL cholesterol and helping to prevent several diseases such as thrombosis, hypertension, inflammatory disease, arrhythmia and coronary heart disease.

The highest concentration of total fatty acids was in the giant water bug (473 mg/100g), while EPA and DHA contents were found in all of Thai aquicolous insects, ranging from 149 to 569 mg/100g and 57 to 264 mg/100g, respectively. This composition is much higher than that found in sand whiting, mackerel, blue fish, sea bream, sea bass and marbled spinefoot. For Thai terricolous insects, EPA was only found in dung beetles (301 mg/100g), while DHA was only found in June beetles (26 mg/100g) and Weaver ants (12 mg/100g). DGLA, arachidonic acid (ARA) and EPA are the precursors for prostaglandins which are products of essential fatty acid metabolism; they are often referred to as eicosanoids. EPA has also been reported to be useful in brain disorders and cancer treatment. DHA is a major component of brain, eye retina and heart muscle, DHA has been considered important for brain and eye development, and also makes a valuable contribution to cardiovascular health. Consumption of DHA at 0.5-0.7 g/day can lower the incidence of heart disease.

Insects as Delicacy: An Album

Agave worm: Also known as the *maguey* worm, these larvae of the *Hypopta agavis* are sometimes included in tequila bottles as proof of authenticity and alcohol content. In Mexico, they are also eaten as part of a meal, and are highly nutritious.

Honeypot ants: have abdomens swollen with a nectar-like substance, which is used to feed other ants, sort of like a "living larder." They are dug up from the ground and eaten raw by aboriginal peoples in Australia.

Leafcutter ants: also known as Hormigas Culonas are usually eaten toasted mainly in South America. In Colombia, they are sold as popcorn at movie theatre.

Bee larvae: especially, are prized in many cultures as tasty morsels. The larvae, when sautéed in butter, taste much like mushroomy bacon. Adult bees may also be eaten, often roasted. In China, ground bees are used as a remedy for a sore throat

Cicadas: primarily found in the Eastern US, live underground for 17 years before emerging and molting into adults. Different species of cicada are also eaten in many Asian countries, such as Japan, Thailand and Malaysia.

Cockroach: contrary to popular belief, cockroaches can actually be very clean and tasty insects, especially if they are fed on fresh fruits and vegetables. They can be eaten toasted, fried or boiled. Madagascar Hissing Cockroaches have a taste and texture like greasy chicken.

Cricket: Eaten fried, sauteed, boiled and roasted. These are amongst the most common insects eaten. Eaten in Mexico, Thailand, Cambodia. Good source of carbohydrates, calcium, potassium, vit. B2, and niacin

Dragon fly: Eaten in Indonesia and China. It can be eaten in adult or larval form. In Indonesia, these are caught by dipping a reed in sticky palm sap and waving it through the air. Often eaten boiled or fried

Grass hopper: In Mexico, these are eaten roasted with chili & lime, and are known as *chapulines*. Tasty grasshoppers are also a Ugandan delicacy, usually prepared fried. They are high in protein and calcium.

Wichetty grub: Eaten by Aborigines in Australia, often roasted in coals or over a fire, wichetty grubs are high in protein and fat. According to Peter Menzel in *Man Eating Bugs*, "Wichetty grub tastes like nut-flavored scrambled eggs and mild mozzarella, wrapped in a phyllo dough pastry."

Hornworm: David George Gordon, author of the *Eat-A-Bug Cookbook*, says that Tomato Hornworms can be fried up much the same as the fruit of the plant on which they feed. They taste a bit like green tomatoes, shrimp, and crab.

Mealworms: are found wherever there is, well, meal! They are the larva of the mealworm beetle. They are often prepared boiled, sauteed, roasted, or fried, and taste like a nutty shrimp

Walking stick: Eaten in Asia and Papua New Guinea, Walking Sticks taste somewhat leafy. Their legs can be used as fish hooks

The giant water bug: is popular in Thai cuisine, both consumed whole (steamed or fried), and as an extract in sauces. Raw bugs have a scent like a green apple. Bit salty, high in protein, vitamin B2 and niacin.

Medicinal use of Insects

Many species of insects, along with a large number of species of plants, have been recognized as possessing curative properties. The Aztecs and several other indigenous groups had knowledge of what might be termed "medicinal insects" (De Asis 1982; Sahagun 1980). Many species of insects have played important roles in the mysticism and magic inherent in many Mexican cultures as well as in the treatment of a variety of illnesses. (Aguirre 1947). Knowledge of medicinal insects and their uses has persisted in many rural areas today, haing been passed down from earlier practitioners of this healing art. Insects are sold in the markets of some towns and various insects parts are said to be useful as diuretics, analgesics, anaesthetics, aphrodisiacs etc. Considering that the number of rural areas where this knowledge survives is reduced each year and that in some regions the diversity of insects is available only during certain seasons of the year, it is important to study the insects associated with the empirical medicine of past and contemporary Mexican cultures. We feel it is imperative to learn about and develop indigenous medicine since it utilizes almost exclusively natural products with minimal side effects.

Various Insects and their Parts used in Medicine

Since early times (thousands of years ago), insects and their products have been used, directly and indirectly. Used singly or in combination with herbs it may be used in different forms. Grass hoppers, *Sphenarium spp., Taenipoda sp, Melanoplus sp.* (Orthtoptera, Acrididae). The hind legs of grasshoppers were crushed and mixed with water, then drunk as a powerful diuretic to treat kidney diseases. The infusion, which is said to have refreshing properties, reduces swelling (De Asis 1982), Rural people in the State of Oaxaca today use grasshoppers to treat certain intestinal disorders, Locusts, Schistocerca spp. These insects were pulverized and eaten as a dietary supplement to alleviate nutritional deficiencies (FAO, 1973) and to fortify the blood. It was also reported to be helpful in cases of postchildbirth anemia and in lung diseases, e.g., asthma and chronic cough. Cricket, Achela ""me.tiea. (Orthoptera, Gryllidae). Crickets legs were prepared like those of grasshoppers and were employed as a diuretic for dropsy (edema) (Barajas 1952; Conconi 1982; De Asis 1982). Bugs" (Hemiptera Pentatomido:e) *Euchislus spp., Edessa spp" Alizie. sp.* and (Stink bugs), (Hemiptera, CorMae), *Acanthocephala spp.*, (Leaf-footed bugsl (Xomitl-Jumiles in Nahuatl), The bugs obtained in these four taxa was applied externally in treating Scrofula and other tubercular diseases and was also used for kidney, liver, and stomach ailments. When alive, these bugs are a powerful analgesic and anaesthetic against toothache and rheumatic and arthritic pain or to alleviate gastrointestinal diseases. It was also used to treat goiter and was recommended for those with a weak constitution and as an aphrodisiac (De Asis 1982; Taylor 1975). Contemporary people of rural areas in the State of Guerrero use them against Bocio disease, perhaps because of the large amount of iodine they contain. Xamues, Pachilis gigas. (Leaf-footed bugs). These insects were roasted and powdered and utilized in whooping cough cases, eating the entire body. This could be because of their nutritional value and the quantity of vitamins they contain. Mealy bugs, can be considered a multi-purpose medicinal and useful insect. In addition to their use as an ointment, varnish, or perfume, whole insect bodies were boiled to produce a sticky mass which was placed over lesions of leprosy and other skin conditions and to treat muscular pain, chronk itching, mange bum, or scars. It aids in the healing of burns through reducing excessive swelling and inflammation and thus is said to be helpful in heat strokes and diseases of fluid imbalance such as dropsy. The mass of boiled mealybugs was sometimes ingested to alleviate the affects of poisonous mushrooms and other fungi, or diarrhea and to dean the teeth . Dactylopius coccus, known as "grana" mealybug, is mostly used as an agent to color or redden tissue or foods. It, too, can be boiled to produce a sticky mass and used, as discussed above, as a skin treatment, a tooth powder to dean teeth and in the treatment of caries. Beetles, CokapteTll, Meloiden, Buprestidae. Derived from the Nahuatl Tefl (fire) and Ocuitin (worm), several species have been used in Mexico as an aphrodisiac in a manner similar to that of the well-known Spanish fly (LyUa vesicatDria). Larvae of these beetles are roasted or crushed, mixed with water then drunk to treat urogenital disorders. It is equally well-known as a stimulant (love potion) for lovers (De Asis 1982). Tlalomitl, a corruption of the Nahuall Tlalli (bone) and Omitl (worm), are actually larvae of several species in the Elateridae. Before being eaten alive or roasted, they are hard, rigid and worm-like in appearance. One species, Strategus juJianus, (Scarabridae, Dynastinoe) known as a llttle bullfight because the male has three homs on its head, is prepared as a drink to increase sexual performance . Butterflies, Lepidoptera. "Meocuilin" is the common name for AegiaJe (Acentrocneme) hesperiaris, (Megathymidae), the white agave worm. It comes from the Nahuatl terms

Metl (Agave) and Ocuilin (worm). Having an appearance of white worms, they are eaten alive for their reputed aphrodisiac properties as well as for stomach disorders and rheumatic diseases. *Palsus spp.* (Hepialidae), known as "gusanilla" (little worm), are said to have aphrodisiac properties. In Oaxaca, Veracruz and Chiapas states where it is eaten alive or roasted, it is used against gastrointestinal diseases such as dysentery, especially in children (Conconi 1982). Also, in rural areas it is used as an ointment for cracked lips or for dry skin. *Bombyx mori* (Bombycidae). The boiled larvae were used in a variety of ailments, e.g., apoplexy, aphasy, bronchitis or pneumonia, and convulsions. The boiled pupae were used to treat hemorrhages and to alleviate polyuria or frequent urination. Excrements of the pupae are eaten to alleviate vomiting and diarrhea brought on by cholera, and to improve circulation. Hymenoptera, several species of ants (Formicidae). Honey ants, *Myrmecosistus spp.* Or necam:catl, derived from the Nahuatl terms for Nectar (honey) and azcatl (ants), are important because of the healing qualities of its honey. Produced and stored in the bodies of certain classes of the worker caste of these ants, the honey was fermented and drunk for its anti-inflammatory and anti-fever properties. The honey was also applied directly as a pomade for eye diseases, cataracts or growths over the iris called pterigions. The fermented drink was considered a sacred drink in religious ceremonies among many cultures, e.g., the Aztecs and Toltecs (Brygoo 1946). The mandibles of worker caste adults *Atta spp.* were used after surgery to close wounds. Several ants were positioned so their bites would pierce the skin on either side of the wound. The heads were then separated with the mandibles acting as sutures. Secretions from the salivary glands were reputed to have antibiotic properties, preventing infections. The venom of ants was used to cure rheumatic diseases. Ants were positioned on the afflicted part of the body, and allowed to sting. The venom penetrated directly into the bloodstream and in this respect resembled an intramuscular injection. Its efficacy in treating rheumatism, arthritis, and poliomyelitis is related to its immunological reaction. Bees, (Apidae) several species itt three genera of Apidae. The bees in this genus were so important to the Maya that they created a god, named A Much Keba, for them. The Maya prepared a sacred drink ("Balche") from the honey. It was also known as 'Water of Youth. if After fermentation, the honey' was drunk and used against internal parasites such as intestinal worms. It was used and still is in Huejutla, Hidalgo for regulating menstruation, decreasing post-childbirth aches, and as a health restorative in the elderly. Apis mellifera, the well-known honey bee, produces abundant honey which was and is applied to the skin for such conditions as excessive scar tissue, rash, and burns. In addition, it was prepared as a plaster or poultice for eye infections. The venom of honey bees has, for more than a century, been utilized intramuscularly through direct stings of live bees to the part of the body afflicted by arthritis, rheumatism, and polineuritis. The frequency, dosage and duration of the treatment varies according to the disease and degree of development, for example, arthritic pain requires large dosages while asthma needs only a small one. Venom is gathered from both snakes and bees in much the same way; it is prepared in different concentrations and applied by injection. Propolis is a resinous, adhesive substance elaborated by bees to serve as a cementing material It is often deposited on the buds of trees and other plant surfaces, The substance is now known to contain many hormones and, together with enzymes from bee saliva is thought to have antibiotic, bactericidal, and bacteriostatic properties, It can be employed as an anae'ihetic and for all kinds of inflammations, even those resulting from tumors. Royal jelly is a white gelatinous product derived from pharingeal glands of worker bees of 5to 14 days of age. The ancient Mexicans used it to reestablish healthy conditions in cases of anaemia, Today it is ingested in very small quantities when it is pure or in capsules or spoon if diluted, and is used for the following diseases: asthenia, anorexia, gastrointestinal ulcers, arteriosclerosis, anaemia, hypo or hypertension, neurasthenia or inhibition of sexual libido.Today these products are available in tablet or capsule form through the health food and wholistic health industries. Certain clinics and hospitals which have "Apitherapy" programs use these products by physiotherapy, ionizations, inhalations, electrophoresis and other treatments.

Conclusion

Recent developments in research and development show edible insects to be a promising alternative for the conventional production of meat, either for direct human consumption or for indirect use as feedstock. Nevertheless, a tremendous amount of work still needs to be done by a wide range of stakeholders over many years to fully realize the potential that insects offer for food and feed security. The great potential these tiny creatures possess, needs to be explored more.

REFERENCES

Aguirre, M., and Collins, M.D. (1993). Lactic Acid Bacteria and Human Clinical Infection. *Journal of Applied Microbiology*, 75(2): 95-107.

Barajas, S., Mendoza, F., and Cogsdon, C.C. (1952). Trombosis intraauriculares en las valvulopatias mitrales. *Arch Inst Cardiol*, 22: 413-452.

Bodenheimer, F.S. (1951). Insects as Human Food. In *Insects as Human Food* (pp. 7-38). Springer Netherlands.

Bornemissza, G.E. (1976): Australian Dung Beetle Project, 1965-1975. *AMRC Rev Aust Meat Res Comm*.

Brygoo, E. (1946). *Essai de bromatologie entomologique: les insectes comestibles*. Trillaud.

Cerritos, R. (2009). Insects as Food: An Ecological, Social and Economical Approach. *CAB Reviews: Perspectives in Agriculture, Veterinary Science, Nutrition and Natural Resources*, 4(027): 1-10.

Conconi, F., Ferrari, M.I.C.H.E.L.E., Ziglio, P.G., Droghetti, P.A.O.L.A., and Codeca, L.U. C.I.A.N.O. (1982). Determination of the Anaerobic Threshold by a Noninvasive Field Test in Runners. *Journal of Applied Physiology*, 52(4): 869-873.

De Asis, L. (1982): *U.S. Patent No. 4,364,174*. Washington, DC: U.S. Patent and Trademark Office.

Data Collected from *The Food Insects Newsletter* (1995) (Vol. 9, No. 2, ed. by Florence V. Dunkel, Montana State University) and *Bugs In the System* by May Berenbaum (Lowa State University, Entomoology Department Febuary 25, 2000 by John Van Dyk)

Foliart, D.E. (1997). Synovitis and Silicone Joint Implants: A Summary of Reported Cases. *Plastic and Reconstructive Surgery*, 99(1), 245-252.

Dufour, D.L. (1987) Insects as Food: A Case Study from the Northwest Amazon. *American Anthropologist*, 89(2): 383.

FAO. (1973). *Guidelines for Small-scale Fruit and Vegetable Processors*. FAO Agricultural Services Bulletin 127. Rome.

Raksakantong, P., Meeso, N., Kubola, J., and Siriamornpun, S. (2010). Fatty Acids and Proximate Composition of Eight Thai Edible Terricolous Insects. *Food Research International*, 43(1), 350-355.

Ramos Elorduy, J. (2005). Insects: A Hopeful Food Source. *In* M.G. Paoletti, ed. *Ecological Implications of Mini livestock; Role of Rodents, Frogs, Snails, and Insects for Sustainable Development*, pp. 263-291. New Hampshire, Science Publishers.

Ramos Elorduy, J., Carbajal Valdés, L.A. and Pino, J.M. (2008). Socio-economic and Cultural Aspects associated with Handling Grasshopper Germplasm in Traditional Markets of Cuautla, Morelos, Mexico. *J. Hum. Ecol.*, 40(1): 85-94.

Sahagun, J., & Harper, J.M. (1980). Parameters Affecting the Performance of a Low-cost Extrusion Cooker. *J. Food Proc. Eng*, 3(4), 199.

Taylor, R.L. (1975). *Butterflies in my Stomach: Insects in Human Nutrition*. Santa Barbara, USA, Woodbridge Press Publishing Company.

Van Huis, A., van Gurp, H. and Dicke, M. (2003). *Het insectenkookboek*. Amsterdam, the Netherlands, Atlas.

Van Lenteren, J., Wäckers, F., Bukovinszkine-Kiss, G. and Winkler, K. (2006). Sugar Resources are vital for Diadegma semiclausum Fecundity under Field Conditions. *Basic and Applied Ecology*, 7(2), 133-140.

Pages: 50-71

Food Technology and Research Advancement
Edited by: **Dr. Avnish Chauhan and Dr. Pawan Kumar 'Bharti'**
ISBN: 978-93-86841-49-0
Edition: **2018**
Published by: **Discovery Publishing House Pvt. Ltd., New Delhi (India)**

5 An Unique Approach to Commercial Fish Farming in West Bengal, Pond Farming of *Chitala chitala* and Variation in Morphology of Alimentary Tracts of Few Small Indigenous Fishes

Subrato Ghosh

ABSTRACT

Extended fields of 15-20 acres, 50-52 acres in area and further above in villages of Moyna Block, Dist. Purba Medinipur, West Bengal are typically lowlands; which when naturally filled with rainwater during monsoon and post-monsoon remains stagnant almost throughout the year at 1.5-2.0 feet depth, making paddy cultivation unsuitable. Embankments are constructed on four sides, water level is further increased upto 5.5 feet depth by drawing in river water or deep tubewell water, fish farming regions are prepared and table-sized major carps are produced therein commercially. Pisciculturists invest a huge amount of money and take these tracts on lease, have adopted proper management practices, *viz.*, preparation of water body before fish seed stocking, bottom soil treatment after an aquacrop, application of supplementary fish feed and lime, produce and harvest grown-up fishes in short periods. Fishes grow rapidly on high quality feed and in enormous space, and are popular as *'Moynar maatther maachh'* in this state. Experiences gained recently about this unique fish farming system, which is unlike to usual trend of fish production in ponds and pond management, have been described here. In the end, some salient features of pond farming of the endangered foodfish *Chitala chitala* have been presented and variations in morphology of alimentary tracts of few small indigenous freshwater fishes of less than 10cm size have been highlighted pictorially.

Key words: Extended fields, fish farming, *Chitala chitala*, major carps, small fishes.

Fishery Extension Officer, Office of the CEO, FFDA, South 24 Parganas, West Bengal (India)

Introduction

We are familiar about farming of the air-breathing catfish *Clarius batrachus*, insectivorous fishes and medium carps traditionally in water-logged paddy fields, about rice-fish integrated farming system in scientific terms in rainfed lowland areas and renovated paddy plots, where simultaneously fish fingerlings are allowed to grow with paddy and retained in trenches/pond refuge after paddy harvest and after monsoon/post-monsoon, when water table in main plot recedes. In estuarine wetlands located 30km eastwards of Kolkata city, brackishwater fishes and shrimps are grown in summer and paddy cropping in practiced in kharif/monsoon season. Through tricropping technology, a crop of brackishwater fishes and shrimps in summer and a freshwater aquacrop along with a paddy crop in kharif season are obtained. Earlier, prevalent practice of trapping fish and prawn in the tide-swept single crop areas and freshwater paddy fields in riverine areas were fully dependant on the natural ingress of fish seed along with water courses in the impounded paddy fields so far as production of fish is concerned. To accelerate the fish yield in such habitats, judicious stocking of selected species of fast growing fish have been increasingly adopted by fish farmers in various parts of India (Natarajan and Ghosh, 1980).

Interestingly, grow-out farming of commercially important major carps is practiced successfully in water-retained extended fields at different villages of Moyna Development Block, Dist. Purba Medinipur, West Bengal. Moyna is a Community Development Block that forms an administrative division in Tamluk Subdivision of Purba Medinipur district of West Bengal. Following the modified-extensive type of husbandry, about 8500 fish farmers produce marketable-sized major carps in this Block, most of them in fields. Under composite fish culture system, Catla (*Catla catla*), Rohu (*Labeo rohita*), Mrigal (*Cirrhinus mrigala*), Silver carp (*Hypophthalmichthys molitrix*) and Grass carp (*Ctenopharyngodon idella*) are the major carps cultured at Moyna due to their high growth rate and consumer preference and further among these, the first three species contribute a lion's share in farmed fish production. Present author made a visit to Moyna town on 11th October, 2016 and obtained authentic information on this activity from three progressive local fish farmers.

Characteristics of Paddy Fields-turned-fish Farming Regions

Fish farming and production of marketable/table-sized fishes at Moyna is an unique system in this state. Grow-out farming of major carps is normally done in stocking ponds elsewhere but most of the extended fields at Moyna act as ponds/water bodies for fish farming. In most of the 81 Mouzas (villages) of this Block, that comes under 11 Gram Panchayats, commercial fish farmers rear fishes in fields of 15-25 acres in area (1 acre =

100 decimal), but, for other resource-rich farmers here, the area of a single plot (locally popular as *'ghery'* or *'maatth'*) may be as vast as 120-140 acres (200 bigha in local dialect, 1.5 bigha = 1 acre); very few of them, the largest ones, are 300-330 acres in area. In most places at Moyna, on both sides of the main roadway and beside other narrow village roads, one can have a view of extended zones of water and water (as if flood-inundated fields) instead of lushy green paddy fields.

Moyna Block is characterized by large extended areas of typical lowlands or saucer- shaped depressions. Here the waterbodies/fish farming regions are formed in depressions in flood-prone areas that are seasonally flooded during the monsoon period and remain submerged for 5-6 months after that (during the wet season). In such areas, land ownership remains with agriculturists. During the wet season and further when freshwater is let into the plots for round-the-year fish farming, the individual land holdings are neither visible nor viable as the area takes the shape of a single large sheet of water (Arthur *et al.*, 2005). Rainwater which is accumulated therein during monsoon and post-monsoon remains stagnant throughout the year at 2.0 feet depth as there is no provision of draining out of water. This makes paddy cultivation quite impossible. Bundhs 8 feet in height are constructed on four sides, water level is further increased upto 5.0 feet depth by drawing in river water and/or deep tubewell water and table-sized major carps are produced therein. Land owners are willingly prepared to provide their land on lease for fish farming and table-sized fish production. Water level may be only waist-height in some parts of a field and deeper in other parts.

Every year, due to heavy rainfall in the rainy season, Moyna basin experiences drainage congestion and water-logged hazard from August-September to December-January. This drainage congestion and resulted standing water in the low-lying agricultural fields has negative effects on agriculture but positive on fish farming activity. From the time when price of freshwater prawns continuously went upward along with major carps, general agro-based people at Moyna transferred low-lying agricultural fields into fish farming grounds, feeling interest to earn much more money and for the betterment of their economic condition. Throughout the year, areas of paddy cultivation remained captured by freshwater aquaculture. Almost 50- 60 villages in this Block like Charandaschak, Baitalchak, Arong Kiarana, Ismalichak, Kripanandapur, Kiarana, Bakcha, Purba-Dakshin Moyna, Paramanandapur, and so forth, are now engaged to culture of *Labeo rohita, Catla catla* and others, in their paddy fields. Giant prawns *Macrobrachium rosenbergii* in the water-logged areas of Bakcha, Arong Kiarana, Kiarana, Ismalichak, Baitalchak, Ramchak, Narikelda are also cultured intensively (Sahu, 2014).

Initially paddy was cultivated in these tracts for 4-6 months and subsequently, after paddy harvest, major carp fingerlings were stocked in these fields after drawing in water if rainwater is insufficient to maintain water table. But since 2006, freshwater fish farming is done only in these plots commercially round the year; only in few fields, still now, fish farming is done and table-sized fishes are produced in 6-7 months and thereafter paddy is cultivated. The sediment characteristics of the soils of Moyna indicated that soil texture of the impoundments were water retentive. At Moyna, the Kangsabati or Kansai river flows adjacent to the farmers' fields; so fish farmers are not always dependent on rain as the river can provide sufficient freshwater in fields from upland areas. A network of canals links the vast waterbodies at this site with river channels and provides water for fish culture and irrigation (Arthur *et al.*, 2005).

Particulars of Fish Farming System

1. Activity of Sri Dipankar Barman

Since 2012, Sri Dipankar Barman is producing table-sized major carps commercially in a 17 acre tract at Vill. Puthputia, which is about 12km far away from Moyna proper. The tract is popularly known as *'Putputia maatth'*. He is running the business in association with his brother-in-law and another close friend. Originally the plot belonged to quite a few agriculturists, who had a share of their own in terms of area in the entire plot. Sri Barman has taken this 17 acre (main water area, excluding bundh) field for fish farming on lease for five years by making payment @ Rs. 34,000/- per 66 decimal (0.66 acre) area per year. Paddy cultivation is no more practiced here. Initially he had to spend Rs. 5,20,000/- to construct bundh (embankment) on all four sides of this field with help of tractors, height of bundh is 8 feet, same is the width. It is a perennial water-retained tract, 5.0-5.5feet in depth; in addition to rainwater, there is facility to let in water from nearby Rupnarayan river via Sankar-aara canal, which is completely fresh/ sweetwater in nature.

Sri Barman mainly stocks advanced fingerlings of *Labeo rohita* and *Cirrhinus mrigala* in this tract, 100-150gm in weight and 6 inches in length. During March, he stocks about 75,000nos of *L. rohita* (80%) and *C. mrigala* (10%), which is @ 3000nos/bigha (1 bigha = 66 decimal), and in addition to this, he stocks 2000nos of *Catla catla* (200-250gm size), 1500nos of each of *Cyprinus carpio* and *Hypophthalmichthys molitrix* (150-200gm) and 500nos of *Ctenopharyngodon idella*. Stocking of fish fingerlings is completed within three weeks, which are procured from fingerling producers in the region who raise fingerlings in ponds. Before stocking, Sri Barman applies Mohua oil cake in his fish farming region to eradicate unwanted fishes and further mustard oilcake as manure. During culture, growing fishes are fed three times in 24 hours (at 8.00am, at 12.30noon and at 5.30pm) with the help of tin-built boats (size: 15feet × 3.5feet, it can hold 2.0-2.5 tonnes of fish feed) or other small boats. In addition to feed mixture comprising mustard oilcake, maize flour, de-oiled rice bran and rice mill by-products, commercially available floating-type pelleted feed is also provided to fishes by Sri Barman. Pelleted feed of 2mm dia is provided initially to fishes of 100-150gm size, feed of 3mm dia to 300-400gm fishes and 4-6mm dia to 500-700gm fishes. Everyday 3kg pelleted feed is provided for every 100kg fish and when feed mixture is applied, it is @ 4kg/100kg fish. Sri Barman uses 'CP 9912' brand fish feed, available in 35kg sacks, Rs. 40-42/-/kg. The 6mm dia feed contains 25% crude protein (min.) and 3% fat, it contains fish meal, soyabean meal, rice bran, broken rice, fish oil, rapeseed meal and Vit-Min. mixture as ingredients.

Sri Barman uses $CaCo_3$ @ 10-12kg/66 decimal water area every month. In July, *i.e.*, within 3.5-4.0 months of farming period, he harvests 50% of the table-sized fishes. *L. rohita* and *C. mrigala* attains 600-650gm body weight, *C. catla* 1500gm, *H. molitrix* 1200gm and *C. carpio* 700-750gm. After harvest, almost equal number of bigger fingerlings, of the number of fishes that have been harvested, are stocked. In end of October, Sri Barman again harvests grown-up fishes for sale, particularly the *L. rohita* and *C. mrigala* of 800-900gm and *C. catla* of 2kg size. About 50,000nos of table-sized fishes are harvested and at the same time, 20,000nos major carp fingerlings are stocked. Harvest is done in October particularly to meet the yearly lease payment that has to be made to original land owners/land donors, and also to fish feed dealers.

2. Activity of Sri Debtosh Moni

Sri Debtosh Moni is another fish farmer who is practicing fish farming in a 13 acre (main water area) field at Vill. Purusottampur in Moyna Block. It is far away from Rupnarayan river, and is near to Keleghai and Chandiya rivers. He prefers to use groundwater instead of river water; in addition to rainwater, he draws up groundwater via deep tube-well to maintain water level (about 6 feet) in his fish farming tract. He is running this business on his own, took the land on lease on payment @ Rs. 27,000/- per 66 decimal per year and has three permanent labourers. He stocks major carp fingerlings in June and harvests in November. As pre-stocking management practice, he initially applies Mohua oilcake in this vast region @ 30kg/66 decimal area (water depth: 1.5 feet). All kinds of predatory and weed fishes are killed. After 17-18 days, mustard oil cake is applied for growth of minute fish-food organisms @ 25kg/66 decimal area. After three days, water level is increased upto 5-6 feet, limestone powder is applied @ 22kg/66 decimal area and netting as well as bottom soil raking is done on the following day.

For every 66 decimal water area, Sri Moni stocks 45-50kg *L. rohita* (50-60gm size), 60-70kg *C. mrigala* (50gm size), 10kg *C. catla* (100-120gm size), 8-10kg *H. molitrix* (100gm size), 25-30 pieces *C. idella* (150-200gm size) and 6-7kg black carp *Mylopharyngodon piceus* (snail and bivalve feeder; 150-200gm size). {Note: In vast tracts where the water depth is 10-12feet, fingerlings of *L. rohita* and *C. catla* are stocked at a higher density, with lesser numbers of bottom-feeder *C. mrigala*}. Sometimes fingerlings are stocked at a higher density. Neither Sri Barman nor Sri Moni uses cow dung in their fish farming fields; $CaCo_3$ (20-22kg/66 decimal area, depending on water quality) and animal bone powder are used by Sri Moni every month during fish culture operation. Sri Moni provides supplementary feed to growing fishes twice in 24 hours, in morning (9.30am) and evening (4.00pm). In morning time, groundnut oilcake (soaked in water for an hour prior to application) is used for two days in a week @ 20kg/day/66 decimal area. Mustard oil cake (soaked in water for 12 hours) is used for other two days of a week in morning @ 12-15kg/day/66 decimal. For the rest three days, rice bran or de-oiled rice bran is used. Everyday, in evening, 3.5kg floating pelleted feed is provided for every 100kg of fish biomass stocked, which is increased to 7.5kg/100kg fish on 4th-5th month of culture. Both these farmers use paddle wheel aerators and pumps (drawing up water from farming zone and forced release upto a distance) to maintain dissolved oxygen level in fish farming area. Instead of fertilizers, Sri Moni uses commercially-available fish growth promoter, which also manages water quality. The deoiled rice bran bought in sacks is heaped and kept at one corner of these fields and covered with polythene sheets; it is used as per requirement.

Netting is done every month to monitor growth and health status of fishes. At time of harvest (almost complete harvest) in November, *L. rohita* attain 400-450gm in weight, *C. catla* 1200-1500gm, *H. molitrix* 2.5kg and *C. idella* about 2kg. Indian major carps and exotic carps are sold to fish traders @ Rs 120-125/-/kg and Rs. 90-100/-/kg respectively. After one such aqua-crop of 5.0-5.5 months duration, water is drawn out, bottom soil is exposed, treated with limestone powder, subsequently other afore-mentioned pre-stocking management practices are followed. By 20th December, fish fingerlings are again liberated in the area for the next crop, table-sized fishes are harvested in April next year and sold. During October-November and again in March-April, Sri Moni has to repay the money that he had borrowed initially from fish feed dealers and other persons. During March-April, he faces water scarcity, and has taken preparations for irrigation technique; but too much ground water is not allowed for use by local Panchayat Samity body for fish farming.

3. Activity of Sri Dibakar Mal

Sri Dibakar Mal is producing exclusively table-sized major carps in a field of 150 acres in area at Vill. Manuakhali, Moyna Block. It is his own business. He opined that almost in every village in this Block, in 70% of the extended fields, fish farming is only done throughout the year and in rest of the areas, paddy cultivation subsequent to fish farming is done. In 2010, he has taken the tract on lease @ Rs. 40,000/-/66 decimal/year for five years. He stocks major carp fingerlings (6-7 inches size; 7-8 pieces/kg) during April-May @ 3000nos/66 decimal area; with 80% of *L. rohita*, 10% *C. catla* and rest 10% comprising *C. mrigala*, *H. molitrix* and *C. idella*. His fish farming territory is very near to Keleghai river, and he draws in river water *via* a canal during April, which, according to him, is freshwater in nature. He prepares supplementary fish feed on his own by mixing ingredients like deoiled rice bran, mustard oil cake, little amount of groundnut oil cake and soyabean dust, which costs Rs. 24/-/kg. He applies 3kg feed daily for every 100kg of fishes stocked. On the 45th day of stocking, his fishes under culture reach 400-500gm size, and he harvests fishes from his pond on every 45th day or every 75th day.

Business Terms made by Pisciculturists with Fish Feed Dealers and Fish Auctioneers

In the context of construction of bundhs on four sides of a vast tract, its lease amount, pre-stocking and post-stocking fish farming management practices, procuring good quality fish feed, netting and other features, fish farmers at Moyna have to bear huge amount of expenditure. Sri Barman has spent Rs. 6,75,000/- for construction of bundhs, bottom soil raking/ploughing and filling his entire tract of 17 acres with water. As source of fund, many fish farmers have to take loan from *Mahajans* and take *Dadan* (imprest money) from local fish auctioneers. As initial investment into fish farming in such vast fields-turned-water bodies, fish farmers make terms and conditions with fish feed dealers and/or fertilizer dealers. Supposedly, if an amount of Rs. 6,00,000/- is required for procurement of fish feed in a total amount of Rs. 20,00,000/- (supposedly) as initial investment, a fish farmer initially pays Rs. 1,50,000/- - Rs. 2,00,000/- (25-40% of total cost of feed) to feed supplier on a condition that the feed dealer has to provide the total amount of fish feed to the farmer that is required for a crop of five months. The fish farmer stocks bigger fingerlings and/or yearlings of major carps, fish feed dealer provides the total feed that is required (*i.e.*, that has been demanded) by the fish farmer, the farmer harvests marketable-sized fishes in short periods, sell those to local fish auctioneers and repays back the money (60-75% of total feed cost) that he has to pay to fish feed supplier.

Fish feed dealers trustfully provides fish feed to fish farmers for extended periods of fish culture even after being paid partially at the beginning; the farmer repays back the total cost of feed slowly in parts after making harvests of fishes at 2.5 months or 4 months interval, which are delivered to fish auctioneers for money.

As source of fund, often fish auctioneers at Moyna are prepared to lent a lumpsome amount of money to fish farmers at the beginning, on a condition that after 3-4 months, the farmer has to bring the entire amount of harvest of table-sized fishes at the disposal of the auctioneer, and even must supply it to him at a lower rate. An established fish auctioneer seeks to provide such imprest money to more number of fish farmers in the region, so that he will be able to built up contacts with more such farmers and marketable-sized fishes will be delivered to him in greater amounts, in comparison to other auctioneers. For fish farmers at Moyna, there is reliable supply of fish fingerlings and fish feed and good market infrastructure exists here, to achieve high production and profit. On account of expansion of fish farming activities, many fish feed dealers have come up in this region recently. Thus in short, it can be said that the fish farmers as renter, in order to be able to get lease of the field-turned-waterbody, takes out a loan from a local fish wholesaler/auctioneer to cover the cost of the lease and required inputs.

Other Salient Features

According to Sri Moni, Sri Mal and Sri Barman, almost in every village of Moyna Block, there exists 2-3nos of such vast tracts of fish farming region, each of which are 50-52 acres in area; even such regions of 80 acres and above will commonly be found. In some cases, fish production in the larger tracts is a partnership business venture of 16-19 fish farmers – cum – large entrepreneurs; for the largest tracts, it is 25-29 fish farmers. Such a kind of entrepreneurial activity and vocation started at Moyna during 2004-2005, slowly flourished in the entire Block and to a lesser extent in adjacent Pingla and Sabang Blocks. There are instances where a resource-rich person in the region is running the fish farming business singly in 2-3 smaller-sized tracts of around 25 acres in area (individually).

Most of the fish farmers follow the partial stocking - partial harvesting strategy. At Moyna, there is market preference for fishes of 500gm in size or just over it. Partial harvesting of major carps, that have been in practice here, provide congenial environment for remaining fishes to grow, and more importantly ensures continuous returns to fish farmers. They retain labourers to manage and guard the fish ponds. In addition to tin-built boats and small wooden boats, fish farmers use indigenous palm tree-trunk canoes for application of fish feed and lime in their farming region. Palm tree trunks, 10-12 feet in length, 2.0 feet and 1.0-1.5 feet in diameter at bottom and upper ends respectively are used, its inner mass is scooped off to give the shape of a canoe/raft. It is sturdy, can support two persons and oar is used to propel it on water.

Rate of fish production in Sri Barman's field and Sri Moni's field has been estimated to be 6.42tonnes and 3.53 tonnes/ha/year respectively. In the 200 acre tracts, *C. catla* reach 2kg size within six months. Everyday, in two trips, table-sized major carps harvested from these fields are brought to local fish auction markets (Moyna market, Annapurna market and Balaipanda market), transported and supplied to distant markets at Asansol, at Farakka, different places of Dist. Bankura (live adult fishes are supplied here mostly as brood fishes for fish seed production), Dist. Purulia, Dist. Nadia, recently fishes are also supplied to Dist. North 24 Parganas (Haringhata, Bongaon, Gobordanga, Kharibari, Baanspota) in West Bengal, even at Dhanbad in Bihar.

From a reference literature (Bera *et al.*, 2014), we have been informed that mainly in 47 Mouzas out of 81 in Moyna Block, extended paddy fields are utilized as fish farming regions. Its area is 5282 hectares. In Mouzas like Paramanandapur, Dakshin Anukha, Bhandar Chak and Dakshin Changra Chak in Moyna Block, there are fields of 125-250 acres in area, where fish farming alone (6-7 months period) and paddy farming sequential to fish production are practiced. The mean water depth is 1.55-1.60mt and fish production from such fields (on average) is 4500kg/ha in six months.

End Note

In West Bengal, freshwater fish farming has upgraded itself from a domestic backyard activity to a highly viable commercial enterprise in recent years. The flexibility in use of local water resources, ensuring assured income, nutritional security and employment opportunity has led the major carp culture of present days to the status of a full-time profession for rural farmers, projecting it as an avenue for sustainable livelihood security and rural socio-economic development (Jena *et al.*, 2007). Advancement and refinement of technologies over the years have made fish farming eminently suitable and significantly contributory to the rural economy both for farmers and entrepreneurs (Radheyshyam, 2007). The fish farming scenario at villages in Moyna Block, a profession that is in vogue extensively, is no exception to this, which is supported by strong traditional knowledge base and scientific inputs in various aspects of management.

Dissemination of scientific skills to end-users through well-focused training assumes great significance in knowledge in commercial aquaculture today. It is believed that for the sake of improvement of fish farmers of Moyna Block in their vocation, discussions on recommended package of practices in increasing fish production and hands-on location-specific training may be organized for them for two weeks at Freshwater Fisheries Research and Training Centre (Government of West Bengal), situated at Kulia, Kalyani, Dist. Nadia, so that they will be well-versed with the principles and practices of analysis of important physico-chemical parameters of water and soil of their fish farming regions, in addition to other aspects of aquaculture. The economics (cost-benefit analysis) involved should be appraised in depth, location-specific needs should be emphasized and addressed.

According to Sri Banaspati Biswas, Training Supervisor, Freshwater Fish Farmers' Development Agency (Government of West Bengal), Meen Bhaban, Dist. Birbhum and senior aquaculture expert, fish farmers at Moyna will be immensely benefitted if they are accepted as beneficiaries under a particular developmental scheme of West Bengal Fisheries Department and floating-type pelleted fish feed is provided to them from Directorate of Fisheries, Government of West Bengal as subsidy. The feed will be fruitfully and judiciously utilized, and will lead to increase in fish yield (Biswas, 2016). Fish health care centre may be established in this region under State Government initiative, and more knowledge should be inculcated among these fish farmers on the recent developments in freshwater aquaculture practices. It will ensure the sustainability of this farming system, profitability and make it more prospectful.

Inundated field as fish farming system

Author (right) with Sri Moni and Sri Mal

Oxygenation of harvested fishes (1)

Oxygenation of harvested fishes (2)

Pond Farming of Freshwater Foodfish *Chitala chitala*

Known by the name 'chital' in Bengali vernacular in West Bengal and regarded as 'State fish' of Uttar Pradesh, the species *Chitala chitala* (Order: Osteoglossiformes; Family: Notopteridae) is a foodfish that commands high market price and high demand, and forms a commercially-important fishery in all major rivers of India. It is rheophilic (preferring to live in fast moving water), distributed in the Ganges-Brahmaputra and Mahanadi river basins, may attain body length in excess of 3.5 feet. Soup prepared from the body muscle and oil prepared out of its sun-dried flesh are administered to patients suffering from measles, a viral disease. It is found in deep and clear waters of floodplain wetlands, stagnant backwaters, large rivers, reservoirs and open-type beels. In rivers, they generally dwell in fairly well-oxygenated waters but in ponds they can adapt themselves in low oxygenated waters owing to their air-breathing habit (Moitra *et al.*, 1986). Deep waters of Gomti, Ganga, Yamuna, Ghaghara and Sharda rivers are the home of *C. chitala*. Its population has come down to 2-5% of what it was in previous occasion (Source: The Times of India, 9th December, 2012).

During March and April 2017, an in-depth survey was made by present author to gain knowledge on the farming principles and management practices of culture of *Chitala chitala* in large ponds. Conversation was made with Sri Dipak Roy, national award winning fish farmer at Malda district; Sri Jibon Ghosh, progressive fish farmer of Alipurduar district; Sri Abdul Sattar and Sri Anisur Rahaman, progressive fish farmers of Kushmandi Block, Dakshin Dinajpur district; Sri Bablu Kumar Ghosh, national award winning fish farmer of North 24 Parganas district, West Bengal.

(i) Seeds of river Brahmaputra

In farm ponds, *C. chitala* fingerlings (4-5 inch) stocked at 1.5-2.0% of total biomass along with bigger fingerlings of major carps attain 2.2-2.5kg in a year. In addition to *A. mola* and *Puntius* sp., they also predate upon fry and advanced-fry stages of silver carp *H. molitrix* residing in upper water column. Adult *A. mola* and spawn of silver carp (price of spawn is lower than that of IMC) are stocked in ponds 15-20 days prior to stocking of *C. chitala* fingerlings. Fish farmer Sri Jibon Ghosh at Dist. Alipurduar in north Bengal purchased naturally-bred *C. chitala* fingerlings from river Brahmaputra (3-4 inch; Rs. 20-25/- each) during June and stocked in carp broodstock ponds; those grew to 2.0-2.2kg in 9-10 months. Their parent stock is assumed to be much superior and weigh 14-15kg, or even more. Sri Ghosh stocked 20-25 pieces *C. chitala* fingerlings in his 1.75 acre carp broodstock pond, which is only 1.5-2.0% of total fishes stocked. High water depth is required in ponds for *C. chitala* farming.

(ii) Pond management

In nature, fertilized eggs of *C. chitala* are deposited over submerged wooden logs in beels and large ponds, or in crevices in old cemented staircase in pond bank underneath water body. Males exhibit parental care, guarding the growing larvae. In broodstock ponds, *C. chitala* can be habituated to feeds like *Glossogobius giuris, Puntius ticto, Puntius sophore* in dead-but-fresh condition. Sri Roy opined that if the 18mm stage larvae, after absorption of yolk sac, are transferred to nursery ponds @ 40-50 lakh per hectare, they will reach to 4-6 inches size within next 45-60 days of rearing. Ponds should be sufficiently productive; a high concentration of zooplankton as well as dissolved oxygen (7.5-8.0ppm) should persist in nursery pond throughout the first 2-3 weeks. Application in three split doses of a mixture of 75kg ground nut oil cake, 25kg cow dung and 5kg single super phosphate per 25 decimal water area can lead to sufficient abundance of zooplankton in nurseries. Pumping and flushing of water upto a distance from pond embankment for continuous ten days (10-12 hours per day) will bring about ideal DO level in pond.

Advanced fry of *C. chitala* can be stocked in farm ponds (1.5-2.5% of the total number) in association with Indian major carps and exotic carps; fingerlings or yearlings of major carps must be 6-7 inches in length. Adults of self-recruiting fishes like *A. mola, P. ticto, P. sophore, Tilapia nilotica* must be stocked in pond 2-3 months in advance, such that young ones of these fishes produced by means of their prolific reproduction naturally may serve as food of growing *C. chitala*. Fingerlings attain about 2.2kg in one year; the 2.5-3.0 inch sized fry stage will attain 1.5kg in polyculture system. In *C. chitala* broodstock ponds, many farmers stock 10,000nos. of adult *T. nilotica* (1M : 2F) and 25kg of *A. mola* and *Puntius* sp. combined; the early stages of *T. nilotica* and adult minnows serve as food of adult *C. chitala*. Natural repository of the 'food/prey' of *C. chitala* is renewed and maintained throughout its broodstock management period. Partial replacement of water (10-15%) is done every fortnight. *C. chitala* brooders may be stocked in 0.08ha water body, which is their breeding tank; wooden planks 27 inches in length and 7 inches wide may be placed inside this pond as substratum for eggs.

(iii) *C. chitala* as policefish

A fish farmer in Assam had stocked fish fingerlings in his pond @ 9000nos/ha; it comprised 30% *Labeo rohita*, 20% *Cirrhinus mrigala*, 30% *Catla catla*, 10% *Hypophthalmichthys molitrix*, 5% *Cyprinus carpio* and the rest 5% comprised fingerlings of *Cirrhinus reba, C. chitala* (4-5 inches) and of *T. nilotica. C. chitala* fingerlings have been pre-determinedly stocked in major carp ponds, as *C. chitala* frequently chases bigger fingerlings of major carps or the yearlings with an intention of predation, although the former fail to get hold of the latter due to large size. Chasing impact of the 'policefish' *C. chitala* has a beneficial impact on growth of major carps in farm ponds. At the end of one year, *L. rohita* and *C. mrigala* attained body weight of 1kg on average, *C. catla* 1.5kg, *H. molitrix* and *C. chitala* 2kg. The farmer fed dead-but-fresh freshwater prawns of small size and less economic importance to growing *C. chitala*.

(iv) Growth in ponds

In 2012, a farmer at Kushmandi Block in Dakshin Dinajpur district, WB had stocked 1700nos. *C. chitala* fingerlings (6-8inches; 50-60gm) in his

130 decimal carp culture pond (5-6 feet deep). At the same time he stocked 1200nos. of *L. rohita* fingerlings, 500nos. *C. catla* and 200nos. *C. mrigala*. Previous to this, he stocked adults of *T. nilotica*. There was provision of letting in freshwater from a nearby beel into this pond *via* sluice gate; fishes like small *Puntius* sp. and *Esomus danricus* gain their entry into pond during water exchange. Farm-made floating-type pelleted feed comprising a mixture of groundnut oil cake, maize dust, rice bran and fish meal was provided to growing major carps. At the end of ten months, he could harvest 3000kg marketable-sized *C. chitala* from this pond (1500 pieces survived, average weight 2kg). His *C. catla* weighed 2.0-2.5kg, *L. rohita* 700-800gm, *C. mrigala* 600-700gm; additionally he could harvest 500kg of *T. nilotica*, average weight being 200gm.

A farmer has succeeded in rearing *Sperata seenghala* and *C. chitala* in polyculture system. Spawn of *H. molitrix*, *Ctenopharyngodon idella* and *Labeo bata* obtained from carp hatchery, which have a fast growth rate but are not high-priced, have been stocked in a nursery pond and reared till fry stage (1.0-1.5 inches) for 16-18 days prior to stocking of *C. chitala* fingerlings. Those were stocked in *C. chitala* pond. He stocked 2500nos. *C. chitala* fingerlings (4-5 inches) and 1000nos. *S. seenghala* juveniles of similar size in his 125-130 decimal pond having 8-10 feet depth. The farmer had taken six ponds on lease for fish farming; he practiced *C. chitala* farming (in monoculture or polyculture system) in two or three of them and the rest of the ponds were utilized for raising live food of *C. chitala, i.e.*, production of fry of above-mentioned carps. He seldom fed early stages of *Anabas testudineus* to *C. chitala*. It likes to chase and predate upon the small fishes or fry stages of carps which inhabit and move on the upper water column/ upper layer of pond, while *S. seenghala* feeds upon small fishes and prawns inhabiting the lower column of pond. Some percentage of carp fry that were released in *C. chitala* pond survives and grows upto adulthood (1.5-2.0kg) in short period of time. Floating-type pelleted feed is provided to them, harvested along with marketable-sized *C. chitala* and *S. seenghala* and sold in market; it fetches an additional income for the farmer.

The farmer sold *C. chitala* of 4-5kg size at Rs. 500-700/- per kg in retail markets, those of 2.0-2.5kg are sold at Rs. 400-450/- per kg. First the bigger ones are selectively harvested, the smaller ones are harvested two months later, by the time which attain an average weight of 3.5kg. A 4.0-4.5kg specimen can devour growing major carps of 200-250gm size. If it is found that some major carps in *C. chitala* pond have grown upto this size, those are brought out and shifted to new pond for further growth. Even if some carps in the nursery pond (earmarked for production of live food of *C. chitala*) grow upto this size, those are allowed to grow upto adulthood. *C. chitala* may escape from culture pond at times of heavy rain and inundated condition; precautions must be taken by the farmer for this.

Officials of Krishi Vigyan Kendra, Murshidabad district had set up a model *C. chitala* farming unit, a 1.50 acre pond had been partitioned into two (one-third and two-third portions) by erecting mosquito net barrier supported by split bamboo. A total 5kg male and 15kg female *T. mossambicus* (adult form) were released in the one-third portion. In addition to this, 3-4 cups of spawn of *H. molitrix* (100ml capacity each) were liberated in this territory. After 21-25 days, *C. chitala* fry of 2.5-3.0 inch size were stocked in the two-third portion. A production rate of 30quintals of marketable-sized *C. chitala* per ha water body per year has been demonstrated. A fish farmer of Bankura district had stocked a few *C. chitala* fingerlings in his carp ponds, which has attained body weight of 2.5kg individually in one year. He sold each of the *C. chitala* at Rs. 750/- (@ Rs. 300/- per kg), which is equivalent to selling price of 7kg of adult *L. rohita*.

(v) Riverine seeds in Bangladesh

At Mymensingh district in Bangladesh, the three-day old (18-20mm size) *C. chitala* larvae are captured from Padma river and Arialetha river, those are counted with the help of large steel spoon and sold to fish farmers. About 7-10 small blackish vertical bands are found on lateral sides of the tender stages. Matured *C. chitala* breeds during June-July in river Padma, fingerlings of 4 inch size are also available in river Padma. According to fish seed collectors, the 20-22 days old *C. chitala* measure 2.0-2.5 inches. If 10,000nos. of *C. chitala* seeds (20mm) are stocked in nurseries of 10 decimal size, then it will reach to about 3 inches within next 22 days. Zooplankton *Daphnia* sp. and *Moina* sp. are fed to them. The nursery ponds are carefully fenced on all four sides with blue mosquito nets in order to avoid predation of frogs and snakes (which is very likely) upon early stages of *C. chitala*. The 2.5-3.0 inch and/or 4-5 inch stages obtained from rivers are counted one by one, kept in large aluminium Hundi (18 inch diameter), green banana leaves are immersed into water and are supplied to fish farmers. *C. chitala* fingerlings aggregate underneath banana leaves inside Hundi; those may be transported to far away distances and remain safe in this condition for 6-7days, but 40-50% water replacement has to be done everyday.

(vi) Stocking density

In monoculture systems in large ponds or well-managed beels, *C. chitala* fingerlings (3-6 inches) must be stocked @ 5-6nos./decimal water area. For every 5 pieces of *C. chitala* fingerlings, 35-40nos. of adult *Tilapia nilotica* (males and females) must be stocked well in advance in culture system. The 1.0-1.5 inch size of this forage fish will be progressively fed by growing *C. chitala*, and availability of the food throughout culture period will be assured. The 18-20mm size will reach to 4-6 inches within 1-2 months of rearing, and then it can be stocked in grow-out systems. In Thailand, *C. chitala* of size 30gm had been reared in submerged-type cages of size one cubic metre for three months; 50 fingerlings had been stocked in each cage. Those were fed a mixture of fish meal and rice bran @ 8% of body weight daily. *C. chitala* attained body weight of 178gm on average at the end of 90 days.

(vii) Many species combined farming

Members of Gajna Fishery Cooperative Society in Hanskhali Block of Nadia district, WB had stocked fingerlings of eight species of major carps in a 5ha pond; those were *C. catla* (3500nos, total wt. 114kg), *H. molitrix* (1000nos, total wt. 35kg), *Aristichthys nobilis* (500nos, total wt. 30kg), *C. idella* (250nos, total wt. 25kg), *L. rohita* (3000nos, total wt. 100kg), *C. mrigala* (1500nos, total wt. 75kg), *L. calbasu* (500nos, total wt. 30kg), *C. carpio var communis* (1000nos, total wt. 50kg). In addition to these, the non-carp species stocked were *Channa striatus* and *C. punctatus* (500nos, total wt. 8kg), *C. chitala* (300nos, total wt. 10kg), *Mystus vittatus* (500nos, total wt. 5kg) and *Pangasius pangasius* (250nos, total wt. 3kg). The pond was manured and fertilized in routinewise manner. At the end of one year culture period, the production obtained of different fishes per hectare water body is accordingly: *C. catla* 3400kg, *H. molitrix* 3000kg, *C. idella* 1200kg, *A. nobilis* 1800kg, *L. rohita* 2500kg, *C. mrigala* 1600kg, *L. calbasu* 400kg, *C. carpio* 2500kg, *Channa* sp. 60kg, *C. chitala* 50kg, *M. vittatus* 18kg, *P. pangasius* 10kg, prawns and crabs 20kg. *C. chitala* in major carp culture pond helps in controlling the weed fishes in pond; thereby it minimizes the loss of feed to the cultured fishes. Also in the process, dissolved oxygen budget is maintained.

(viii) Farming in ponds of FPG and SHG

Under the initiative of Assistant Director of Fisheries, Coochbehar district, WB during 2000-2011, *C. chitala* fingerlings have been provided to members of Arampur Fishermen Cooperative Society in Tufanganj-I Block, Haribolhat Janapriyo Mohila Group in Sitai Block, Rampur Anchal Fishermen Cooperative Society in Tufanganj-II Block, Guriahati Fish Production Group in Coochbehar-I Block, Ankur Swayambhar Group in Coochbehar-II Block, Bamanhat Fish Production Group in Dinhata-II Block, Ashokbari Fishermen Cooperative Society in Mathabhanga-I Block, Nishiganj Fishermen Cooperative Society in Mathabhanga-II Block, Balasi Youth Swanirbhar Gosthi in Mathabhanga-II Block. The practice and technology of semi-intensive *C. chitala* farming was discussed with the members of different Groups, thereafter potassium permanganate treated *C. chitala* fingerlings (3-4 inches) were liberated in their ponds.

(ix) Freshwater prawn as food

During April-May 2006, two fish farmers at Vill. Chapahat, Kushmandi Block, Dakshin Dinajpur district had stocked 35nos. of *C. chitala* fingerlings (5-6 inches) in a 225 decimal carp culture pond, which were purchased from *Goldar* of Malda district, each costing Rs. 45/-. They were mainly carp fingerling producers, stocked 400kg of fry of *L. rohita, C. catla, C. mrigala* and *C. carpio* in the pond, all of 2.5-3.0 inch size. Bigger fingerlings (15-16nos. weighing 1kg; 5-6 inch size) are selectively harvested after 60-75 days, and again 1 quintal of carp fry is released. In this way it is continued following the multiple stocking – multiple harvesting strategy. At the end of one year, *C. chitala* in the pond attained body weight of 3.0-3.5kg individually, 30 nos. could be harvested. Those were sold at Dalkhola fish market @ Rs 650/- per kg. According to the farmers, the advanced fry of major carps that were stocked in the pond are the yearlings, *i.e.*, spawn produced in previous year. *C. chitala* grew by devouring a small amount of major carp fry, as because there was abundant natural stock of the small-sized, slow-moving whitish prawn *Macrobrachium lamarrei* in the pond. These prawns are 3.0-4.5cm in length, light in weight and are highly preferred by growing *C. chitala* as food. Thus *C. chitala* did not caused much damage to the quantity of growing fry stages of IMC in the pond. Initially when the 9-10 months old finger-sized IMC are harvested from a separate pond and stocked in this culture pond, along with it, *M. lamarrei* enters in pond, reproduce and proliferate in number. These naturally-occurring small prawns are preferred by common people also, sold at Rs. 40/- per 100gm in village retail markets.

The consumer requirement of *C. chitala* is primarily met from the capture fishery of rivers, floodplain wetlands and wetlands locally known as jheels and beels. There is a strong need to develop package of practices for its controlled farming in big ponds in order to ensure its regular supply (Jahan, 2015; Kohinoor, 2012; Sarkar *et al.*, 2006). The fish is now rarely to be found, but was considered 'majestic' even 35-40 years back.

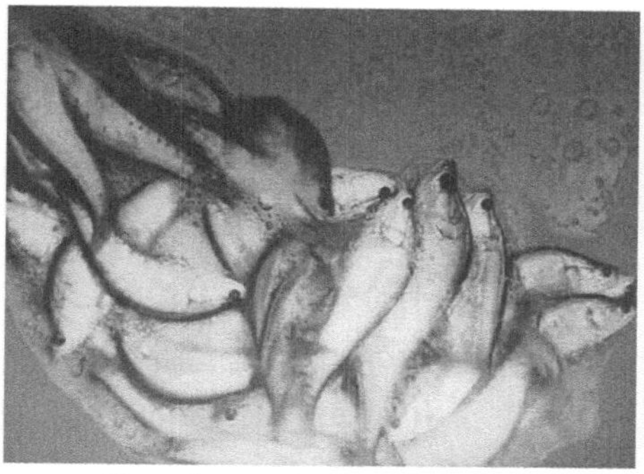

Fingerlings of *Chitala chitala*

Fertilized eggs of *Chitala chitala*

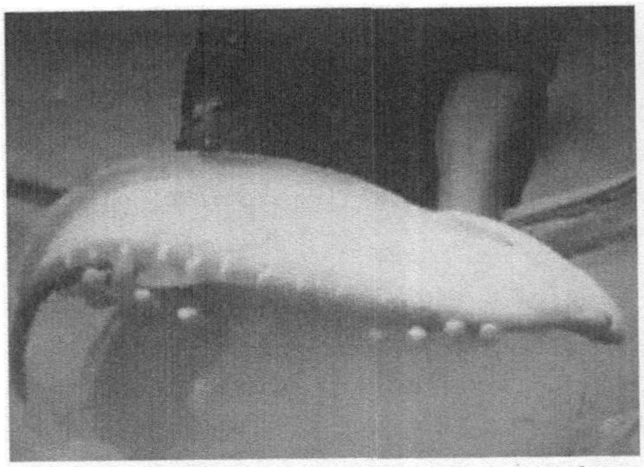

Chitala chitala harvested from a pond

Matured *Chitala chitala* (6kg size)

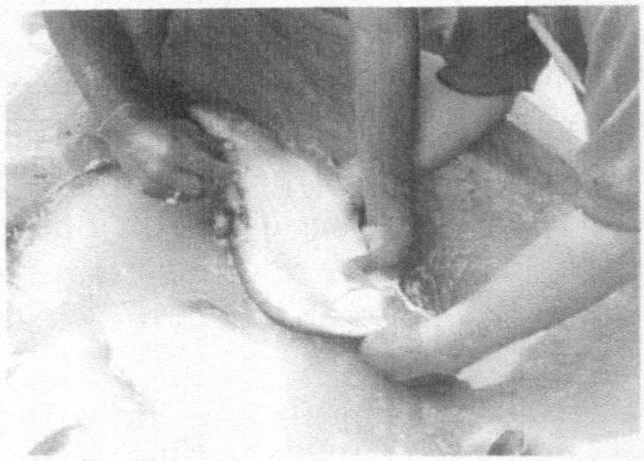

Induced breeding at ICAR-NBFGR, Lucknow

Pond reared *Chitala chitala*

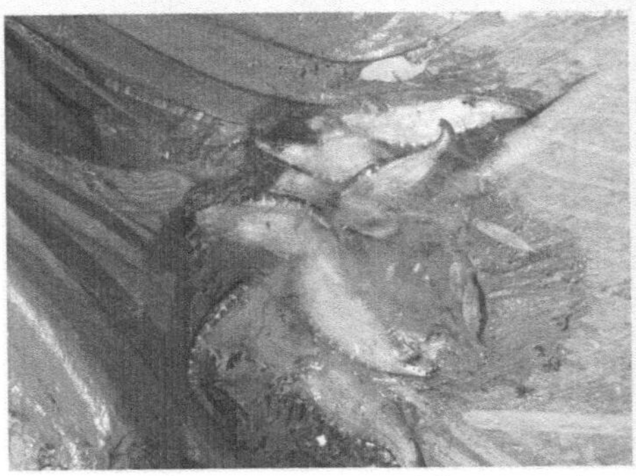

Chitala chitala harvested from pond

Chitala chitala in aquarium (1.5-2.0kg)

Morphology of Alimentary Tracts of Small Freshwater Fishes

In curiosity, during March-April 2017, author made a small investigation into the variations in morphology of alimentary tracts of few small indigenous freshwater fishes, which commonly occur in nature and are not more than 9cm size. The particulars of the observations are mentioned here in tabular form.

Name of Fish	Length of Fish	Length of Intestine	Particulars
Chanda nama	8.2cm	3.7cm	Short thick-walled intestine, stomach absent
Salmostoma bacaila	8.6cm	8.4cm	Tube-like intestine, stomach absent
Sperata seenghala	8.6cm	3.2cm	Short thick-walled intestine, prominent cardiac stomach present
Puntius ticto	8.5cm	14.4cm	Short, slender intestine, stomach absent
Colisa fasciatus	9.8cm	37.0cm	Small bulb-like stomach, two pyloric caeca, thread like long intestine
Amblypharyngodon mola	7.2cm	23.5cm	Stomach absent, long thread-like intestine
Mystus vittatus	8.8cm	4.2cm	Short thick-walled intestine, prominent stomach present

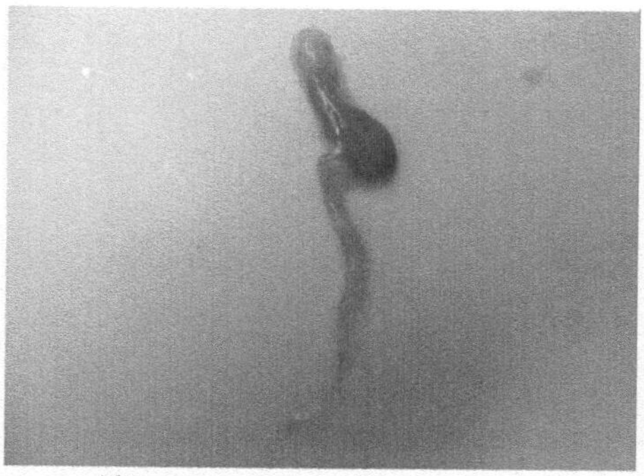

Alimentary tract of *S. seenghala*

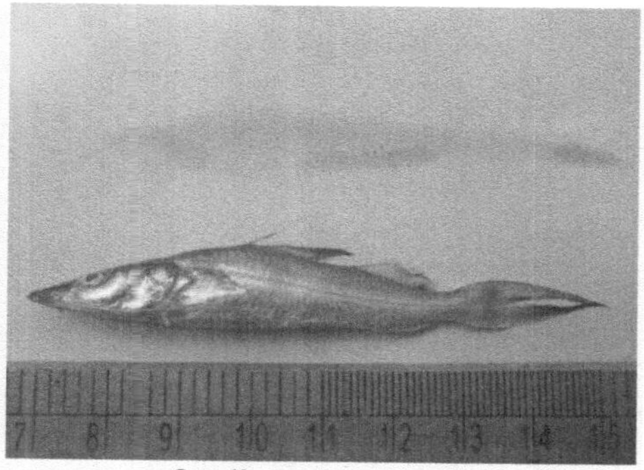

Small-sized *S. seenghala*

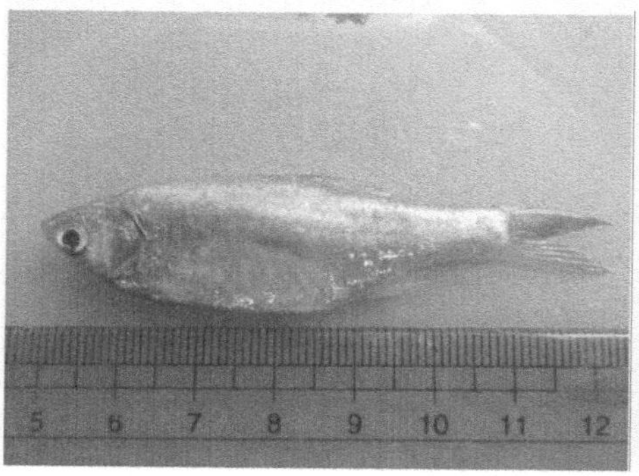

Amblypharyngodon mola

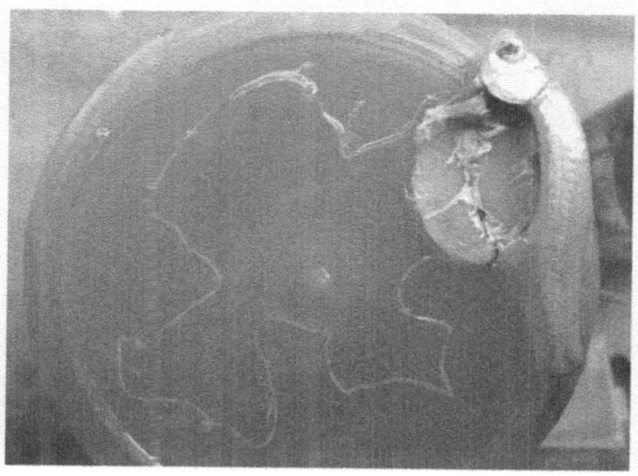

Displayed intestine of *A. mola* (1)

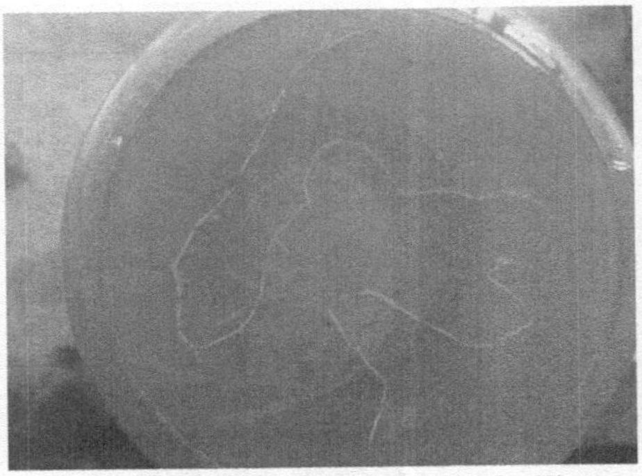

Displayed intestine of *A. mola* (2)

Chanda nama

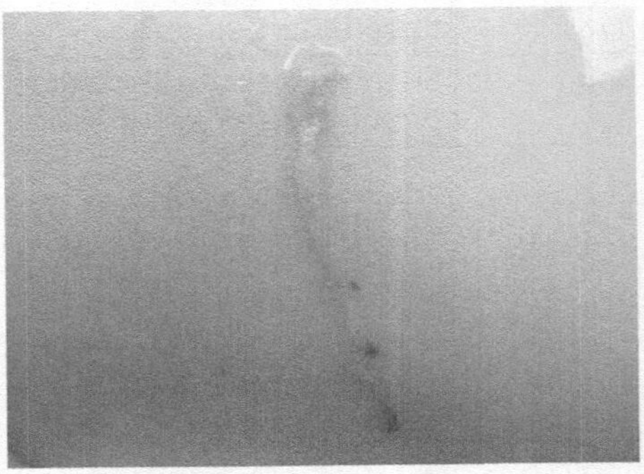

Alimentary tract of *Chanda nama* (1)

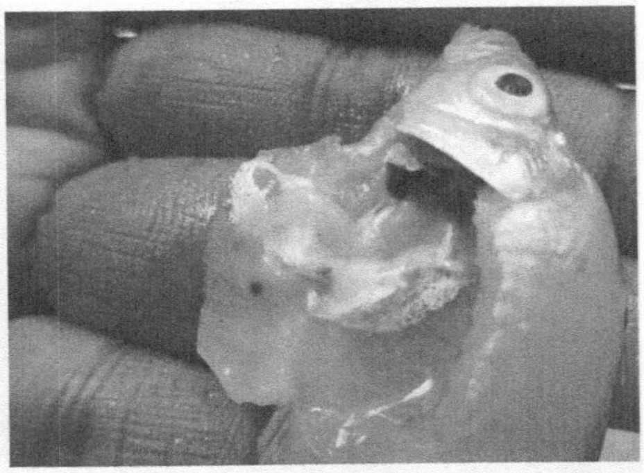

Alimentary tract of *C. nama* (another view)

Salmostoma bacaila

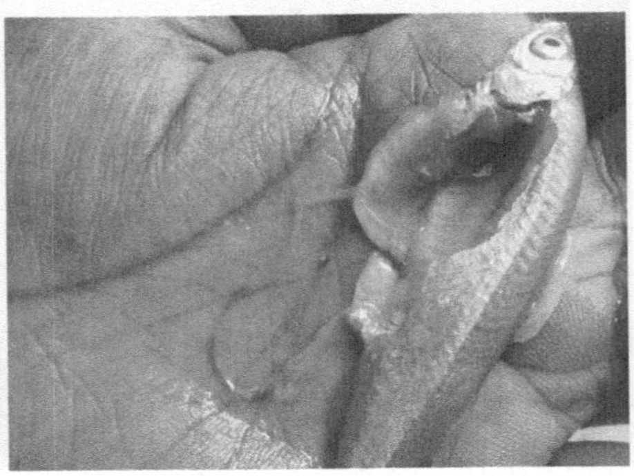

Intestine of *S. bacaila*

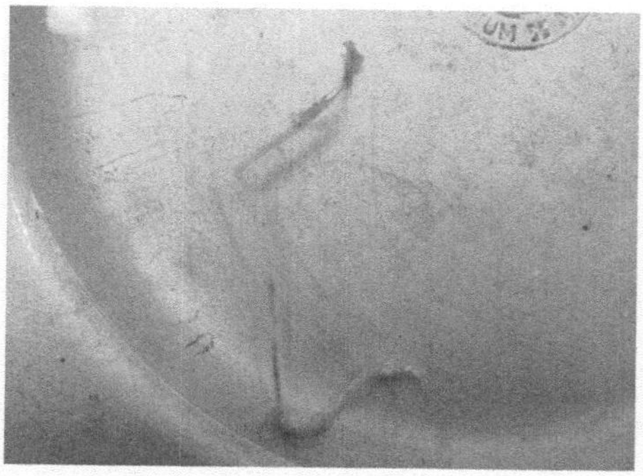

Displayed intestine of *S. bacaila*

Colisa fasciatus

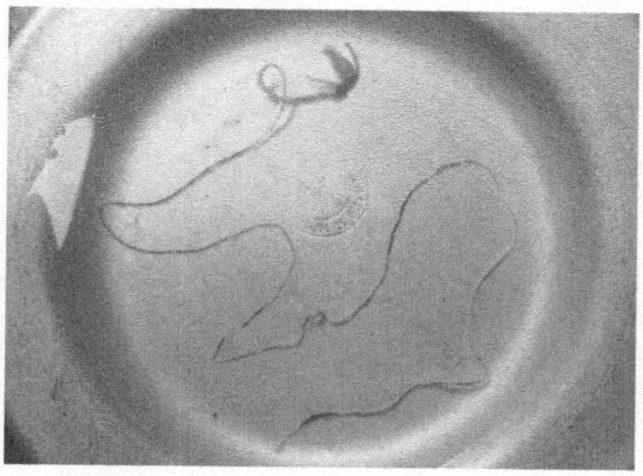

Displayed intestine of *C. fasciatus*

Puntius ticto

Displayed intestine of *P. ticto*

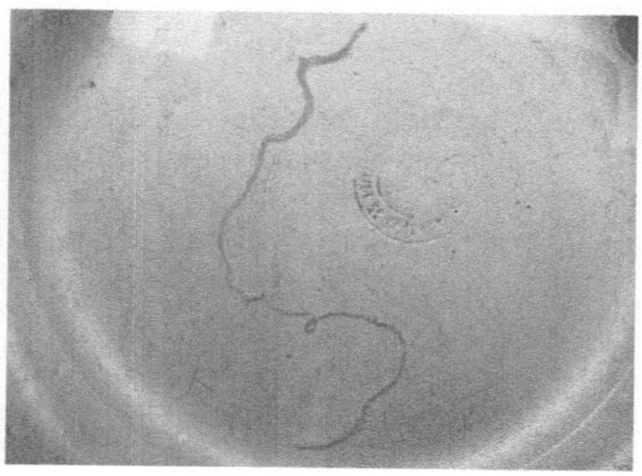

Intestine of *P. ticto* (another view)

Mystus vittatus

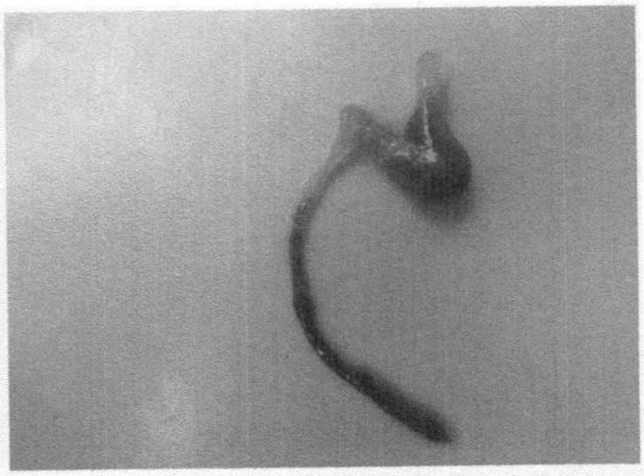

Diplayed alimentary tract of *M. vittatus*

Alimentary tract of *M. vittatus*

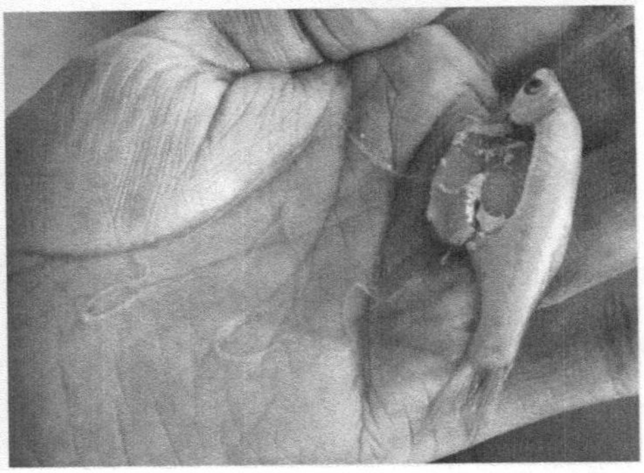

Intestine of *A. mola* on hand

Photographs: Subrato Ghosh

REFERENCES

Arthur, R. I., Bhaumik, U., Pandit, P. K., Saha, S., Garaway, C. J. and Ghosh, T. (2005): *FMSP Project Document R8292* (Funded by the UK Department for International Development, 2005), 1-98.

Bera, T. K., Patra, B. C. and Bhattacharjee, M. (2014): *Research Journal of Animal, Veterinary and Fishery Sciences*, 2(7): 1-5.

Biswas, B. (2016): Fish Farming in Moyna Fields (Bengali Version), *Panchayati Raj*, 7: 28-30.

Ghosh, T.K., Moitra, A., Kunwar, G.K. and Munshi, J.S.D. (1986): Bimodal Oxygen uptake in a Freshwater Air-breathing Fish *Notopterus chitala, Japanese Journal of Ichthyology*, 33(3): 280-285.

Jahan, D.A., Rasid, J., Khan, Md. M. and Mahmud, Y. (2015): Early Embryonic and Larval Development of Threatened Humped Featherback *Chitala chitala* (Ham), *Trends in Fisheries Research*, 4(2): 1-7.

Jena, J.K., Das, P.C. and Sarangi, N. (2007): Composite Fish Culture in Freshwater Ponds, *Indian Farming*, 56(10): 25-28.

Kohinoor, A.H.M., Jahan, D.A., Khan, M.M., Islam, M.S. and Hussain, M.G. (2012): Reproductive Biology of Featherback *Notopterus chitala* Cultured in a Pond of Bangladesh, *Int. J. Agril. Res. Innov. & Tech.*, 2 (1): 26-31.

Natarajan, A.V. and Ghosh, A. (1980): *Bull. ICAR-Central Inland Fisheries Research Institute, Barrackpore, India*, 32: 1-10.

Radheyshyam (2007): Principles of Rural Aquaculture, *ICAR Sponsored Short Course in New Initiatives in Aquaculture Extension* (ICAR-CIFA Publication, Bhubaneswar), 12-21.

Sahu, A.S. (2014): *Geography Journal*, ID 401324, 1-9.

Sarkar, U.K., Deepak, P.K., Negi, R.S., Singh, S. and Kapoor, D. (2006): Captive Breeding of Endangered Fish *Chitala chitala* for species Conservation and Sustainable Utilization, *Biodiversity and Conservation (Springer Publication)*, 15: 3679-3589.

Pages: 72-88

Food Technology and Research Advancement
Edited by: **Dr. Avnish Chauhan and Dr. Pawan Kumar 'Bharti'**
ISBN: 978-93-86841-49-0
Edition: **2018**
Published by: **Discovery Publishing House Pvt. Ltd., New Delhi (India)**

6

Quinoa
The Super Food

Priyanka Shukla

Introduction

Quinoa (from Quechua *kinwa* or *kinuwa*) is the common name for *Chenopodium quinoa*, a flowering plant in the amaranth family Amaranthaceae. It is an herbaceous annual plant grown as a grain crop primarily for its edible seeds. Because it is not a grass, it is a pseudocereal rather than a true cereal. Quinoa is closely related to the edible plants beetroot, spinach, and amaranth (*Amaranthus spp.*), another pseudocereal which it closely resembles.

After harvest, the seeds are processed to remove the outer coating that contains bitter-tasting saponins. They are gluten-free. Generally, the seeds are cooked the same way as rice and can be used in a wide range of dishes. The leaves are sometimes eaten as a leaf vegetable, much like amaranth, but commercial availability of quinoa greens is limited.

When cooked, the nutrient composition is comparable to common cereals like wheat and rice, supplying a moderate amount of dietary fiber and minerals. Quinoa is a complete source of protein, and contains all nine essential amino acids. The Food and Agriculture Organization of the United Nations declared 2013 to be the "International Year of Quinoa".

History

Quinoa originated in the Andean region of Peru, Bolivia, Ecuador, Colombia and Chile, and was domesticated 3,000 to 4,000 years ago for human consumption in the Lake Titicaca basin of Peru and Bolivia, though archaeological evidence shows a non-domesticated association with pastoral herding 5,200 to 7,000 years ago.

National Institute of Food Technology, Entrepreneurship and Management, Kundli - 131 028 (Haryana) (India)

Description of the Plant

Quinoa Plant before Flowering

It is a dicotyledonous annual plant, usually about 1-2 m (3.3-6.6 ft) high. It has broad, generally powdery, hairy, lobed leaves, normally arranged alternately. The woody central stem is branched or unbranched depending on the variety and may be green, red or purple. The flowering panicles arise from the top of the plant or from leaf axils along the stem. Each panicle has a central axis from which a secondary axis emerges either with flowers (amaranthiform) or bearing a tertiary axis carrying the flowers (glomeruliform).The green hypogynous flowers have a simple perianth and are generally self-fertilizing. The fruits (seeds) are about 2 mm (0.08 in) in diameter and of various colors—from white to red or black, depending on the cultivar.

Distribution

It is believed to have been domesticated in the Peruvian Andes from wild or weed populations of the same species. There are non-cultivated quinoa plants (*Chenopodium quinoa* var. *melanospermum*) that grow in the area it is cultivated; these may either be related to wild predecessors, or they could be descendants of cultivated plants. Currently, quinoa cultivation occurs in more than 50 countries, including France, England, Sweden, Denmark, Holland, and Italy. Quinoa is also being developed successfully in Kenya, India, and the United States, and it continues to grow in popularity as a health food in North America, Europe, Australia, and Japan.

Due to quinoa's adaptability to different environments as well as its dietary benefits, it has the potential to lessen dependence on staples such as wheat and rice. It can also have benefits for the local environment. Because of these properties, quinoa can potentially be grown in food deserts or places that suffer from food insecurity.

Processing/Manufacturing

Quinoa is ready for harvest when the leaves have fallen and only the dried seed heads remain. Seeds can be simply stripped upwards off of the stalk with a gloved hand. In the case of frost, a seed past the green stage will probably not be damaged, and harvesting can happen a day or two later. However, extremely hot weather and warm nights can prevent fruit set. Near germination, the weather needs to be watched, since rain can cause the dry seeds to germinate. If the heads are not completely dry, they can be harvested when the seed can barely be indented with a fingernail. These seeds should be thoroughly dried before storage.

Quinoa should be cleaned with screens, by winnowing, with a fan, or with other blowing devices. It is important to dry the crop, which can be done with trays in the hot sun or near an indoor heat source so that it doesn't mold in storage. The seeds should be stirred occasionally until as dry as possible, then they can be stored in an airtight container in a cool, dry place.

Quinoa grains have a bitter saponin coating that deters birds and insects from eating them and that needs to be removed before consumption. This can either be accomplished by polishing – which removes the saponin coat but also refines it like white rice, white flour, or pearled barley – or washed in a three-step process that cleans the saponin without removing vital nutrients. Polished quinoa has half the fiber of washed quinoa, along with lower protein, vitamin, and mineral levels. The saponin that is removed has commercial uses as pharmaceutical steroids, soaps, detergents, shampoos, cosmetics, and synthetic hormones.

There are ongoing breeding attempts to develop saponin-free quinoa varieties. Currently, quinoa can be classified as sweet (saponin-free or containing less than 0.11 percent saponin) or bitter (more than 0.11 percent saponin). While the sweet varieties require less processing before market, they may be more susceptible to bird production.

Once processed and properly dried, quinoa can last for several years stored in a dry kitchen cabinet.

Financial Analysis

A gram of quinoa seeds will sow around 50 feet (15 m) of the row, with an acre requiring about a pound of seed.

From 1992 to2010, cultivated area of quinoa in the main producing countries (Bolivia, Peru, and Ecuador) almost doubled while production almost tripled. In 2009, production in the Andean region reached approximately 70,000 tons. (FAO) In 2013, the United States imported nearly 70 million pounds of quinoa, mostly from Peru and Bolivia.

The price of quinoa has also increased dramatically, nearly tripling between 2006 and 2013 due to high demand in the United States and Europe. Prices started to drop in 2015 indicating a better balance of supply and demand, but there is nevertheless a strong market for quinoa even today.

Quinoa leaves can be eaten as a leaf, like an amaranth, though the current commercial availability is limited. In addition, the thinning from quinoa production can be incorporated into salads. Quinoa leaves can also be used for livestock feed.

Grain quinoa can be used in side dishes similarly to rice, flaked as a breakfast cereal, added to snack foods and pasta, in multigrain infant cereals, and in ground flour. Because quinoa is gluten free, it reduces bread volume by more than 10 percent when baked.

Starch grains in quinoa are very small, much like those in taro, and it contains less amylose than most commercial starches. It can be used for cream substitutes and dusting in some candy applications.

Because it is hardy and can grow anywhere from sea level to 4,000 meters above sea level, quinoa could be beneficial to improve food security in at-risk regions.

Saponins and Oxalic Acid

Red quinoa, cooked

Quinoa's outer seed coat (pericarp) is rich in bitter saponins, natural detergent molecules found throughout the plant kingdom. Saponins are comprised of a steroidal or triterpenoid aglycone (mainly oleanolic acid, heder-agenin, phytolaccagenic acid, and serjanic acid), with one or more sugar moieties. Sugars can be linked to the aglycone at the C-3 and C-28 positions. The major sugar moities include glucose, galactose, arabinose, glucuronic acid, and xylose. Saponin chemistry of quinoa seeds is highly diverse. Madl and others (2006) identified 19 previously reported and 68 novel saponin compounds in quinoa using nano-HPLC electrospray ionization multistage tandem mass spectrometry (nLC-ESI-MS/MS) from a complex triterpene saponin crude extract of quinoa seed coats. Saponins possess several common properties, including high foaming capacity in aqueous solutions, hemolytic activity when in direct contact with blood cells, and the formation of complexes with cholesterol and other steroidal components of cell membranes. Therefore, they are useful for crop protection from microbial infection and insect/bird herbivory, which facilitates organic production of this crop. The synthesis of secondary metabolites, including saponins, is a response to environmental factors and part of an adaptative strategy for abiotic stress tolerance. Triterpenoid saponins are synthesized via the isoprenoid pathway, leading to the formation of triterpenoid skeletons such as oleanane, ursane, lupeol, or dammarane. Subsequent structural modifications, including oxidation, substitution, and glycosylation, are mediated by various enzymes.

Since saponins interfere with quinoa's palatability and digestibility, they must be removed before consumption.

Some varieties of quinoa have been bred to contain lower saponin content, termed "sweet" quinoa Most of the grain sold commercially has been processed to remove this coating. This bitterness has beneficial effects during cultivation, as it deters birds and therefore the plant requires minimal protection.[14] The genetic control of bitterness involves quantitative inheritance.[13] Although lowering the saponin content through selective breeding to produce sweeter, more palatable varieties is complicated by ~10% cross-pollination, it is a major goal of quinoa breeding programs, which may include genetic engineering.

The toxicity category rating of the saponins in quinoa treats them as mild eye and respiratory irritants and as a low gastrointestinal irritant. In South America, the saponins have many uses, including their use as a detergent for clothing and washing, and as a folk medicine antiseptic for skin injuries.

Additionally, high levels of oxalic acid are in the leaves and stems of all species of the *Chenopodium* genus, and in the related genera of the Amaranthaceae family. The risks associated with quinoa are minimal, provided it is properly prepared and the leaves are not eaten to excess.

Nutritional Quality of Quinoa

Quinoa has an excellent balance between oil, fat, and protein and has a unique composition of amino acids (Table 6.1). One of the key essential amino acids, lysine, which is relatively uncommon within the plant kingdom, comes very close to the standards set by the FAO for human nutritional needs. Table 6.2 compares several major grains with quinoa. Quinoa compares favorably with all the grains and has a good balance between protein and carbohydrates. The pericarp of the seed contains as much as 6% saponins. The saponins are plant glycosides which are probably utilized by the plant as a predator deterrent. These compounds, which are bitter tasting, must be removed prior to consumption. Saponins may interfere with digestion by directly interacting with the digestive enzymes, preventing absorption of nutrients. Removal of the saponins can be accomplished by rinsing the quinoa in cold water or mechanically rubbing the outer layer from the seed. An improved variety called "sajama" has been develolped in Bolivia; it is free of saponins and can be processed directly for food (FAO, 1989). There are agreat number of color varieties found in quinoa. The colors are probably due to habitat (eco-type) differences. Table 6.3 illustrates the nutritional variation among the varieties of quinoa. Additional benefits of quinoa are the mild, pleasant taste and ease of preparation. It is usually cooked like rice and has a very mild taste with a texture similar to cooked barley. In addition, quinoa can be eaten like a hot breakfast cereal, as a side dish in dinner, or put in soups, salads, pilafs and desserts. With the increasing availability of quinoa many unique cooking methods are being developed, multiplying the ways this food can be prepared. With all these benefits, quinoa may allow greater versatility in meeting the nutritional needs of humans on long-term space missions.

Protein

Quinoa's protein quantity depends on the variety, with a protein range of 10.4 to 17.0 percent of its edible portion. While generally higher in protein quantity than most grains, quinoa is known more for its protein quality. Protein is made up of amino acids, of which eight are considered essential for both children and adults. As shown in table 6.1, when compared to the FAO's recommended essential amino acid scoring pattern for 3 to 10 year old children, quinoa exceeds the recommendation for all eight essential amino acids. In contrast to quinoa, most grains are low in the essential amino acid lysine, while most legumes are low in sulphuric amino acids methionine and cysteine.

Table 6.1: Essential amino acid profile (g]16g nitrogen) of field-grown quinoa compared with wheat, soybean and the FAO standard amino acid profile for human nutrition[19]

Amino Acid	Quinoa	Wheat	Soybean	FAO
Isoleucine	4.0	3.8	4.7	4.0
Leucine	6.8	6.6	7.0	7.0
Lysine	5.1	2.5	6.3	5.5
Phenylalanine	4.6	4.5	4.6	–
Tyrosine	3.8	3.0	3.6	–
Phenylalanine plus Tyrosine	8.4	7.5	8.2	6.0
Cyst(e)ine	2.4	2.2	1.4	–
Methionine	2.2	1.7	1.4	–
Cystine plus Methionine	4.6	3.9	2.8	3.5
Threonine	3.7	2.9	3.9	4.0
Tryptophan	1.2	1.3	1.2	1.0
Valine	4.8	4.7	4.9	5.0

Dietary Fibre

A recent study of four quinoa varieties found the dietary fibre in raw quinoa to range from about 13.6 to 16.0 grams per 100 grams dry weight.Most of the dietary fibre was insoluble, with a range of 12.0 to 14.4 grams compared to 1.4 to 1.6 grams of soluble fibre per 100 grams dry weight. Similar to quinoa's total protein value, its dietary fibre value is generally higher than that of most grains, but lower than that of legumes. Dietary fibre is the indigestible portion of plant foods, and it is important for good digestion and to prevent against constipation.

Fat

As shown in table 6.2, quinoa contains more fat (6.3 g) per 100 grams dry weight than beans (1.1 g), maize (4.7 g), rice (2.2 g) and wheat (2.3 g).

Fat is an important source of calories, and aids in the absorption of fat soluble vitamins. Of quinoa's total fat content, over 50 percent comes from essential polyunsaturated fatty acids linoleic (omega-6) and linolenic (omega-3) acid. Linoleic and linolenic acid are considered essential fatty acids because they cannot be produced by the body. Quinoa's fatty acids have been shown to maintain their quality because of quinoa's naturally high value of vitamin E, which acts as a natural antioxidant.

Table 6.2: Nutritional analysis of field-grown quinoa compared with various grains

Crop	% Water	% Crude Protein	% Fat	% Carbohydrate	% Fiber	% Ash
Barley	9.0	14.7	1.1	67.8	2.5	5.5
Buckwheat	10.7	18.5	4.9	43.5	18.2	4.2
Corn	13.5	8.7	3.9	70.9	1.7	1.2
Millet	11.0	11.9	4.0	68.6	2.0	2.0
Oats	13.5	11.1	4.6	57.6	10.3	2.9
Quinoa	12.6	13.8	5.0	59.7	4.1	3.4
Rice	11.0	7.3	0.4	80.4	0.4	0.5
Rye	13.5	11.5	1.2	69.6	2.6	1.5
Wheat	10.9	13.0	1.6	70.0	2.7	1.8

Table 6.3: Nutritional analysis of several varieties of quinoa

Composition	Red	White	Yellow
Carbohydrate	68.4	74.3	68.5
Protein	15.35	14.05	15.95
Fat	7.5	7.15	6.15
Ash	3.05	2.4	3.65
Saponin	3.7	3.4	3.9

Minerals

On average quinoa is a better source of minerals than most grains as shown in table 6.4. Quinoa is especially a good source of iron, magnesium and zinc when compared to the daily mineral recommendations. A lack of iron is often one of the most common nutrition deficiencies. However quinoa, like all plant foods, does contain certain non-nutritive components that can reduce its mineral content and absorption. Most notable are its saponins, which are found on the outer layer of the quinoa seed and are usually removed during processing to remove their bitter taste. Quinoa is also high in the compound oxalate, which can bind to minerals such as calcium and magnesium, reducing their absorption in the body.

Table 6.4: Mineral content of Quinoa and selected foods, mg/100g dry weight

Minerals	Quinoa	Maize	Rice	Wheat
Calcium	148.7	17.1	6.9	50.3
Iron	13.2	2.1	0.7	3.8
Magnesium	249.6	137.1	73.5	169.4
Phosphorus	383.7	292.6	137.8	467.7
Potassium	926.7	377.1	118.3	578.3
Zinc	4.4	2.9	0.6	4.7

Source: Koziol (1992)

Vitamins

Quinoa is also a good source of B vitamins riboflavin and folic acid compared to other grains, similar in amounts of thiamine, but lower in niacin on average as shown in table 6.5. It also contains significant amounts of vitamin E, though the quantity seems to decline after processing and cooking. In general, quinoa's vitamin content is not affected by removing its saponins as the vitamins are not found in the pericarp of the quinoa seed.

Table 6.5: Vitamin content of Quinoa and selected foods, mg/100 g dry weight

Vitamins	Quinoa	Maize	Rice	Wheat
Thiamine	0.2-04	0.42	0.06	0.45-0.49
Riboflavin	0.2-0.3	0.1	0.06	0.17
Foilc acid	0.0781	0.026	0.02	0.078
Niacin	0.5-0.7	1.8	1.9	5.5

Phytosterols

Though the phytosterol content of quinoa seeds has not received much attention, quinoa seeds contain phytosterol levels up to 118 mg/100 g quinoa seed, whereby the major constituents were β- sitosterol, campesterol, brassicasterol, and stigmasterol (Villacres and others 2013). It was found that ´ quinoa seeds contain β-sitosterol (63.7 mg/100 g), campesterol (15.6 mg/100 g), and stigmasterol (3.2 mg/100 g), and these levels were higher than those found in barley, rye, millet, and maize Phytosterols are lipophilic compounds structurally similar to cholesterol. Epidemiological evidence, intervention studies, and meta-analyses have consistently concluded significant hypocholesterolemic effects of phytosterols in humans. Phytosterols lower serum cholesterol levels by competing for cholesterol intestinal absorption, and possibly also by decreasing atherogenic lipoprotein production in the liver and intestines. Furthermore, phytosterols have demonstrated anti-inflammatory, antioxidative, and anticarcinogenic effects.

Table 6.6: Nutritional analysis of cooked Quinoa

Quinoa, cooked 0.75 cap 185.00 grams				Calories: 222 GI: Low
Nutrition	**Amount**	**DRI/DV (%)**	**Nutrition Density**	**World's Healthiest Foods Rating**
Manganese	1.17 mg	59	4.7	Very good
Phosphorus	281.20 mg	40	3.3	Good
Copper	0.36 mg	40	3.2	Good
Magnesium	118.40 mg	30	2.4	Good
Fiber	5.18 g	21	1.7	Good
Folate	77.70 mcg	19	1.6	Good
Zinc	2.02 MG	18	1.5	Good

World's Healthiest Foods Rating	Rule
Excellent	DRI/DV>=75% OR Density>=7.6 AND DRI/DV/DV>=10%
Very good	DRI/DV>=50% OR Density>=3.4 AND DRI/DV>=5%
Good	DRI/DV/>=25% or Density>=1.5 AND DRI/DV>=2.5%

This chart graphically details the %DV that a serving of Quinoa provides for each of the nutrients.

Selection and Storage of Quinoa

Quinoa is generally available in prepackaged containers as well as bulk bins. Just as with any other food that you may purchase in the bulk section, make sure that the bins containing the quinoa are covered and that the store has a good product turnover so as to ensure its maximal freshness. Whether purchasing quinoa in bulk or in a packaged container, make sure that there is no evidence of moisture. When deciding upon the amount to purchase, remember that quinoa expands during the cooking process to several times its original size. If you cannot find it in your local supermarket, look for it at natural foods stores, which usually carry it.

The most common type of quinoa you will find in the store has an off-white color but red and black quinoa is becoming more available. You may even be able to find a tri-color mixture sold in packages or bulk bins.

Store quinoa in an airtight container. It will keep for a longer period of time, approximately three to six months, if stored in the refrigerator.

Preparation and Cooking of Quinoa

Tips for Preparing Quinoa

Processing methods used in the commercial milling of quinoa usually remove most of the saponins found in the outer coat of the quinoa seeds. Because the quinoa saponins are largely responsible for its bitter taste, many people chose to rinse and rub the seeds after purchase to remove any bitter taste that may remain in the seeds. An effective method to do so is to place the quinoa seeds in a fine-meshed strainer and run cold water over the quinoa while gently rubbing the seeds together in your hands. After completing this process, you can taste a few seeds to determine if a bitter taste remains. If it does, simply continue this rinsing and rubbing process until you no longer taste a bitter residue.

The Healthiest Way of Cooking Quinoa

To cook the quinoa, add one part of the grain to two parts liquid in a saucepan. After the mixture is brought to a boil, reduce the heat to simmer and cover. One cup of quinoa cooked in this method usually takes 15 minutes to prepare. When cooking is complete, you will notice that the grains have become translucent, and the white germ has partially detached itself, appearing like a white-spiraled tail. If you desire the quinoa to have a nuttier flavor, you can dry roast it before cooking; to dry roast, place it in a skillet over medium-low heat and stir constantly for five minutes.

Quinoa is a perfect food to include on a gluten-free diet, since it not only lacks gluten but doesn't even belong to the same plant family as wheat, oats, barley, or rye. Some studies also show quinoa flour to have higher-than-expected digestibility. Both of these factors would be expected to decrease the risk of an adverse reaction to quinoa—especially in comparison to a cereal grass like wheat. While it is possible to make baked goods and pastas out of 100% quinoa flour, most companies combine quinoa flour with other flours (like tapioca flour or rice flour) or with oatmeal to produce a lighter texture. (Products made with 100% quinoa flour typically have a heavy and dense texture, sometimes referred to as "truffle-like.") When combined with rice flour or tapioca flour, however, quinoa-based products definitely qualify as gluten-free and should help reduce risk of adverse reactions.

Individual Concerns

Quinoa is not a commonly allergenic food. Because quinoa does not belong to the plant family containing wheat, oats, barley, and rye, it is also a gluten-free food. Some studies also show a higher-than-expected digestibility for quinoa, making it a food less likely to produce adverse reactions.

Health Benefits

Overall Nutrient Richness

Perhaps the most striking health benefit provided by quinoa is its overall nutrient richness. When the nutrient composition of this food is analyzed in depth, the results are unusual and striking. While quinoa can be eaten in the same way as a grain, or ground into flour like is so commonly done with grains, it lacks some important nutritional shortcomings of grains.

One of the shortcomings overcome by quinoa involves its protein content. Most grains are considered to be inadequate as total protein sources because they lack adequate amounts of the amino acids lysine and isoleucine. The relatively low level of both lysine and isoleucine in the protein of grains is what causes these amino acids to be considered as the limiting amino acids (LAAs) in grains. In other words, these LAAs prevent grains from serving as complete protein sources in our diet. By contrast, quinoa has significantly greater amounts of both lysine and isoleucine (especially lysine), and these greater amounts of lysine and isoleucine allow the protein in quinoa to serve as a complete protein source.

In terms of fat content, quinoa once again overcomes some of the shortcomings of most grains. Since it takes nearly 350 calories' worth of whole wheat to provide 1 gram of fat, whole wheat is not generally regarded as a significant source of fat, including essential fatty acids or heart-healthy monounsaturated fats (like oleic acid). By contrast, since it only takes 63 calories' worth of quinoa to provide 1 gram of fat, quinoa is typically considered to be a valuable source of certain health-supportive fats. About 28% of quinoa's fatty acids come in the form of oleic acid, a heart-healthy monounsaturated fat, and about 5% come in the form of alpha-linolenic acid or ALA—the omega-3 fatty acid most commonly found in plants and associated with decreased risk of inflammation-related disease.

Neither quinoa nor any grains qualify as good vitamin E sources in our WH Foods rating system. However, in the case of quinoa, or rating system does not do full justice to the fact that quinoa contains significant amounts of certain tocopherols (vitamin E family members) largely absent from most grains. For example, one cup of quinoa provides 2.2 milligrams of gamma-tocopherol—a form of vitamin E that has been more closely associated with certain anti-inflammatory benefits in health research. Quinoa is also a good source of RDA nutrients like folate, zinc, and phosphorus in contrast to whole wheat, which does not qualify as a good source in our rating system.

Quinoa is an equally impressive food in terms of its overall phytonutrient benefits. In many Central and South American countries, the leaves of the quinoa plant are valued for their betacyanin pigments, which provide some of their bright reddish shades. But even the seeds themselves can be phytonutrient-rich and can provide significant amounts of antioxidants like ferulic, coumaric, hydroxybenzoic, and vanillic acid.

The antioxidant flavonoids quercetin and kaempferol are also especially plentiful in quinoa. In fact, the concentration of these two flavonoids in quinoa can sometimes be greater than their concentration of high-flavonoid berries like cranberry or lingonberry.

Considered in combination, these diverse nutrient benefits of quinoa give it uniqueness among grain-related foods. For us, this high overall level of nourishment provided by quinoa may qualify as its greatest health benefit.

Anti-Inflammatory Benefits

Most of the quinoa studies that we've seen in this area have been animal studies. However, we believe that the preliminary indications for humans are very promising. Research has shown the ability of daily quinoa intake to lower levels of inflammation in fat (adipose) tissue in rats and in the linings of their intestine as well.

We're not surprised at either of these results because a wide range of anti-inflammatory nutrients is already known to be present in quinoa. This list of anti-inflammatory nutrients includes phenolic acids (including hydroxycinnamic and hydroxybenzoic acids), members of the vitamin E family like gamma-tocopherol, and cell wall polysaccharides like arabinans and rhamnogalacturonans.

Somewhat more controversial in this anti-inflammatory nutrient list are the saponins found in quinoa. Saponins are the bitter tasting, water-soluble phytonutrients found in the outer seed coat layer of quinoa. (More specifically, the saponins found in quinoa are derived from hederagenin, oleanic acid, phytolaccagenic acid, and serjanic acid.) The quinoa saponins have been shown to have both anti-inflammatory and antioxidant properties. However, soaking, boiling, and milling can reduce their presence, and, in general, this reduced presence is usually regarded as a good thing since it can make the quinoa much more enjoyable for most people to eat. In research to date, the relationship between and anti-inflammatory benefits of quinoa and saponin levels has yet to be clarified. However, even though more research is needed in this particular phytonutrient area, the list of anti-inflammatory nutrients in quinoa remains impressive.

Other Benefits

We have yet to see large-scale human studies on intake of quinoa and risk of type 2 diabetes or risk of cardiovascular disease. However, we would expect such studies to show significantly reduced risks. With respect to type 2 diabetes, quinoa simply has too many things in common with other foods known to decrease risk. At the top of the list here would be its fiber and protein content. Quinoa is a good source of fiber—one of the key macronutrients needed for health blood sugar regulation. It also provides outstanding protein quality, even in comparison to commonly-eaten whole grains. Strong intake of protein and fiber are two dietary essentials for regulation of blood sugar. Because chronic, unwanted inflammation is also a key risk factor for development of type 2 diabetes, the diverse range of anti-inflammatory nutrients found in quinoa also make it a great candidate for diabetes risk reduction.

Animal studies have already demonstrated the ability of quinoa to lower total cholesterol and help maintain levels of HDL cholesterol (the "good" cholesterol). While we would expect these results in humans as well, we would also expect the anti-inflammatory nutrients in quinoa to help protect human blood vessels from inflammatory damage. Protection of this kind would also provide reduced risk of many cardiovascular diseases, including atherosclerosis. We expect to see future, large-scale human studies demonstrating the benefits of quinoa for risk reduction in this area of cardiovascular disease.

The antioxidant and anti-inflammatory phytonutrients in quinoa also make it a likely candidate for cancer risk reduction in humans. Given the preliminary animal results involving the digestive tract, risk reduction for colon cancer may turn out to be a special area of interest.

A final area of likely benefit involves decreased risk of allergy—especially for individuals who have adverse reactions to certain grains and seek practical alternatives. Already, several public organizations have recommended quinoa as a substitute for wheat whenever the avoidance of this gluten-containing grain is required. The low-allergy potential of quinoa—coupled with its relatively high digestibility—has also made it a food of special interest in the diet of children and toddlers.

What's New about Quinoa

- The Food and Agricultural Organization of the United Nations (FAO) has officially declared that the year 2013 be recognized as "The International Year of the Quinoa." Proposed by the government of Bolivia and receiving strong support from many Central and South American countries, quinoa has now been singled out by the FAO as a food with "high nutritive value," impressive biodiversity, and an important role to play in the achievement of food security worldwide. We realize that quinoa remains unfamiliar to many people, especially in the practical sense of cooking and recipes. But we hope that situation will change, given the remarkable nature of this easily-prepared, nutrient-rich food.

- Researchers have recently taken a close look at certain antioxidant phytonutrients in quinoa, and two flavonoid—quercetin and kaempferol—are now known to be provided by quinoa in especially concentrated amounts. In fact, the concentration of these two flavonoids in quinoa can sometimes be greater than their concentration in high-flavonoid berries like cranberry or lingonberry.
- Recent studies are providing us with a greatly expanded list of anti-inflammatory phytonutrients in quinoa. This unique combination of anti-inflammatory compounds in quinoa may be the key to understanding preliminary animal studies that show decreased risk of inflammation-related problems (including obesity) when animals are fed quinoa on a daily basis. The list of anti-inflammatory phytonutrients in quinoa is now known to include: polysaccharides like arabinans and rhamnogalacturonans; hydroxycinnamic and hydroxybenzoic acids; flavonoids like quercetin and kaempferol; and saponins including molecules derived from oleanic acid, hederagenin and serjanic acid. Small amounts of the anti-inflammatory omega-3 fatty acid, alpha-linolenic acid (ALA), are also provided by quinoa.
- In comparison to cereal grasses like wheat, quinoa is higher in fat content and can provide valuable amounts of heart-healthy fats like monounsaturated fat (in the form of oleic acid). Quinoa can also provide small amounts of the omega-3 fatty acid, alpha-linolenic acid (ALA). Given this higher fat content, researchers initially assumed that quinoa would be more susceptible to oxidation and resulting nutrient damage. However, recent studies have shown that quinoa does not get oxidized as rapidly as might be expected given its higher fat content. This finding is great news from a nutritional standpoint. The processes of boiling, simmering, and steaming quinoa do not appear to significantly compromise the quality of quinoa's fatty acids, allowing us to enjoy its cooked texture and flavor while maintaining this nutrient benefit. Food scientists have speculated that it is the diverse array of antioxidants found in quinoa—including various members of the vitamin E family like alpha-, beta-, gamma- and delta-tocopherol as well as flavonoids like quercetin and kaempferol—that contribute to this oxidative protection.

Summary

Chenopodium quinoa is being considered as a new crop for the Controlled Ecological Life Support System (CELSS) because of its high protein values (12-18%) and unique amino acid composition. Lysine, an essential amino acid that is deficient in many grain crops, is found in quinoa approaching Food and Agriculture Organization of the United Nations (FAO) standards set for humans. This "new" crop, rich in protein and with desirable proportions of important amino acids, may provide greater versatility in meeting the needs of humans on long-term space missions.

REFERENCES

1. Abugoch James, L.E. (2009) Quinoa (Chenopodium quinoa Willd.). Advances in Food and Nutrition Research.
2. *Barbara Pickersgill (August 31, 2007). "Domestication of Plants in the Americas: Insights from Mendelian and Molecular Genetics". Annals of Botany. 100 (5): 925-40. PMC 2759216. PMID 17766847. doi:10.1093/aob/mcm193.*
3. Bhargava A, Shukla S and Ohri D. Chenopodium quinoa - An Indian Perspective. Industrial Crops and Products, Volume 23, Issue 1, January 2006, Pages 73-87. 2006.
4. *"Biopesticides Registration Action Document: Saponins of Chenopodium quinoa" (PDF). EPA. 2009.*
5. Brady K, Ho CT, Rosen RT *et al*. Effects of Processing on the Nutraceutical Profile of Quinoa. od Chemistry, Volume 100, Issue 3, 2007, Pages 1209-1216. 2007.
6. Cammareri M, Consiglio MF, Pecchia P, Corea G, Lanzotti V, Ibeas JI, Tava A, Conicella C. 2008. Molecular Characterization of β-amyrin Synthase from Aster Sedifolius L. and Triterpenoid Saponin Analysis. Plant Sci 175(3): 255-61.
7. De Bruin, A.: Investigation of the Food Value of Quinua and Cafiihua Seed. J. Food Science, Vol. 29, No. 6, pp. 872-876, 1964.
8. Del Castillo V, Lescano G, and Armada M. [Foods Formulation for People with Celiac Disease based on Quinoa (Chenopoduim quinoa), Cereal Flours and Starches Mixtures]. Arch Latinoam Nutr. 2009 Sep; 59(3): 332-6. Spanish. 2009.
9. Dini I, Tenore GC, and Dini A. Antioxidant Compound Contents and Antioxidant Activity before and after Cooking in Sweet and Bitter Chenopodium Quinoa Seeds. LWT - Food Science and Technology, Volume 43, Issue 3, April 2010, Pages 447-451. 2010.
10. Fuentes, F.F.; Martínez, E.A.; Hinrischen, P.V.; Jellen, E.N.; Maughan, P.J. (10 May 2008). "Assessment of Genetic Diversity Patterns in Chilean quinoa (Chenopodium quinoaWilld.) germplasm using Multiplex Fluorescent Microsatellite" (PDF). Springer Science+Business Media. Retrieved 14 February 2016.
11. *Heiser Jr., Charles B. & Nelson, David C. (September 1974). "On the Origin of the Cultivated Chenopods (Chenopodium)". Genetics. 78 (1): 503-5. PMC 1213209/.PMID 4442716.*
12. *"International Year of Quinoa 2013". Food and Agricultural Organisation of the United Nations. Retrieved 18 August 2015.*
13. James LEA. Chapter 1: Quinoa (Chenopodium quinoa Willd.): Composition, Chemistry, Nutritional, and Functional Properties. Advances in Food and Nutrition Research, Volume 58, 2009, Pages 1-31. 2009.
14. *Jarvis, David E.; Ho, Yung Shwen; Lightfoot, Damien J.; Schmöckel, Sandra M.; Li, Bo; Borm, Theo J. A.; Ohyanagi, Hajime; Mineta, Katsuhiko; Michell, Craig T. (2017-02-08). "The Genome of Chenopodium quinoa". Nature. Advance online Publication (7641): 1-6. Bibcode:2017Natur.542..307J. ISSN 1476-4687. doi:10.1038/nature21370.*
15. Johnson, D.L.; and Croissant, R.: Quinoa Production in Colorado. Service in Action, No. 112, Colorado State Univ., Cooperative Extension, Fort Collins, Colo., 1985.
16. *Johnson DL, Ward SM (1993). "Quinoa". Department of Horticulture, Purdue University; Obtained from Johnson, D.L. and S.M. Ward. 1993. Quinoa. p. 219-221. In: J. Janick and J.E. Simon (eds.), New Crops. Wiley, New York. Retrieved 21 May 2013.*

17. Johnson, R.; and Aguilera, R.: Processing Varieties of Oilseeds (Lupine and Quinoa). Report to Natural Fibers and Food Protein Commission of Texas ... Texas A & M University, 1980.

18. *Kolata, Alan L. (2009). "Quinoa" (PDF). Quinoa: Production, Consumption and Social Value in Historical Context. Department of Anthropology, The University of Chicago.*

19. Koziol, M. (1992) Chemical Composition and Nutritional Evaluation of Quinoa (Chenopodium quinoa Willd.). Journal of Food Composition and Analysis. 5, 35-68.

20. Madl T, Sterk H, Mittelbach M, Rechberger GN. 2006. Tandem Mass Spectrometric Analysis of a Complex Triterpene saponin Mixture of Chenopodium quinoa. J Am Society Mass Spec 17(6): 795-806.

21. Marangoni F, Poli A. 2010. Phytosterols and Cardiovascular Health. Pharmacol Res 61: 193-9.

22. *Masterbroek, H.D.; Limburg, H.; Gilles, T.; Marvin, H. J. (2000). Occurrence of Sapogenins in Leaves and Seeds of Quinoa (Chenopodium quinoa Willd). New York, NY: Journal of the Science of Food and Agriculture. pp. 152-156.*

23. National Research Council. (1989) Lost Crops of the Incas: little known Plants of the Andes with Promise for World-wide Cultivation. Washington, DC: National Academy Press.

24. Ng, S., Anderson, A., Cokera, J. and Ondrusa, M. (2007) Characterization of Lipid Oxidation Products in Quinoa (Chenopodium quinoa). Food Chem. 101(1), 185-192.

25. *"Quinoa 101: What You Need to Know".*

26. *"Quinoa". Alternative Field Crops Manual. University of Wisconsin Extension and University of Minnesota. January 20, 2000.*

27. Ramakrishna A, Ravishankar GA. 2011. Influence of Abiotic Stress Signals on Secondary Metabolites in Plants. Plant Signal Behav 6(11): 1720-31.

28. *Reinhard Lieberei, Christoph Reissdorff & Wolfgang Franke (2007). Nutzpflanzenkunde. Georg Thieme Verlag. ASIN 3135304078.*

29. Ryan E, Galvin K, O'Connor TP, Maguire AR, O'Brien NM. 2007. Phytosterol, Squalene, Tocopherol Content and Fatty Acid Profile of Selected Seeds, Grains, and Legumes. Plant Food Hum Nutr 62: 85-91.

30. Repo-Carrasco, R., Espinoza, C. and Jacobsen, S.E. (2003) Nutritional Value and use of the Andean Crops Quinoa (Chenopodium Quinoa Willd.) and Kañiwa (Chenopodium pallidicaule). Food Reviews International. Vol. 19, Nos. 1 & 2, 179-189.

31. Reyes Montaño, E.A., Ávila Torres, D.P. and Guevara Pulido, J.O. (2006) Componente nutricional de diferentes variedades de quinua de la región Andina. AVANCES Investigación en Ingeniería.5, 86-97.

32. Stuardo M, San Martin R. 2008. Antifungal Properties of Quinoa (Chenopodium quinoa Willd) Alkali Treated Saponins against Botrytis Cinerea. Ind Crops Prod 27: 296-302.

33. *Siener, Roswitha; Honow, Ruth; Seidler, Ana; Voss, Susanne; Hesse, Albrecht (2006). Oxalate contents of species of the Polygonaceae, Amaranthaceae and Chenopodiaceae families. Food Chemistry, Volume 98 Issue 2. pp. 220-224. ISSN 0308-8146. doi:10.1016/j.foodchem.2005.05.059.*

34. Teofilo Laime Ajacopa, Diccionario Bilingüe Iskay simipi yuyayk'ancha, La Paz, 2007 (Quechua-Spanish dictionary)

35. *"The Plant List: A Working List of All Plant Species". Retrieved May 1, 2014.*

36. *The Lost Crops of the Incas: Little-Known Plants of the Andes with Promise for Worldwide Cultivation. U.S. National Research Council, Advisory Committee on Technology Innovation, National Academies. 1989.*

37. *Vaughn, JG; Geissler, CA (2009). The New Oxford Book of Food Plants. Oxford University Press. ISBN 019954946X.*

38. Vidueiros SM, Fernandez I, Bertero HD *et al*. Effect of Quinoa (Chenopodium quinoa, W) on the Intestinal mucosa of Growing Wistar Rats. FASEB J, Apr. 2012; 26: 1033.4. 2012.

39. Villacres E, P ´ astor G, Quelal MB, Zambrano I, Morales SH. 2013. Effect of ´ Processing on the Content of Fatty Acids, Tocopherols and Sterols in the Oils of Quinoa (Chenopodium Quinoa Willd), lupine (Lupinus mutablis Sweet), Amaranth (Amaranthus caudatus L.) and sangorache (Amaranthus quitensis L.). Global Adv Res J Food Sci Technol 2(4): 44-53.

40. Watanabe I, Ibuki A, Yi-Chum C *et al*. Composition of quinoa Protein Fractions. Journal of the Japanese Society for Food Science and Technology (Nippon Shokuhin Kagaku Kogaku Kaishi)50. 11 (2003): 546-549. 2003.

41. Yendo ACA, De Costa F, Gosmann G, Fett-Neto AG. 2010. Production of Plant Bioactive triterpenoid saponins: elicitation Strategies and Target Genes to improve yields. Mol Biotechnol 46: 94-104.

42. *"11 Proven Health Benefits of Quinoa". www.healthline.com.*

Pages: 89-109
Food Technology and Research Advancement
Edited by: Dr. Avnish Chauhan and Dr. Pawan Kumar 'Bharti'
ISBN: 978-93-86841-49-0
Edition: 2018
Published by: Discovery Publishing House Pvt. Ltd., New Delhi (India)

7

Mitigation Strategies for Fodder Scarcity

S.S. Kadam; Mohd. Arif; R.R. Dhutmal and Ashok Kumar

Introduction

India consists about 15 per cent of world's cattle population. It ranks first in the world in milk production which produces about 146.3 million tonnes of milk. However, the productivity of the individual animal is very low. This is due to inadequate supply of feed and fodder. It is estimated that about 60 to 65 per cent expenses are incurred on only feed and fodders. (Hegde, 2010). Since the cost of the concentrate feed is increasing day by day, fodder based cheaper strategies are required to reduce the cost on livestock rearing. The plant part either in green, dry, hay or in silage form is called as fodder. Fodder is the cheapest source than concentrate feed. It provides nutrients such as carbohydrate, proteins, mineral matter and vitamins such as A and D.It contains about 70 to 80 per cent water hence in little extent it fulfils the water need of the animal especially during the dry season. Due to water content in green fodders the nutrients get solubilised hence the digestibility gets improved. The lush green fodders are relished by the animals and thereby palatability is also increased due to feeding of the green fodders to the animals..Secondly the fodders can be stored or preserved and fed to the animals throughout the year. In short the success of Dairying business depends on the availability of the fodders.

The fodder crops are broadly classified as seasonal fodder crops which complete their life cycle in particular season includes kharif, Rabi and summer season crops. They are again classified as cereal fodders viz.Maize, Jowar, Bajra, Oat and Barley. Legume fodders comprise Cowpea, Guar, Moth bean etc. The perennial crops are those fodder crops which remains in the field for more than one year. The perennial crops are again classified as cereals/ Grasses viz.Napier, Hybrid Napier, Guinea, Para grass etc. Legume

Rajasthan College of Agriculture, MPUA&T, Udaipur - 313 001

perennials include Lucerne, Berseem, Stylosanthes, Subabbol, and Dashrath etc. The study of classification of fodder crops is important to include the fodder crops in yearly planning/cropping system so as to provide the balanced nutrients to the animals. Cereals are rich in carbohydrate provide energy to the animals and legume are rich in proteins which maintains the productivity of the animals.

Present Scenario of Fodders

Table 7.1: Scenario of fodder requirement and availability (million tonnes)

Year	Supply		Demand		Deficit (%)	
	Green	Dry	Green	Dry	Green	Dry
1995	379	421	947	526	60(568)	20(105)
2000	385	428	988	549	61(604)	22(121)
2005	390	443	1025	569	62(635)	22(126)
2010	395	451	1061	589	63(666)	24(138)
2015	401	466	1097	609	64(696)	23(143)
2020	406	473	1134	630	64(728)	25(1137)
2025	411	488	1170	650	65(759)	25(162)

Source: Draft report of working group on Animal husbandry and Dairying for five year plan 2002-2007, Govt. of India, Planning Commission)

Although the fodders are cheapest source of the nutrient supply there is wide gap between the actual availability and its requirement (planning commission Report, 2007) which is depicted in the above table. It indicates during the year 2010 there is availability of green and dry fodders is 395 MT and 451 MT as against the requirement of about 1061 MT and 589 MT respectively. It indicates there is shortage of 666 MT (63 per cent) of green fodder and 138 MT (24 per cent) shortage of the dry fodders in our country. In the state like Maharashtra where there is severe drought situation at present the shortage of green fodders rise up to 74 per cent green fodders and 34 per cent dry fodders.

Causes of fodder scarcity:

1. Less area under cultivation of fodder crops -in India it is reported that only 4.7 per cent of total cultivable land that is 7.2 mha is under fodder crop cultivation. Due to less area under cultivation of fodder the total production is very low.
2. Small farmers and Marginal farmers - there is large numbers of small and marginal farmers who cannot part their land for fodder cultivation on cost of production of the food crops for their subsistence. Also there is tendency of the farmers to grow cash crops instead of cultivating the fodder crops.

3. Lack of Scientific knowledge about fodder cultivation and forage preservation methods - those farmers are growing the fodders do not adopt the scientific methods of fodder cultivation viz.selection of variety, line sowing/planting, fertilizer and irrigation management, harvesting management etc which affects the forage yield drastically. Also those farmers produce the excess green fodders do not know the scientific methods of preservation of the green fodders. Hence during the drought there is acute shortage of the green fodders
4. Uncontrolled grazing - the Indian grasslands are deteriorating due to continuous grazing or uncontrolled grazing by the unlimited herd. Due to which some of the valuable grass species are disappearing from the grasslands also soil erosion is the serious problem in these deteriorated grassland.
5. Unavailability of quality seed/rooted slips - the farmers are not getting the quality fodder seed and rooted slips in time hence the production of fodder is low in our country.

Strategies to mitigate the fodder Scarcity:

1. Fodder preservation (Silage making and hay making)
2. Agro forestry approach (Silvi-pasture, Horti-pasture, Agro-horti, Agri-horti-silvi-pasture systems)
3. Controlled grazing (Rotational and deferred grazing)
4. Massive cultivation of fodder trees
5. Wasteland to grassland
6. Adoption of improved methods of fodder cultivation
7. Promotion of techniques of treatment to crop residues
8. Hydroponics fodder production
9. Alternative sources of fodder viz.sugarcane tops &vegetable waste
10. Extension approach

Fodder Requirement and Planning for One Year

To overcome the fodder scarcity problem especially during the severe drought if occurred in future the farmers should have planning of fodders in advance and accordingly one can follow the above mentioned strategies as per the resources available. For annual planning of the fodder requirement livestock owner should take into consideration the number of small and large animals, their per day green as well as dry fodder requirement and availability of irrigated land etc.This planning will help the farmers to mitigate the fodder scarcity by adopting various measures such as silage making, hay preparation, hydroponics or by agro forestry approaches without much efforts.

Requirement of fodders for 10 milch animals -

1. Green fodder/annum

   @30 kg per day ×10 animals = 300

   For one month 300 × 30 days = 9 MT

   For one year 09 × 12 months = 108 MT

2. Dry fodders/annum

   @10 kg per day × 10 × 30 × 12 = 36 MT

For production of 108 MT green fodders and 36 MT dry fodders at least 02 acres of minimum land is required which should be under cultivation of legume and cereal fodder crops in equal proportion so as to provide the nutrients to the animals in balanced proportion round the year.

Similarly the green and dry fodder requirement of the small stall fed animals like sheep and goat required for one year should be calculated in advance to overcome the fodder scarcity situation in future.

1. Preservation of fodder

(a) Silage Making

Preservation of green fodders under anaerobic condition or air tightened situation is called as silage. During rainy season there is ample quantity of the greens/grasses available. At the end of mansoon that is in the month of October-November these excess grasses should be cut and stored in air tightened condition scientifically for silage making. Its quality can be improved by adding molasses and urea solution.

Crops rich in carbohydrate are generally selected for the silage making. Cereal crops like Maize, Jowar, Bajra, Oat and grasses like Hybrid Napier due its more CHO content give good quality silage. The crops selected for silage making should be cut before flowering so as to get the maximum nutrients. Delayed harvesting will yield the poor quality silage and early harvesting of such crops will produce less biomass. After harvesting of the crop it should be dried in sun to have moisture content up to 55 to 60 per cent. It will be then chopped into small pieces 2.5 to 4.0 cm long with the help of chaff cutter which prevent about 30 per cent of fodder wastage. Then these chaffed green is put in silo structure. Every time during the filling of silo pit it should be pressed so as to remove the air from the silo pit. To prevent the entry of water and air inside the silo pit it should be covered with polythene sheet and sealed with cow dung slurry mixed with soil. Silage becomes ready for feeding within 60 to 65 days after sealing of pit. It can be opened during the shortage of green fodders. It is also called as pickle of fodder.

For silage making various silo structures are in use commonly used structure is Bunker Silo useful to the farmers who have large number of animals. About 10×10×06 cu.feet silo structure can store about 10 to 12 MT of green fodders. Due to its high construction cost, unavailability of sufficient fodders and more laborious the bunker silo are not popular among the farmers. Hence Bombay Veterinary College initiated silage making in Plastic bags and plastic drums especially to the farmers having very small herd size of about 4 to 5 animals. These store about 450 kg and 150 kg green material respectively. The selected crop after proper drying is cut into small pieces of 3-4 cm long and the copped material is placed in the plastic bags, by pressing to remove the air. The silage prepared in this way can be stored without losing the nutritive value at least for one year. Plastic silage bags are economical alternative to traditional silage preparation methods such as pits and other silo when related harvest and storage losses are considered. This method of silage making allows the farmers to store silage anywhere they need it and can be easily transported to the cattle shed thus it saves the labour cost on transportation, for removal of silage and its feeding. Also there is no spoilage of silage material once opened for feeding to the animals because it can be easily opened and sealed as and when required. However, much of silage in pit or bunker silo has been found to be spoiled due to poor sealing and exposure to air every day when the silage is removed for feeding.

Bunker silo

Plastic bag for silage

Table 7.2: Nutritive analysis of silage

Sr. No.	Parameter (%)	DHN-6 Fodder	Maize Bran	Composite Silage
1.	Moisture	62.74	61.21	60-70
2.	Crude protein	9.03	7.65	8.8-12.09
3.	Ether extract	0.86	3.07	1.3-3.3
4.	Crude fiber	27.80	15.24	17-26
5.	Total Ash	9.55	2.03	6-8
6.	NFE	52.76	71.11	48-60

Source: BVC RKVY Report 2011-12

From the table it is found that DHN-6 variety of Hybrid Napier produced 9.03 crude proteins which are at par with the crude protein generally observed in fresh green Hybrid Napier (9.0 to 11.0).Hence excess fodders produced during rainy season can be stored and utilized in the form of silage without much nutrient loss.

Also it was found that poor quality fodder crops viz.Para grass (Bracharia mutica) can be enriched by making composite silage that is mixing with DHN-6 and maize bran. Compo site silage includes the silage prepared from more than two fodder crops. Generally cereal crops rich in carbohydrates are mixed with legume fodder crops which are rich in proteins. Composite silage prepared by mixing of such crops are nutritious. While making the composite silage 70-80 per cent green part should be from cereal crops and 20-30 per cent part should be from legume or vegetable waste. The most economically feasible results are obtained when low quality components (vegetables and fruit waste) are added into more qualitative components like Maize up to 30 per cent. High quality of silage can be obtained from whole plant of Maize (45 per cent), Maize grain (25 per cent) and fresh alfalfa (30 per cent)

Advantages of Silage:

1. Stable composition of the feed i.e. silage for a longer period up to five years.
2. The plants can be harvested at optimal phase of the development and are efficiently used by the livestock.
3. More economical use of the plants with high yield of green mass.
4. Better utilization of land with 2-3 crops in year.
5. Silage is the boon to overcome the fodder scarcity.

(b) Hay Making

A method of conserving green crops in dried form is known as hay making. The aim of hay making is to reduce the moisture content of green crops up to 15-20 per cent to inhibit the action of plant and microbial enzymes. Thus a green crop in mature stage is preserved for long period which can be fed to the animals during the fodder scarcity. Selection of crop and harvesting at proper time are also important to get nutritive hay. Generally the legume hay has got special importance in dairy industry because it contains higher percentage of of digestible nutrients, more proteins, minerals like calcium and vitamins such as D and E.The legume hay are palatable than the nonlegume hay. Among the various legume fodder crops lucerne, berssem, soybean and cowpea are considered the best for good quality hay. on leguminous hay is prepared from grasses and cereal crops like Oat, Barley etc.They are low in proteins and minerals, but rich in carbohydrate.For making good quality of hay such crops should be harvested at milk stage.

2. Agro forestry approach

Agro forestry is playing the greatest role in maintaining the resource base and increasing overall productivity in the rainfed areas in general and the arid and semi-arid regions in particular. Agro forestry land use increases livelihood security and reduces vulnerability to climate and environmental change. There are ample evidence to show that the overall (biomass) productivity, soil fertility improvement, soil conservation, nutrient cycling, micro-climate improvement, and carbon sequestration potential of an agro forestry system is generally greater than that of an annual system. Agro forestry has an important role in reducing vulnerability, increasing resilience of farming systems and buffering households against climate-related risks. It also provides for ecosystem services - water, soil health, and biodiversity. Therefore, agro forestry will be required to contribute substantially to meet the demands of rising population for food, fruits, fuel wood, timber, fodder, bio fuel, and bio-energy. Agro forestry systems on arable lands envisage growing of trees and woody perennials on terrace risers, terrace edges, field bunds, as intercrops, and as alley cropping. Agro forestry practices for non arable degraded lands such as boulder riverbeds, torrents, landslide, shifting cultivation areas, waterlogged soils, control of desertification, mine spoil rehabilitation, and treatment of saline and alkaline lands have been developed and demonstrated. Agro forestry land use in conjunction with soil water conservation and animal husbandry need to be emphasized

Agro forestry is indeed the best land management system which fulfils the five F that are fruit, fodder, fuel wood, furniture and food also which brings harmony between forestry and agriculture. The agro forestry system protects crops and forages, increase their production and helps to conserve soil and moisture by reducing the erosion. The agro forestry system consist silvi- pasture, horti-pasture, agri-silvi- horti- pasture system and agri-horti systems.

(a) Silvi-pasture

This is simultaneous growing of trees under-storey herbaceous vegetation of forage value on the same place of land and in the agricultural system. Such silvipastoral farming system has been practised in arid and semi-arid parts. The trees as a group offer wood, fuel, oils, industrial raw materials, medicinal principles, shade, aesthetic pleasure and pollution suppression, control of soil erosion and above all leaf and pods as forage to domestic animals. The biodynamic of the sivipastoral system involves four major distinct live forms viz.the herbaceous vegetation (for the most part grasses), the tree component, the domesticated animals surviving on the foregoing vegetation and man who controls the other three components. In addition, soil and climate have their own roles to play and complicate the diversity. Establishing the suitable components of such systems deserve considerations. Silvipasture is very useful for developing feed resources in wastelands eg. Acacia spp. + Cencrhrus ciliaris.

(b) *Horti-pasture*

The pasture is developed particularly in the dry land fruit crops/ orchards are known as hortipasture system.Viz. Custard apple and Guinea grass or Ber (Ziziphus mauritiana) and cenchrus ciliaris etc

(c) *Agri-Horti-Silvi-Pasture*

In this type of agro forestry system various agronomical crops such as proso millet, horticultural crops like Aonla, and forest trees like Teak and pasture like Stylosanthes are grown together.

(d) *Agro-horticulture system*

It includes growing of agronomical crops along with horticultural fruit trees.

Common Agro forestry Fodder Production Models

A number of fodder production systems have been designed to produce sufficient foliage for livestock feeding particularly during the dry season. These production systems include various types of agroforestry-silvipastoral systems, where trees, animals and pastures are deliberately combined to obtain benefits and services.

(i) Fodder bank systems - Trees are planted as close as 1 m × 1 m and are cut regularly to induce maximum herbage production. The cut herbage is usually carried to animal feeding stalls; sometimes sheep or goats are brought to the plots and allowed to forage on the cut branches of naturally-growing fodder. The system is called fodder bank, which provides reserve fodder when it is in short supply, usually in the dry season.

(ii) Protein bank - This is a type of fodder bank which intentionally chooses trees, shrubs legumes with high protein-containing leaf biomass. Commonly used species include L. leucocephala and G. sepium.

(iii) Three-strata forage system - This is another type of fodder bank; it involves the planting of forages, shrubs and trees to form three canopy layers or strata in a unit of land. Pasture grasses, vines and herbs occupy the lower strata; shrubs occupy the middle strata and trees occupy the upper strata. The combination of grasses and trees can ensure year-round supply of fodder.

(iv) Live fence or boundary systems - Single or double rows of fodder trees are planted along farm boundaries. The trees have the dual purpose of providing fodder and serving as live fence posts. If intended to enclose animals, the trees are usually planted densely, as

in hedges, to prevent animals from getting out. In some cases, thorny species are planted as thick hedges to prevent livestock from straying into crop plots and also to fence them off from wild animals.

(v) Hedge row intercropping systems - Fodder trees, mostly leguminous are planted as hedges in single, double or triple rows. The spaces in between hedge rows are planted with pasture grasses. As in fodder banks, herbage may be cut and carried to animal feeding stalls. The more common practice is to let the animals forage on cut tree branches and pasture grasses.

(vi) Tree plantation + animal grazing systems - The understory of tree plantations is utilized as grazing area for cattle, sheep, and goats. The plantation may be of forest trees, fruit trees, coconuts, oil palms, or rubber. The livestock is allowed to graze freely on improved pasture grasses planted under trees.

(vii) Indigenous cut-and-carry systems - As the name implies, the fodder is cut and carried to animal stalls. Farmers have a long been practicing this system. Indigenous legumes such as Ficus, Acacia, Leucaena, Gliricidia, and Albizia are the most preferred fodder tree species. (Mathukia *et al.*, 2016).

3. Controlled grazing systems

Uncontrolled grazing of the grasslands is one of the reasons of the degradation of ours pasture land. Due to which some valuable species of the grasses are disappearing slowly. Hence it is necessary to formulate the policies to maintain the village pastureland by adopting controlled grazing. In India the following two controlled grazing systems could be possible.

(a) *Rotational Grazing*

In this type of grazing system the grassland is divided into four equal compartments. According to the area of pasture land available the limited number of animals is allowed to graze the paddock in rotational manner one after another so as to get rest period for each compartment/paddock.

(b) *Deferred Grazing*

In this type of grazing system the grassland is divided into four equal compartments. Three compartments are grazed in rotational manner and fourth compartment is kept closed till the seed formation. The closed compartment is opened just before falling of the seeds in that particular compartment. By this grazing due to fall of the seeds a valuable species of the particular grass are conserved.

4. Massive cultivation of fodder trees

Fodder trees are playing an important role in reducing the fodder shortage problem in India. In most parts of our country after the end of rainy season, animals suffer badly due to lack of protein rich diet since availability of fodder become scarce. The situation becomes serious during the dry season under rainfed conditions, when generally no crop can be grown and natural pasture, grasses, and weeds become unproductive. Farmers either feed their animals withthe low-quality hay of the stored crop residues or they travel long distances to gather green grasses or fodders. In such circumstance, shrubs and fodder trees are able to withstand the drought, stay green, and provide a nutritious fodder for livestock.. Alarming shortages of forage in our country can be solved partially by planting fodder trees capable of sustained production of palatable forage high in protein and total digestible nutrients. Through the plantation of these species on degraded lands under silvi-pastoral systems. Oaks, Grewia optiva, Celtis australis in Western Himalaya, and Ficus spp., Alnus nepalensis and Bauhinia spp., in Eastern Himalayas have been used as important fodder trees. Lopping of Prosopis cineraria (Khejri) in western Rajasthan, A. lebbeck, Albizia procera, A. indica in northern and central India for leaf fodder, use of pods of A. nilotica and P. juliflora for fodder are common practices since old days. Most of these species are important source of fodder during lean period as well. Advantages of tree fodder are that trees can be grown on steep, rocky mountain slopes, in arid, saline, or water-logged soils, and in areas with severe climatic conditions. Furthermore, trees do not need heavy inputs of fertilizer, irrigation, labor, pesticides, etc., as are generally needed to grow conventional fodder crops. Trees use and recycle nutrients that are beyond the reach of grasses and other herbaceous plants. Trees that accumulate nitrogen enhance forage quality. Their relative deep root system can exploit deep moisture resources and using this and other strategies,trees are more tolerant to dry periods than pasture.(Mathukia *et al.*,2016). Also the scarcity fodder trees like Subabool, Dashrath and Anjan tree etc which require very less water during their growth and development should be grown on large scale along the road, on bunds, along the farm fencing, on wasteland which would be useful during the scarcity of fodder as well as during the acute shortage of water when other fodder crops cannot be cultivated. Hence massive fodder tree plantation programmes should be conducted at village level on panchayat land or community land or wastelands.

5. Converting Wasteland into Grassland

In India the area under cultivated fodder crops is only 4.7 per cent that is 7.2 mha which is the major cause of t he forage scarcity. Hence fallow, wasteland terrace risers, bunds etc.should necessarily be brought under cultivation of grasses such as Sewan grass, Marvel, Anjan grass, Rhodes grass etc.to meet the forage requirement as well as these grasses prevent soil erosion and hence are suitable to grow on the bunds (biological bund).

6. Promotion of technique for treatment of crop residues

(a) Urea treatment

After harvesting of the food crops its crop residue like straw is either burnt or fed to the animals as such without any treatment. Rice straw available in large quantities due to staple food of large masses fed to the animals as such which has created number of health problems in cattle due to its high oxalic content of about 1 to 3 per cent. Urea treatment with such poor quality rice straw will help to enrich the fodder and reduce the scarcity of fodder at some extent. Also it will help to lower down the oxalic content in rice straw.

Generally 4 per cent urea treatment is recommended. After treatment the straw is arranged in uniform layers one above another and covered with polythene sheet which become ready for feeding after 21 days. The crude protein content in rice straw increase from 4 per cent to 12 per cent due to this treatment. Thus enrichment of other coarse straw also can be done by using urea solution.

(b) Urea Molasses Mineral Blocks

These blocks are prepared from different ingredients such as molasses, rice bran, urea, cement, salt, dicalcium phosphate, trace elements and water. These provide proteins, minerals to the animals and most useful during the scarcity of fodders in drought period. Now days these blocks are supplied at drought relief camps instead of bulk quantity of dry and green fodders to save the cost and convenient to transport these blocks from remote area.

7. Adoption of improved methods of fodder production

Adoption of scientific methods of cultivation include selection of the high yielding fodder variety of crop, line sowing at appropriate distance, use of recommended manure and fertilizer dose, irrigation management and harvesting of the crop at right stage to get sufficient nutrients to the animals.

8. Hydroponics fodder production

Hydroponic is one of the new emerging technologies of fodder production without soil medium. It is commonly used in maize, barley and Lucerne fodder crops. Government also encouraged the farmers to adopt this technology to face the fodder deficit problem during severe drought situation.

Hybrid Napier

Advantages of Hydroponics Technology

Sr. No.	Attributes	Conventional Fodder Production	Hydroponics Fodder Production
1.	Area	10,000 sq.m	50 sq.m
2.	Land fertility	Essential	Not essential
3.	Fertilizers	Required	Not required
4.	Water req.	High	Very low
5.	Labor req,	More	Less
6.	Growth period	45-60 days	7-8 days
7.	Fodder yield dependency	On climate	Controlled condition
8.	Fodder production	36 MT	36 MT

Source: ICAR Extension Folder, 2011

Improved methods of fodder production

Sr. No.	Fodder Crop	Varieties	Sowing/planting	Fertilizer dose NPK (kg/ha)	Harvesting Stage	Green Fodder yield (t/ha)
1.	Jowar	Ruchira, MP chari, Maldandi 35-1	30 cm	80:40:40	70-90 DAS	35-45
2.	Maize	African tall, Ganga-2	30 cm	120:60:60	65-70 DAS	45-50
3.	Hybrid Napier	CO-3, CO-4, DHN-6	60×60 cm	50:50:50 as basal dose & 25kg/ha N at each cutting	First cut 2.5 MAP & next 45-50 days interval	175-180
4.	Para grass	—	30×30 cm	30:30:30 &20kg N at each cutting	First cut 2.5 MAP & 30 days interval	125-150
5.	Guinea grass	Bundl guinea-1 & 2, Hamil	60×60 cm	30:30:30 and 25 kg N each cutting	First-2.5 MAP & 40 days interval	50-60
6.	Lucerne	Anand, Sirsa, NDRI selection	30 cm	20:100:40	60-65 DAS & next cut 30 days interval	70-80
7.	Berseem	Wardan, Meskavi, BL-1	25-30 cm	20:80:40	First cut 60 DAS and next 30 days interval	50-60
8.	Subabool	K-8, Hawai	1×1 m	25:50:0	First 5-6 MAP and next 50 days	60-70
9.	Dashrath	—	60×60 cm	25:50:0	First 4-5 MAP and next cut 45 days	50-60

DAS – Days after sowing, MAP – Month after planting

9. Alternate source of fodders during acute shortage

During acute shortage of fodder especially during the drought sugarcane tops and vegetable waste can be fed to the animals to maintain their health and keep them alive. However, feeding by the sugarcane tops should not be the regular practice since it contains high oxalic content which come in contact with the calcium in bones of animal form calcium oxalates which is leached through urine. Due to more leaching of the ca from animal body after few years the animal become weak and unproductive. Hence while feeding the sugarcane tops the animal should also provided with calcium through separate mineral mixture.

10. Strengthening extension activities

The farmers should be made aware about the importance of fodder in animal health and production. The farmer should be encouraged to allot some area for cultivation of quality fodders also they should be encouraged to adopt the preservation of excess fodder appear during rainy season. Awareness program should be conducted through organizing training programs, field trips, farmer rally etc. Since there are little hopes to increase separate area for quality forage production, the farmers should be encouraged to cultivate the fodder trees or take massive cultivation of scarcity fodder trees on wastelands or along the roads and follow the agro forestry approaches including silvi-pasture and horti-pasture to get multiple produces from the same land with proper utilization of the resources The livestock owners should also be trained to enrich the by-products and crop residues produced on their farm as a feed for animals. The rooted slips and seeds of high yielding varieties of fodder crop should be made available to the farmers.

Review of Research Work

1. An experiment was conducted during 2001-02 to 2004-05 to study the effect of pruning intensities on productivity of ber based horti pasture systems under semi-arid rainfed conditions. Ram and Kumar (2011) found that pruning of secondary branches of ber at 20 cm length from base recorded significantly higher dry forage (4.3 t/ha) of pasture as compared to pruning at 60 cm length. Among the pasture combinations, intercropping of guinea grass with *stylosanthes hamata* produced significantly higher dry forage (6.34 t/ha) than other sole and combined pasture under investigation.
2. Shukla *et al* (2011) based on two year of study at IGFRI, Jhansi concluded that dry forage yield (2.25 t/ha) and growth of bael tree var.NB-9 in terms of collar diameter (2.89 cm) was highest when staggered trench method of moisture conservation was applied.

Table 7.3: Effect of pruning levels of Ber (*Zizrohus mauritiana*) and grass – legume intercropping on dry forage yield in ber based horti-pasture system (pooled data of 4 years)

Treatment	Dry Forage yield (t/ha)		
	Grass	Legume	Total (t/ha)
Pruning length(cm)			
20	3.6	0.7	4.3
40	3.3	0.7	4.0
60	3.2	0.6	3.8
CD (p=0.05)	0.3	0.1	0.4
Grass + legume intercropping			
Guinea + Stylosanthes	5.6	0.7	6.3
Guinea + Stylo+ Dinanath	5.4	0.8	5.1
Dinanath + Stylo	2.4	0.9	3.3
Natural Pasture	1.1	0.3	1.3
CD (0.05)	0.4	0.1	0.5

Source: Ram and Kumar, 2011

Table 7.4: Performance of bael based horti-pastoral system with moisture conservation measures

Treatments	Growth of CISH B-2 (collar diameter in cm	Growth of var.NB-9	Forage Yield (dry) t/ha
Staggered trench	2.75	2.89	2.25
Stone mulch	2.49	2.81	1.78
Water retaining chemical	2.59	2.39	1.71
Control	1.99	1.64	1.51
Sole bael	2.48	2.33	–
Anjan & Stylo pasture	–	–	**1.91**
Mean	2.46	2.41	1.83

Source: Shukla *et al.*2011

3. Mahanta and Pachauri (2005) observed that nutrient content in three different varieties in the form of silage and in fresh green fodder were at par. It indicated that there were no losses of nutrients during preservation of green sorghum fodder.

Table 7.5: Proximate analysis of three varieties of sorghum as green and silage (on% DM basis)

Attributes	HC-136	HD-15	J.sel-10
Green			
OM	94.14	90.90	93.99
Crude protein	5.38	8.20	6.09
EE	1.69	1.78	1.52
NDF	65.53	66.18	67.19
ADF	36.54	35.35	37.50
Cellulose	31.28	29.14	32.32
Total ash	5.86	9.10	6.09
Silage			
OM	92.35	89.82	86.37
Crude protein	5.24	7.43	5.87
EE	2.13	2.16	2.03
NDF	80.87	81.96	79.89
ADF	48.96	51.00	50.35
Cellulose	39.38	39.27	38.84
Total Ash	7.65	10.18	13.63
PH	4.2	3.8	4.1
Lactic acid	6.12	7.30	6.88
NH_3N	8.41	7.36	9.10

Source: Mahanta and Pachauri, 2005

4. Gupta *et al.* (2005) studied the harvesting stages of different cereal crops and relative nutrient content. It was observed that harvesting of these fodder crops at the right stage gave maximum nutrient content.

Table 7.6: Comparative nutritional quality of non-legume fodders

Fodder Crop	Harvesting Stage	Crude Protein (%)	Dry matter Digestibility (%)
Maize	55-65 DAS	8-11	68-0
Bajra	50-55 DAS	7-10	62.5
Sorghum	70-80DAS	7-8	60.5
Teosinte	80-85DAS	7-9	62.5
Hybrid Napier	First cut at 1 mt ht and subsequent 30 days interval	7-11	60.5
Guinea grass	First at 1 m ht and 25-30 days interval	8-10	60.5

Source: Gupta *et al.*, 2005

5. Premratne and Premlal (2006) conducted experiment at Veterinary Research Institute, Gannoruwa, peradeniya, Srilanka and compared nutritive value of NB-21 and CO-3 varieties of Hybrid Napier. It was observed that CO-3 was superior over NB-21 in nutritional aspects.

Table 7.7: Nutritional comparison of NB-21 and CO-3 grasses

Nutritional Ingredients	Value (Dry matter basis)	
	NB-21	CO-3
Crude protein	10-11	15-16
Crude fibre	27-30	34-37
Acid detergent fibre	39-41	42-47
Neutral detergent fibre	60-65	74-78
Crude Fat	5.7-6.2	6.2-6.9
Ash	8.2-10.7	9.5-12.8
Lignin	9-13	6-8
Calcium	0.17	0.11
Potassium	0.47	0.42
Magnesium	0.21	0.36

Source: Premratne and Premlal, 2006

6. Datt (2008) found that vegetable waste was the good source of different nutrents such as Crude protein, ether extract, crude fibre and ash content. Therefore it could be an alternative source of the fodder.

Table 7.8: Proximate analysis of vegetable waste

Name	Per cent Composition (Dry matter basis)			
	CP	EE	CF	Ash
Cabbage waste	10.12	2.91	13.82	12.40
Cauliflower	18.12	4.92	14.50	10.38
Brinjal	17.42	3.10	22.55	7.82
Pumpkin	15.12	3.98	14.79	5.42
Bottle gourd	16.05	2.55	15.69	7.59
Raddish	12.8	2.10	9.98	14.30

Source: Datt, 2008

7. From the below table it was found that nutritive value of maize is higher in hydroponics over conventional maize fodder production at ICAR Research Complex, Goa.

Table 7.9: Comparison between nutritional value of conventional maize fodder and hydroponics maize fodder

Nutrients	Conventional	Hydroponics
CP	10.67	13.57
EE	2.27	3.49
CF	25.92	14.07
NFE	51.78	66.72
Total ash	9.36	3.84
Acid insoluble ash	1.40	0.33

Source: ICAR Extension Folder, 2011

8. Horti-pasture

Tiwari *et al.* (1999) found that Ber (Zizyphus spp,) based horti-pasture has proved renumerative in Thar desert on farmer's field. Ber tree were planted at spacing 6x6 m and grass Cenchrus ciliaris was introduced betwwen the rows after third year.On an average dry grass production was 1.55 t/ha/year.The fruit,leaf fodder and fuel wood production from ber tree was 2.77,1.87 and 2.84 t/ha/year respectively.

Table 7.10: Improved horti-pasture (Ber+cenchrus ciliaris) on farmer's field

Year	Dry grass(t/ha)	Tree Products (t/ha)		
		Fuel Wood	Leaf Fodder	Fruit Yield
1.	1.50	3.10	2.13	3.10
2.	1.67	2.74	1.80	2.74
3.	1.42	2.46	1.71	2.49
4.	1.66	2.49	1.63	2.85
5.	1.48	2.43	2.01	2.80
6.	1.57	2.63	1.94	2.67
Average	1.55	2.64	1.87	2.77

Source: Tewari *et al.*,1999

Tewari *et al* (2001) demonstrated that agroforestry,particularly improved jujube based horti-pasture system can be major source of livelihood in many parts of arid region.

Table 7.11: Economics returns (In terms of gross income)from jujube based horti-pastoral system

Particular	Production(t/ha)	Returns (Rs.)
Dry grass	1.55	3100
Fuel wood	2.64	2640
Leaf fodder	1.87	7480
Fruits	2.77	33240
Total	–	46640

Source: Tewari *et al.*2001

9. Silvi-pasture

In an improved silvi-pasture *Hardwickia binata* was taken as tree component at 3×3 m spacing with *Cenchrus ciliaris* grass.Results of nine year study have been depicted in the following table. Harsh *et al.*(1992) found that average carrying capacity of the practice was 4.1 sheep/ha/year against 3.7 for sole *C.ciliaris* pasture and 1.6 for sole *H.binata* plantation.In this type of improved silvipasture practice,in addition to grass+top feed production to the tune of 3.06 t/ha/year,0.26 t/ha/year of fuel wood is also obtained.

Table 7.12: Production potential of *Hardwickia binata* + *Cenchrus ciliaris* based improved silvi-pasture

Year of Plantation	Grass (t/ha)	Leaf Fodder (t/ha)	Total Fodder yield(t/ha)	Carrying Capacity (Sheep/ha/year)
1.	0.82	–	0.82	1.9
2.	1.23	–	1.23	2.9
3.	1.64	–	1.64	3.9
4.	2.05	–	2.05	4.9
5.	1.64	–	1.64	3.9
6.	1.64	–	1.64	3.9
7.	1.24	2.31	3.55	8.5
8.	0.84	0.66	1.50	3.6
9.	0.84	0.66	1.50	3.6
Average	1.33	0.40	1.73	4.1

Source: Harsh *et al.*1992

10. Silvi-pasture

From the following table Tiwari *et al.* (1999) evealed that maximum herbage biomass production of 3.9 t/ha was recorded in Prosopis cineraria based silvipasture system with maximum carrying capacity of 4.5 sheep/ha/year which is followed by the Zizyphus spp, based silvipasture system.

Table 7.13

Silvipasture	Herbage Biomass (t/ha)	Herb spp. Richness (nos.)	Herb spp. Diversity	Palatable Herb (%)	Carrying Capacity (Sheep/ ha/Year)
Prosopis cineraria based	3.9	2	0.41	50.0	4.5
Zizyphus spp. based	2.3	7	2.31	42.8	2.3
Acacia senegal based	1.2	2	0.59	50.0	1.4
Acacia tortlis based	1.5	1	0.00	0.00	0.00

Source: Tiwari *et al.*1999

Also from the following table the forage production under agro forestry tree species indicate that under Prosopis cineraria and Tecomena undulata tree species produced maximum herbage biomass of 1.5 t/ha and minimum under Acacia senegal.

Table 7.14: Estimated forage production with agro forestry trees species in arid region of western Rajasthan

Tree species	Forage yield (kg/ha)
P.cineraria	1500
Zizyphus spp	1500
Tecomella undulate	1500
Albizzia lebbek	1400
A. Senegal	600

Source: Tiwari *et al.* 1999

Conclusion

The possibilities for increase in good arable area under fodder production are remote as there is immense pressure on the land for grain crops, cash crops and other varied uses. There will be further shrinkage in the area under forage production and natural grasslands in future. The yield levels in cultivated forage crops are already approaching to plateau.Therfore fodder scarcity can be minimised by adopting agro forestry approach scientifically for higher forage biomass either on degraded wastelands, forest land or range land, enriching the available crop residue and adopting the fodder preservation technologies viz.Silage and Hay making.

REFERENCES

BVC, Rashtriya Krishi Vikas Yojana Annual Report 2011-2012: 2

Datt (2008). Proximate Composition of some Important Horticultural Crop Residues. Danisco Animal Nutrition.

Gupta, B.K., Bharadwaj, B.L. and A.K.Ahuja (2005). Nutritional Value of Forage Crops of Punjab. Punjab Agricultural University Publication.

Harsh, L.N, Tewari, J.C., Burman, U and Sharma, S.K. (1992). Agroforestry in Arid Region. *Indian Farming*, 45: 32-37.

Hegde, N.G. (2010). Forage Resource Development in India. Souvenir of IGFRI Foundation Day: pp. 8.

ICAR Extension Folder (2011). Technology for Production and Feeding of Hydroponics Green Fodder: 45.

Mahanta, S.K. and Pachauri, V.C.(2005). Nutritional Evaluation of Two Promising Varieties of Forage Sorghum in Sheep Fed as Silage. *Asian Aust.J.Anim.Sci.* 18(12): 1715-1720.

Mathukia, R.K, Sagarka, B.K. and Panara, D.M. (2016). Fodder Production through Agroforestry: A Boon for Profitable Dairy Farming. Innovare Journal of Agriculture Science, 4 (2).

Planning Commission Report (2007). Draft Report of Working Group on Animal Husbandry and Dairying.

Premratne, S. and Premlal, G. (2006). Hybrid Napier Var. CO-3: A Resourceful Fodder Grass for Dairy. *The Journal of Agricultural Sciences*. 2 (1): 22-33

Ram, S.N. and Sunil Kumar (2011). Effect of Pruning on Productivity and Economics of Ber based Horti-pasture System. *Indian J.Dryland Agric.Res. & Dev.*, 26(2): 86-90

Shukla, A.N., Sunil Kumar and Ram, S.N.(2011). Performance of Bael (*Aegle marmelos*) based Hortipasture System for Sustaining Productivity in Semiarid Agro-ecosystem. *Range mgmt and Agro Forestry*: 431.

Tewari, J.C., Bohra, M.D. and Harsh, L.N. (1999). Structure and Production Function of Traditional Extensive Agroforestry System and Scope of Intensive Agroforestry in that Desert. *Indian Journal of Agroforestry* 1(1): 81-94.

Tewari, J.C. Tripathi, D. and Narain, P. (2001). Jujube: A Multipurpose Tree for Arid Land Farming System. *The Botanica,* 51: 121-126.

Pages: 110-123

Food Technology and Research Advancement
Edited by: Dr. Avnish Chauhan and Dr. Pawan Kumar 'Bharti'
ISBN: 978-93-86841-49-0
Edition: 2018
Published by: Discovery Publishing House Pvt. Ltd., New Delhi (India)

8

Developmental Biology of *Pseudodiaptomus serricaudatus* (crustacea: copepoda) Reared at Different Temperatures and Algal Diets in the Laboratory

G. Padmavati

ABSTRACT

Post-embryonic development and biochemical composition of the calanoid copepod, *Pseudodiaptomus serricaudatus* is described. The development proceeded in general calanoid pattern except that there are only five-live nauplii stages, the first naupliar stage (N1) being suppressed. The clutch size was positively related to the body size of adult female (*t-test*, $p<0.001$). The relationship between development time and temperature was described by Bêlehrádek's functions. The development time of *P. serricaudatus* with respect to different temperatures viz. 25±0.5°C and 28±0.5 °C and different feeds (*Chaetoceros, Isochrysis* and *Nannochloropsis*) affected significantly (one-way ANOVA, $p<0.01$). The generation length, as sum of development time from egg to adult (CVI) was 12.7 and 12.4 days at 25 °C and 11.9 and 12.4 days at 28 °C with *Chaetoceros peruvianus* feed and 20.2 and 24.0 days at 25 °C and 15.1 and 14.6 days at 28 °C respectively with *Isochrysis* feed. Copepodite growth was retarded with *Nannochloropsis* feed. This study is the first report on successful rearing of *P. serricaudatus* from eggs to adults under controlled laboratory conditions from coastal waters of Visakhapatnam, Bay of Bengal. Biochemical composition of this copepod (protein: 42.8%; lipid: 6.7% of DW) in this study suggest that *P. serricaudatus* can be utilized effectively as a live feed for marine finfish and shellfish larvae.

Key words: Developmental biology, calaonoid copepod, *Pseudodiaptomus serricaudatus*, Bay of Bengal, India.

Department of Ocean Studies and Marine Biology, Pondicherry University, Port Blair - 744 112, Andaman and Nicobar Island (India)

Introduction

Pseudodiaptomus serricaudatus (Scott, T. 1894) a planktonic copepod occurs commonly in brackish water environment such as lower reaches of rivers, coastal lagoons and neritic waters (Padmavati 1992) in tropical and temperate regions. Females carry the eggs in an egg mass attached to the genital somite until the nauplii hatch out. Species of the genera *Pseudodiaptomus* contributes substantially to the total zooplankton standing stock and represent an important prey item in the diets of invertebrates (Froneman, 2001) and fish larvae (Froneman and Vorwerk, 2003). Although attempts to use this species as live feed for aquaculture seem to be successful (Doi *et al.*, 1997), constraints in propagation techniques lie in the poor understanding of its biology. Information about stage-to-stage developmental rates of this copepod is currently lacking from the Indian Ocean, largely because of difficulties in resolving discrete cohorts in seasonal field samples (Padmavati and Ikeda, 2002). To date, only a limited attempt on development of other species of *Pseudodiaptomus* has been made (Ummerkutty 1964; Uye *et al.*, 1983; Pillai, 1976). There is apparently no study on reproductive biology of this species from coastal waters of Visakhapatnam, Bay of Bengal. Hence, to fill this lacuna, it was considered necessary to undertake a study on developmental biology of *P. serricaudatus*. This paper describes the developmental biology and biochemical composition of *P. serricaudatus*. In this study, the effect of different temperatures and algal diets on egg production and development by *P. serricaudatus* was evaluated under controlled laboratory conditions.

Materials and Methods

Live specimens of zooplankton were collected from Lawson's Bay Station (17 °N 83°E) from the coastal waters of Visakhapatnam coast, Bay of Bengal (Fig. 8.1) through oblique hauls by a zooplankton net having mesh size of 250µm. Upon the retrieval of the net, the contents in the cod-end were diluted in 5 liter plastic containers filled with surface seawater and transported to the land laboratory. At the laboratory, gravid females of *Pseudodiaptomus serricaudatus* (Copepoda: Calanoida) with egg sacs carrying eggs were sorted out from other zooplankton and placed individually in 15ml glass vials filled with filtered seawater, and the containers were placed at 25±0.5°C and 28±0.5 °C °C in incubators under dark conditions. These temperatures represent typical conditions for *Pseudodiaptomus serricaudatus* in the coastal waters of Visakhapatnam coast, Bay of Bengal (Rao and Durve, 1992).

Laboratory grown phytoplankton cultures such as, *Chaetoceros peruvianus, Isochrysis galbana* and *Nannochloropsis salina* were provided as food at a concentration of 3.0~ 3.5 × 10^6 cells ml^{-1} to these copepods. Batches of newly hatched nauplii thus obtained were placed in 15 ml glass vials, and maintained at 25±0.5°C and 28±0.5 °C. Effects of temperature and different feeds on the survival and growth of nauplii and copepodite stages were recorded. Body length of copepodite stages was expressed in terms of Prosome length (from the anterior point of rostrum to the posterior later edge of the last prosome segment) of each copepodite stage was measured to the nearest 0.01 mm under a dissecting microscope fitted with an eye-piece micrometer. Biochemical composition such as protein and lipid content of this copepod was calculated as a percentage of dry weight (Omori and Ikeda, 1984). Protein content was determined by MicroKjeldahl method. Lipid content was estimated by Folch *et al.*, 1957).

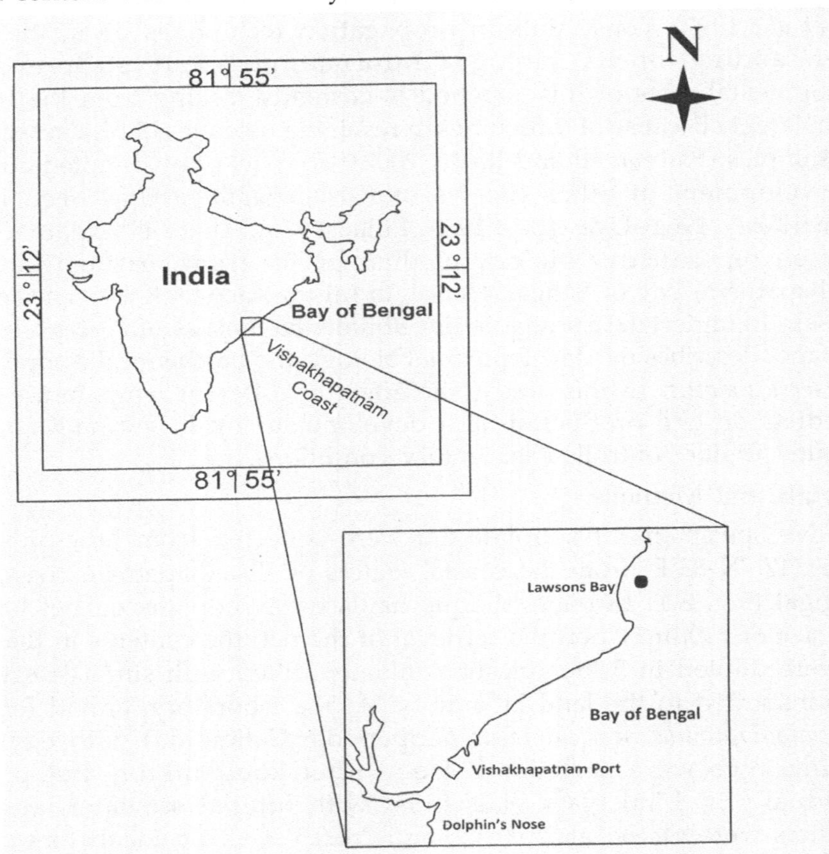

Fig. 8.1: Location of the sampling station (•)

Results

Egg sac of *P. serricaudatus* was spherical in shape (0.2±0.04 mm; Fig. 8.2). The mean clutch size varied from 16.6 to 15.8mm. The number of eggs per female egg sac ranged from 6 to 33 (Fig. 8.2) and increased with increasing female prosome length. The clutch size was positively correlated to the body size of adult female (r2=1, $p<0.001$; Fig. 8.3). The effect of temperature on egg hatchability was significant (*t*-test, $p<0.05$) (Table 8.1). Nauplii production at both 25 and 28°C was high with *Chaetoceros* feed and low with *Nannochloropsis* (Fig. 8.4). The effect of feed on nauplii production was significant (one-way ANOVA, $p<0.01$).

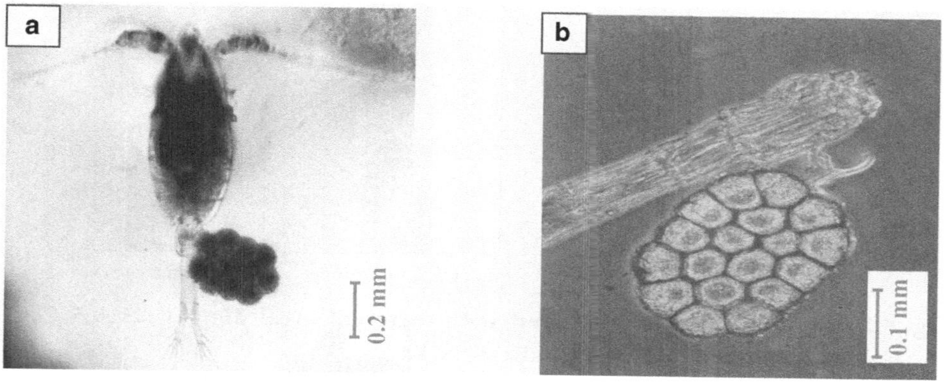

Fig. 8.2: *P.serricaudatus* (a) Gravid female carrying egg sac (b) Egg sac

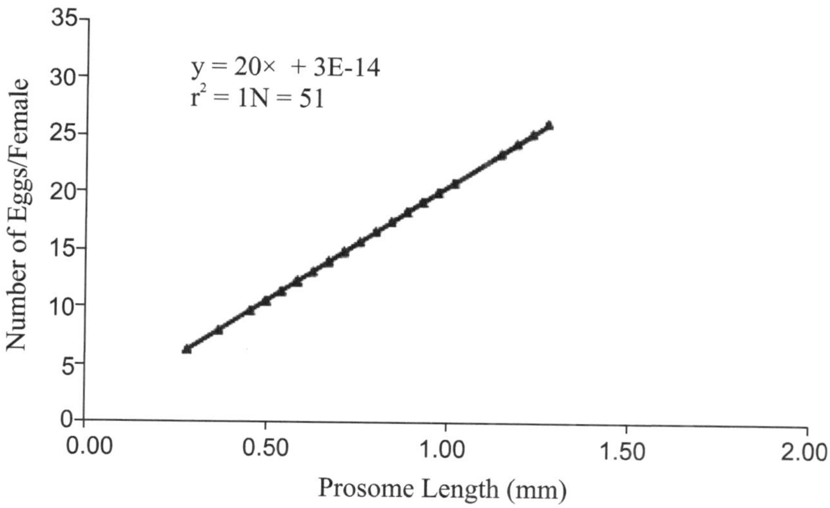

Fig. 8.3: Relationship between clutch size and prosome length of adult ♀ of *P.serricaudatus* using the females from stock culture.

The life cycle of egg-sac carrying calanoid copepod *P. serricaudatus* in this study comprised 5 nauplii and 5 copepodite stages. There were only five-live nauplii stages, the first N1 being suppressed. *P. serricaudatus* carried the eggs in an egg mass attached to the genital somite until the nauplii (N-II) hatched out. The first nauplii brooded within the egg sac.

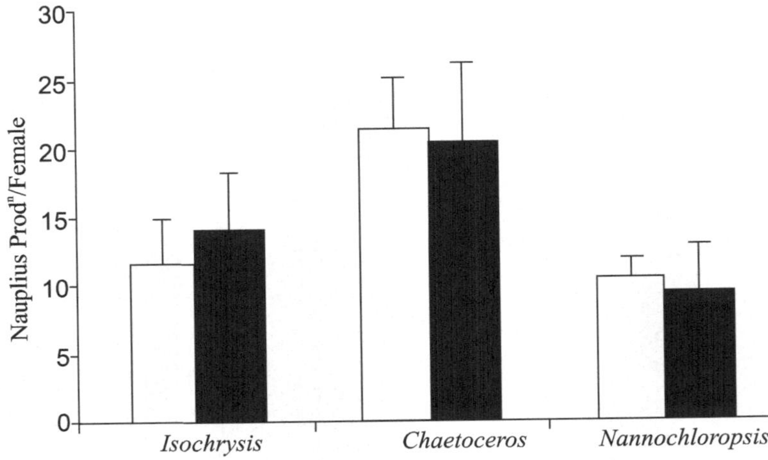

Fig. 8.4: Nauplius Production/♀ fed with different algal diets at 25±0.5°C (□) and 28±0.5°C (■). Bars indicate SD

Nauplius II (NII): Average size 0.16 ± 0.01 mm. The posterior tip was bifurcated with the right lobe slightly at a higher level than the left one. Antennule is 3-segmented, the segments bearing one, two and five setae respectively. In Antennae, the protopodite is 2 segmented, the endopodite 1-segmented and exopodite 6-segmented. The segmentation of basal protopodite and endopodite was similar to that of antennae, exopodite however being only 4-segmented.

Nauplius III (NIII): The posterior tip tapered more acutely. In caudal armature a short seta was added towards the left lobe. There was no change in the first and second segments of antennules. But the third segment carries seven setae. Rudiments of maxillules were formed and represented by two spines.

Nauplius IV (NIV): The body shape was more elongated than in NIII. Body length was 0.22 ± 0.01 mm. In the caudal armature there were four setae on each lobe. The spinous seta was the longest and stout. There were eleven setae on the terminal segment of antennules. Maxillule was bilobed structure bearing three setae.

Nauplius V (NV): Length of the body was 0.26 ± 0.01 mm. The body showed traces of segmentation. The caudal armature differed from that of fourth stage by having one shorter seta on the right lobe. There were thirteen setae on the terminal segment of antennules. A rudimentary lobular maxilla with two setae was present beyond maxillle.

Nauplius VI (NVI): Body length was 0.28 ± 0.02 mm. The last segment of antennules carried sixteen setae. Rudiments of Maxillipede and 1st and 2nd swimming legs (P1 and P2) appeared.

Table 8.1(a-c): Development time of eggs, total nauplii and each copepodite stages of *P. seirricaudatus* reared in the laboratory at two different temperatures (25 °C & 28 °C), with three different algal diets. Mean ± SD with the number of specimens in parentheses

8.1a. With *Chaetoceros* Feed

Temp. (°C)	Eggs (days)	N2-N6 (days)	C1 (days)	C2 (days)	C3 (days)	C4 (days)	C5 (days)	Eggs-C6 (days)
25±0.5	1.1±0.3 (295)	3.1±0.3 (192)	2.2±0.4 (152)	2.0±0.7 (133)	1.8±0.6 (107)	1.5±0.4 (75)	(♀) 2.2±0.4 (32) (♂) 5.0±0.8(33)	CVI♀12.7±1.7 * (30) CVI ♂ 12.4±1.6* (27)
28±0.5	1.0±0.4 (305)	3.1±0.4 (193)	2.3±0.3 (163)	1.9±0.4 (160)	1.7±0.5 (123)	1.5±0.5 (110)	(♀) 2.3±0.5 (44) (♂) 1.8±0.4 (33)	CVI ♀ 11.9±1.7* (32) CVI ♂ 12.4±2.0* (25)

* $p<0.05$

8.1b. With *Isochrysis* Feed

Temp. (°C)	Eggs (days)	N2-N6 (days)	C1 (days)	C2 (days)	C3 (days)	C4 (days)	C5 (days)	Eggs-C6 (days)
25±0.5	1.9±0.5* (84)	4.5±1.1 (45)	2.3±0.5 (21)	2.6±0.7 (17)	2.1±0.6 (13)	1.8±0.4 (11)	(♀) 4.0±0.7 (6) (♂) 5.0±0.8(3)	CVI♀ 20.2±1.7* (4) CVI ♂ 24.0±0.8* (2)
28±0.5	1.2±0.4* (241)	4.4±0.7 (123)	1.9±0.3 (96)	2.2±0.4 (89)	1.6±0.5 (67)	1.5±0.9 (30)	(♀) 3.3±0.5 (11) (♂) 2.8±0.4 (15)	CVI ♀ 15.1±2.2* (6) C6VI ♂ 14.6±1.4 *(7)

* $p<0.05$

8.1c. With *Nannochloropsis* Feed

Temp. (°C)	Eggs (days)	N2-N6 (days)	C1 (days)	C2 (days)	C3 (days)	C4 (days)	C5 (days)	Eggs-C6 (days)
25±0.5	2.0±0.4* (37)	5.0±0.3 (19)	3.5±0.1 (2)	–	–	–	–	–
28±0.5	2.0±0.3* (29)	4.7±0.3 (11)	3.0±0.1 (1)	–	–	–	–	–

* $p<0.05$

Copepodite I: There was a dramatic change in the morphology from the last naupliar stage to the first copepodite stage (C1). The body length was 0.44 ± 0.11 mm. The body was composed of a prosome of four segments and an urosome of two segments. Antennule composed of nine segments. Two pair of swimming legs and five pairs of caudal setae was present on each ramus.

Copepodite II: Body length was 0.51 ± 0.04 mm. An additional segment was formed in the prosome and bears 3 pairs of swimming legs and five pairs of caudal setae on each ramus. Urosome had two segments as in C1. Antennule composed of fourteen segments.

Copepodite III: Body length was 0.61 ± 0.01 mm. The body was composed of a prosome of five segments and a urosome of two segments. Four pairs of biramous swimming legs and five pairs of caudal setae on each ramus. Antennule composed of 21 segments.

Copepodite IV: This stage was characterized by the presence of 5 pairs of swimming legs and 5 setae on each caudal rami. Urosome of both male and female had 3 segments. Body length of male was 0.73 ± 0.04 mm and female 0.81 ± 0.02. The fifth swimming legs (P5) were asymmetrical in male (♂) and symmetrical in female (♀). Antennule composed of 21 segments in both sexes.

Copepodite V: Urosome was 3- segmented in female and 4- segmented in male. Body length of male was 0.9 ± 0.04 mm and female 1.0 ± 0.05. All four pairs of swimming legs were well developed and 5 setae on each caudal rami. In female P5 is 2-segmented. In male right P5 was larger than the left. Antennule composed of 18 segments in ♀ and 20 segments in ♂.

Copepodite VI (Adult): Body length of male was 1.1 ± 0.11 mm and female 1.2 ± 0.21 mm. Urosome was 4- segmented in female and 5-segmented in male. Complete development, modification of antennules and fifth legs was found. Antennule composed of 19 segments in ♀ and 23 segments in ♂. The genital segment of ♀ was asymmetrical. 5th thoracic segment lined with serrated spinules that are clearly visible in lateral view. The genital segment is prolonged into a sheath and its posterior margin bears a row of spines. 1st and 2nd urosomal segment bears fine spinules on dorsal end. 5 setae on each caudal rami. No spines on the Th-segments in ♂. P5 was asymmetrical and last segment of right leg sickle-shaped (Figs. 8.5 & 8.6).

A reduction in the prosome length was seen for copepodites stages (C1-C6) of *P. serricaudatus* raised at 28°C (Fig. 8.7). Specimen raised at 28°C were smaller than at 25°C but the difference in body length for most stages between two temperatures tested in this study was not significant (one-way ANOVA, $p>0.05$) could be due to the temperature range (25-28°C) of this study was not wide enough to induce significant effect of temperature on prosome length.

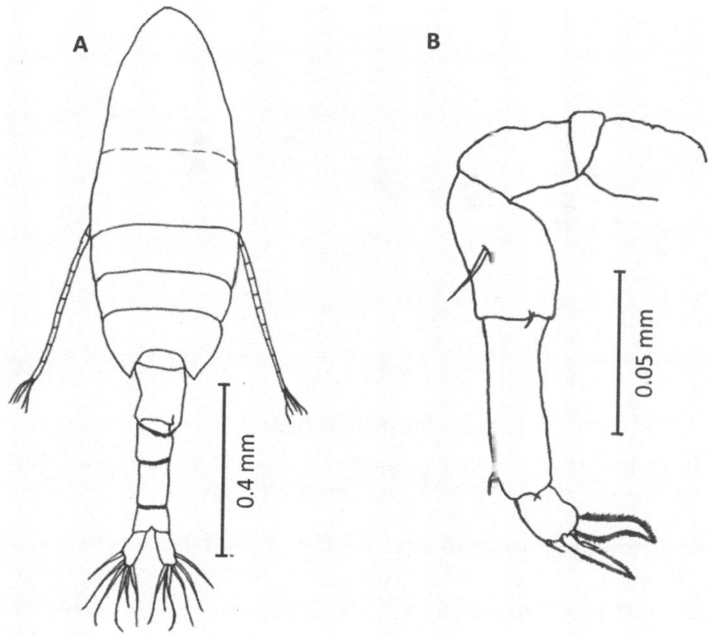

Fig. 8.5: ***P. serricaudatus*** **A; ♀ doral; B; ♀ P5**

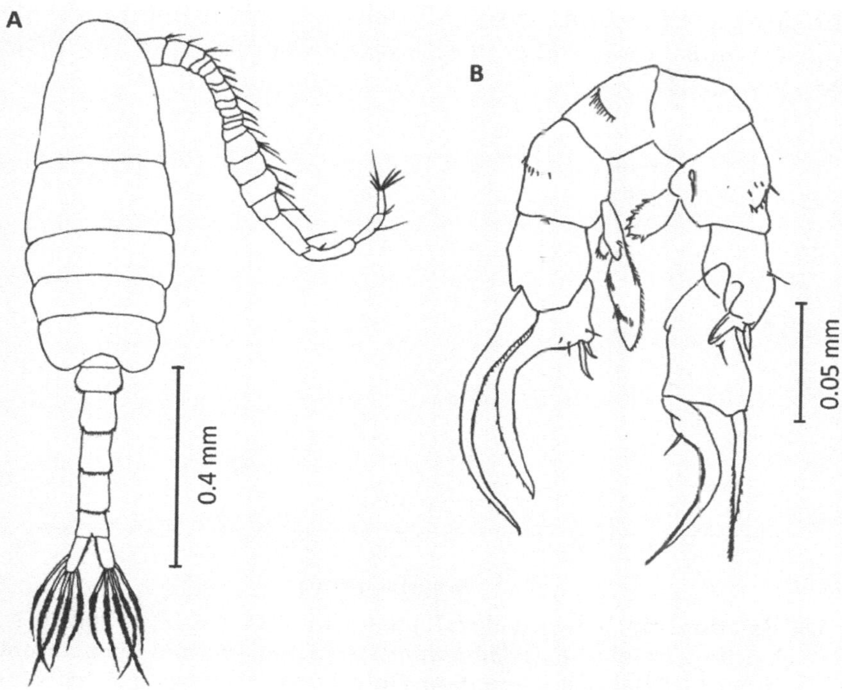

Fig. 8.6: ***P. serricaudatus*** **A; ♂ doral; B; ♂ P5**

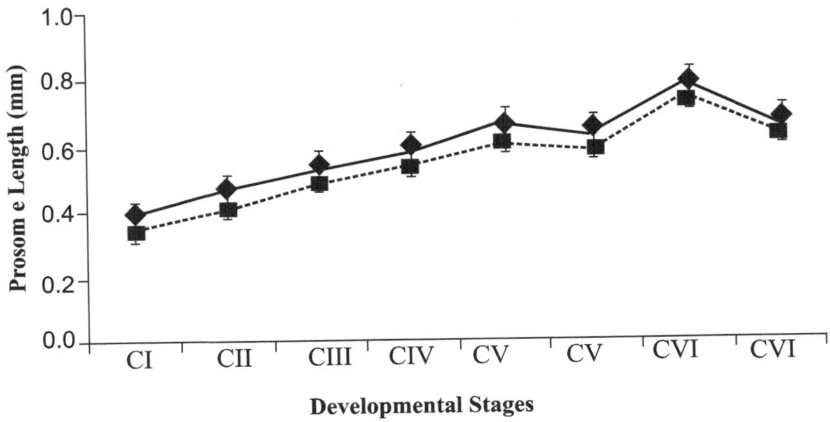

Fig. 8.7: Prosome length of each copepodite stage of *P. serricaudatus* raised in the laboratory 25±0.5°C (◆) and 28±0.5°C (■)

The development time from egg to N2 (egg hatching time), C1 (naupliar development time), C5 and C6 (generation time) were fitted to the Bêlehrádek function; D= a (T-α) $^{-2.05}$ (Figs. 8.8-8.10). Where D is the development time, 'T' is temperature, 'a' and 'α' are constant (McLaren and Corkett, 1969). Thus the predicted development time from the Bêlehrádek equation from this study fell well within the ranges derived from field population for other *pseudodiaptomid* species such as *P. annandalei* (Golez *et al.*, 2004).

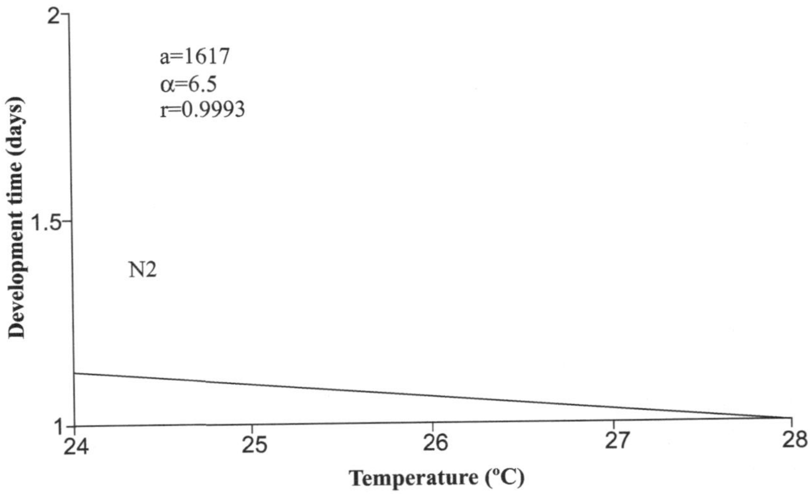

Fig. 8.8: Relationship between development time (days) from egg to N2 (egg hatching time) of *Pseudodiaptomus serricaudatus* and temperature (T°C) fitted to Bêlehrádek equation D= a (T-α) $^{-2.05}$ shows egg hatching time (egg to N2) decreased with increasing temperature

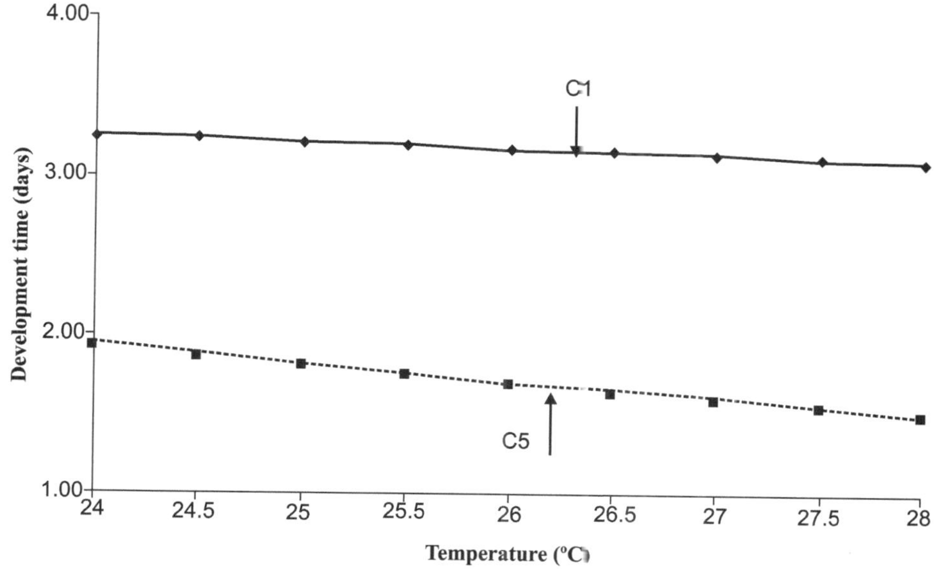

Fig. 8.9: Relationship between development time (days) from N2 to C1 (Naupliar development time) and C5 (Copepodite development time) of *P. serricaudatus* and temperature (T °C) fitted to Bêlehrádek equation D= a (T-α) $^{-2.05}$

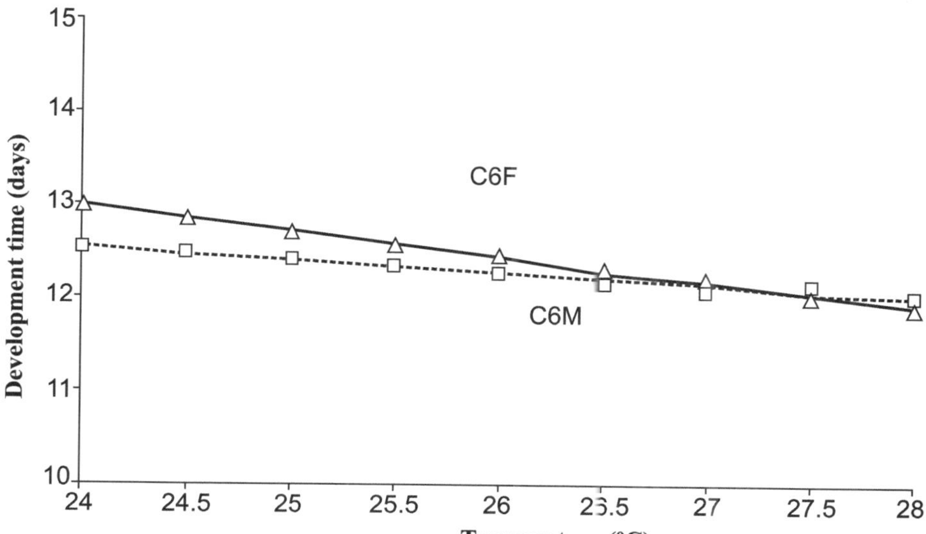

Fig. 8.10: Relationship between development time (days) from C5 to C6 of *P. serricaudatus* and temperature (T°C) fitted to Bêlehrádek equation D= a (T-α) $^{-2.05}$

The generation length, as sum of development time from egg to adult (C6) was 12.7 and 12.4 days for females and males (C6♀ and C6 ♂) at 25°C and 11.9 and 12,4 days for females and males at 28 °C and 20.2 and 24.0 days for females and males (C6♀ and C6 ♂) at 25°C and 15.1 and 14.6 days for females and males at 28°C respectively. Copepod survival to maturity from late nauplii at 25°C and 28°C was greater with a diet of *Chaetoceros* and *Isochrysis* while the survival was nil with *Nannochloropsis* feed (Table 8.1a-c).

The number of specimens that reached to C6 (adult stage) was 57 with with *Chaetoceros* algal diet (Table 8.1a) while the number of specimens reached C6 was only 19 with *Isochrysis* feed (Table 8.1b). With *Nannochloropsis* feed the newly hatched nauplii were grown only upto CI stage (only two individuals) and could not able to survive and grow further (Table 8.1c).

Discussion

The effect of temperature on egg hatchability was significant (*t*-test, $p<0.05$) and the duration of nauplii (N2-N6) and C5 stages was longer in the tested temperatures (25 & 28°C) as found in this study has been reported earlier for calanoid copepods (Padmavati & Ikeda, 2002). The development of *P. serricaudatus* proceeded in the general calanoid pattern except that there were only five free-living naupliar stages. The suppression of first naupliar stage (NI) and the egg hatching into a stage which was morphologically similar to the second nauplius (NII) stage of other pseudodiaptomid species as observed in this study has been reported earlier for other diaptomid species such as *Pseudodiaptomus aurivilli* and *P. euryhalinus* (Jerling and Wooldridge, 1991; Ummerkutty, 1964; Grice, 1969).

Distinct changes in the body form of *P. serricaudatus* occurred during transition from the last naupliar stage (NVI) to the first copepodid stage (CI) as observed in this study has been reported earlier for other diaptomids (Ummerkutty, 1964; Golez *et al.*, 2004). Of the three effective diets used to rear copepods, *Chaetoceros peruvianus* and *Isochrysis galbana* which contain high proportion of Docosahexaenoic acid (DHA) and Highly Unsaturated Fatty Acids (HUFA) might have utilized by this copepod for the growth and fecundity as observed in this study has been reported ealier (Jónasdottir, 1994) while *Nannochloropsis* with very high proportion of Eicosapentaenoid acid (EPA) which might not be a suitable diet for *P. seirricaudatus* and looks like *P. serricaudas* was unable to digest this phytoplankton species in this study (Norsker and Støttrup 1994). Uye *et al.* 1982 reported that copepod nauplii generally consume smaller (<30µm) particle but it was not so in this study as the copepodite of this copepod could not be able to survive beyond C1 stage with small sized *Nannochloropsis* algal diet. The rate of development of *P. serricaudas* was dependent on both temperature and food quality as observed in this study has been reported earlier for other calanoid copepods (McLaren and Corkett 1981; Uye and Kasahara, 1982; Ban 1994; Padmavati and Ikeda, 2002, Gopakumar G and Santhosi I, 2009).

The egg production rate for *P. serricaudatus* was low compared to an earlier study for other *Pseudodiaptomus* species (Uye, 1997) could be related to the type of spawning and the fecundity of egg-sac carrying copepods which is limited by the number of eggs in the sac (Corkett, 1970). The clutch size was positively correlated to the body size of adult female as found in this study has been reported earlier for other diaptomids (Uye and Kasahara, 1982). Under conditions of sufficient food supply, the prosome length of copepods are known to be largely a function of temperature (Mauchline, 1998; Padmavati and Ikeda, 2002) and the higher the temperature the smaller the length as observed in this study has been reported earlier (Uye *et al.*, 1983; Ban, 1994).

Biochemical constituent based on species level such as *Pseudodiaptomus serricaudatus* as estimated in this study provided a more realistic assessment than copepods as a whole (Hunter, 1982). Protein content of this copepod was high (42.8% of dry weight) while the Lipid fraction was low (6.7% of dry weight). Protein constituted the major fraction in terms of dry weight indicating that protein is the main energy reserve for this copepod. It is therefore evident that this copepod can be utilized as nutritional live feed for aquaculture.

Conclusion

The present study is the first report on developmental biology of calanoid copepod from the coastal waters of Visakhapatnam, Bay of Bengal. This study demonstrated clearly that laboratory-rearing is a powerful approach to fill the gaps in our knowledge on developmental patterns and generation length of copepods. Protein constituted the major fraction of biochemical composition in terms of dry weight indicating that copepods can be utilized as nutritional live feed for aquaculture.

REFERENCES

Ban, S. 1994. Effect of Temperature and Food Concentration on Post-embryonic Development, Egg Production and Adult Body Size of Calanoid Copepod *Eurytemora affinis*. *Journal of Plankton Research* 16: 721-735.

Corkett, C.J. 1970. Relationships between Development Rate of Eggs and Older Stages of Copepods. *Journal of Marine Biological Association of UK* 50: 161-168.

Doi, M.J.D., M.S. Toledo, N. Golez,, M. De los Santos and A. Ohno. 1997. Preliminary Investigation of Feeding Performance of Larvae of Early Red-spotted Grouper, *Epinephelus coioides* Reared with Mixed Zooplankton. *Hydrobiologia* 358: 259-263.

Folch, J.M, Lees, M., Sloane Stanley, G.H. 1956. A Simple method for the Isolation and Purification of Total Lipids from Animal Tissues *Journal of Biological Chemistry*, 226: 497-509.

Froneman, P.W. 2001. Feeding Ecology of the Mysid, *Mesopodopsis wooldridgei,* in a Temperate Estuary along the Eastern Seaboard of South Africa. *Journal of Plankton Research* 23: 999-1008.

Froneman, P.W. and P. Vorwerk. 2003. Predation Impacts of Juvenile *Gilchristella aestuaria* (Clupeidae) and *Atherina breviceps* (Atherinidae) on the Zooplankton in the Temperate Kariega Estuary, South Africa. *African Journal of Aquatic Science* 28: 35-41.

Golez, M.S.N., T. Takashi, T. Ishimarl, and A. Ohno. 2004. Post-embryonic Development and Reproduction of *Pseudodiaptomus annandalei* (Copepoda: Calanoida). *Plankton Biology and Ecology* 54(1): 15-25.

Gopakumar, G., and I. Santhosi. 2009. Use of Copepods as Live Feed for Larviculture of Damselfishes. *Asian Fisheries Science* 22: 1-6.

Grice, G.D. 1969. The Development Stages of *Pseudodiaptomus coronatus* Williams (Copepoda Calanoida). *Crustaceana* 16: 291-301.

Jerling, H.L., and T.H. Wooldridge. 1991. Population Dynamics and Estimates of Production for the Calanoid Copepod *Pseudodiaptomus hessei* in a Warm Temperate Estuary. *Estuarine, Coastal and Shelf Science* 33: 121-135.

Jónasdottir, S.H.1994. Effects of Food Quality on the Reproductive Success of Acartia Tonsa and Acartia Hudsonica: Laboratory Observations. *Mar. Biol.* 121: 67-81.

Mauchline, J. 1998. The Biology of Calanoid Copepods. *Elsevier,* San Diego 33: 1-710.

McLaren, I.A., and C.J. Corkett. 1981. Temperature-dependent Growth and Production by a Marine Copepod. *Canadian Journal of Fisheries Aquatic Science* 38: 77-83.

McLaren, I.A.C.J., E. Corkett, and J. Zillioux. 1969. Temperature Adaptations of Copepod Eggs from the Arctic to the Tropics. *Biology Bulletin* 137: 486-493.

Norsker, N.H., and J.G. Støttrup. 1994. The Importance of Dietary HUFAs for Fecundity and HUFA Content in the Harpacticoid, *Tisbe holothuria* Humes. *Aquaculture* 125: 155-166.

Omori, M., and T. Ikeda. 1984. *Methods in Marine zooplankton* Ecology. John Wiley and Sons, New York.

Padmavati, G. 1992. Zooplankton Ecology of the Estuarine, near Shore and Adjacent Coastal Waters of Goa. *Ph.D. Thesis,* Berhampur University: 175 pp.

Padmavati, G., and T. Ikeda. 2002. Development of *Metridia pacifica* (Crustacea: Copepoda) Reared at different Temperatures in the Laboratory. *Plankton Biology and Ecology* 49(2): 93-96.

Pillai, P.P., 1976. A Review of the Calanoid Copepod Family Pseudodiaptomidae with Remarks on the Taxonomy and Distribution of the species from the Indian Ocean. *J Marine Biological Association of India* 18(2): 242-265.

Rao, N.G., and V.S. Durve. 1992. Structure and Dynamics of Zooplankton Community in Lake Rangasagar, Udaipur, India. *Journal of Environmental of Biology* 13(3): 343-355.

Scott, A. 1894. Addition to the Fauna of the Firth of Forth. Report of the Fishery Board for Scotland 13: 231-271.

Ummerkutty, A.N.P. 1964. Studies on Indian Copepopds 6. The Post-embryonic Development of Two Calanoid Copepods, *Pseudodiaptomus aurivilli* Cleve and *Labidocera bengalensis* Krishnaswamy. *Journal of Marine Biological Association India* 6(1): 48-60.

Uye, S. 1997. Population Dynamics and Production of the Planktonic Copepods in a Eutrophic inlet of the Inland Sea of Japan. IV *Pseudodiaptomus marinus,* the Egg-carrying Calanoid. *Marine Biology* 128: 415-421.

Uye S., Y. Iwai, and S. Kasahara. 1982. Reproductive Biology of *Pseudiaptomus marinus* (Copepoda: Calanoida) in the Inland Sea of Japan. *Bulletin of the Plankton Society of Japan* 29(1): 25-35.

Uye, S., Y. Iwai, and S. Kasahara. 1983. Growth and Production of the inshore Marine Copepod *Pseudodiaptomus marinus* in the Central Part of the Inland Sea of Japan. *Marine Biology* 73:91-98.

Pages: 124-156

Food Technology and Research Advancement
Edited by: **Dr. Avnish Chauhan and Dr. Pawan Kumar 'Bharti'**
ISBN: 978-93-86841-49-0
Edition: **2018**
Published by: **Discovery Publishing House Pvt. Ltd., New Delhi (India)**

9

Microgreens

A Noval Approach of Food and Nutritional Security

M. Siva; G. Ranganna; M.M. Nagaraju; T. Thomson; G. Koteswararao; T. Kranthikumar and M. Surendrababu

ABSTRACT

Microgreens became popular in 20 years ago in the middle of 1990s in California and the first use of the word "microgreens" was documented in 1998. Microgreens are older than sprouts and much younger than baby greens. Microgreens are usually 1-3 inches in height, harvested at 7-14 days after germination, depending upon species. Microgreens differ from "sprouts" in that microgreens germinate in soil and require natural or artificial sunlight for growth, whereas sprouts germinate in water. Microgreens frequently called "vegetable confetti and considered as latest nutritional miracle-food. Microgreens are young, tender greens that are used to enhance the color, texture or flavor of salads or to garnish a wide variety of main dishes. Therefore, microgreens can be served as a new ingredient in salad, soups and sandwiches to brighten up a wide variety of main dishes. Microgreens boast two compensatory nutrients, namely phytonutrients and chlorophyll. Chlorophyll has antiseptic and anti inflammatory properties and guards against health diseases and can cure some types of anemia. Microgreens are having more plant sugars, more plant starches, more plant fibers, more vitamins, more minerals, more enzymes, and more phytonutrients. Phytochemicals, also called phytonutrients, are a broad range of substances in plants (phyto means plants or plant based) that promote health, prevent disease, and likely even help cure disease, including cancers. Hence these are considered as 'functional foods' or 'super foods'. Microgreens had the highest

College of Horticulture, Dr. YSR Horticultural University, Venkataramannagudem - 534101 West Godavari, Andhra Pradesh (India)

concentrations of ascorbic acid (vitamin C), tocopherols (vitamin E), phylloquinone (vitamin K), and beta-carotene (a vitamin A precursor), plus other related carotenoids in the cotyledons higher levels of vitamins and carotenoids-about five times greater than their mature plant counterparts, an indication that microgreens may be worth the trouble of delivering them fresh during their short lives. The microgreens can be grown in flat trays, filled with good organic potting mix or vermiculite. Then seeds are sown in lines and moisture it. Sprinkle the water with seeds top of the media. Provide high light 12 and 16 hours with low humidity. Germination after 7-9 days in appearance of 1st set of true leaves stage harvesting was followed by Sharpe knifes. Microgreens are cut above from media surface and packing without roots depending on the species and sold with the stem and attached cotyledons (seed leaves). Vegetable crops which can be grown as microgreens are Amaranth, Fennel, Arugula, Kale, Kohlrabi, Basil, Beet, Broccoli, Mustard, Cabbage, Onion, Carrot, Parsley, Celery, Popcorn, Chives, Radish, Collards, Spinach, pea and Swiss chard.

Key words: Vegetables, Microgreens, Food security, Nutritional security

Introduction

Microgreens are an exotic genre of edible greens appearing in upscale markets and restaurants which have gained popularity as a new culinary trend over the past few years. They are tender immature greens produced from the seeds of vegetables and herbs, having two fully developed cotyledon leaves with or without the emergence of a rudimentary pair of first true leaves. They are older than sprouts and much younger than baby greens. Microgreens became popular in the middle of 1990s in California and the first use of the word "microgreens" was documented in 1998. Microgreens are usually 1-3 inches in height, harvested at 7-14 days after germination, depending on the species, and sold with the stem and attached cotyledons (seed leaves). Frequently called "vegetable confetti," microgreens are young, tender greens that are used to enhance the color, texture, or flavor of salads, or to garnish a wide variety of main dishes (Murphy *et al.*, 2010; Treadwell *et al.*, 2010; Lee *et al.*, 2009).

Defination of Microgreens

It refers to microgreens are larger than a sprout and have produced at least two true leaves after expansion of the seedling leaves or cotyledons called a microgreens. They range in size from 13 to 1 ½" long, including the stem and leaves. A Microgreen has a single central stem which has been cut just above the soil line during harvesting. It has two fully developed cotyledon leaves and usually one pair very small, partially developed true leaves. The typical stem and leaf configuration for micro greens is about 1" to 1½" in height, and ½" to 1" in width across the top.

What are microgreens

Microgreens are young and tender edible seedlings produced using the seeds of different species of vegetables, herbaceous plants, aromatic herbs and wild edible plants. Depending on the species that has been used, they can be harvested 7-21 days after germination when the cotyledonary leaves have fully developed and the first true leaves have emerged (Xiao, 2013). Microgreens are harvested by cutting the single seedlings just above the soil line when their height is 3 to 9 cm without the rootlets. The edible portion is constituted by the single stem, the cotyledonary leaves and often by the emerging first true leaves. In some cases, when small and tender also the integuments of the seeds that remain attached to the cotyledons may be considered edible. Despite small in size microgreens also known as "vegetable confetti" (Treadwell *et al.*, 2010) or "microherbs" when referring to aromatic herbs, can provide a wide variety of intense flavors, bright colors and a good texture; therefore, they may be proposed as a new ingredient to enhance and garnish drinks, salads, appetizers, main and second courses, soups, sandwiches and desserts (Treadwell *et al.*, 2010; Xiao *et al.*, 2012). Microgreens represent a new category of vegetables with different traits as compared to the already known sprouts and the common fresh-cut leafy vegetables, also known as baby leaf vegetables. Moreover, they should not be confused with mini vegetables, also known as miniature, petite, and Lilliputian vegetables that can be produced by means of specific cultivation techniques (high plant density or anticipated harvest) or refer to genetic material at reduced growth and development.

Sprouts: germinated seeds with emerging root

Microgreens: 2-3 inches in height; 7-21 days (harvest stem, cotyledons, and emerging true leaves)

Baby greens: 4-6 inches in height; 21- 40 days.

Mature greens: > 6 inches in height; 40-60 days.

Reasons to Grow Microgreens

- Healthy Microgreens are extremely dense in vital enzymes, minerals and vitamins and chlorophyll. There are many foods you could eat that are fresher.
- Delicious Enjoy a dazzling array of new flavors. Plants are at their absolute peak of flavor intensity at the Microgreens stage of life.
- Different Your friends and family will be amazed at this new and exciting way to eat. Microgreens are perfect as a complete salad, additions to traditional salad, on sandwiches, in soups, as garnishes and much more.
- Easy & Fun Microgreens can be grown hydroponically with virtually no mess.
- It is perfect for countertop gardening. Our step by step kits take the guesswork out of growing.

Nutritional Properties of Microgreens

It has become an urban legend that Microgreens possess high concentrations of various nutritional and beneficial compounds. Numerous articles and websites claim that Microgreens are the latest nutritional miracle-food. The fact is, there have been no studies done on Microgreens to substantiate any of these claims so at this point it is all just wishful thinking; new-age mumbo jumbo. It would, of course, be to our benefit to claim that Microgreens are some kind of super-food. Most likely, have been said to contain particularly high concentrations of a certain chemo-protective compound, Sulphoraphane Glucosinolate (SGS). If at some point there are reliable nutritional studies done on microgreens, and they do show high values, Fresh Origins will be very pleased to promote it. A microgreens have a content of antioxidant compounds even ten times higher (Xiao *et al.,* 2012). For instance, in the case of the red cabbage, comparing the amount of the above-mentioned vitamins in the microgreens with those reported in the literature for the same species harvested at a regular ripening stage, microgreens showed an average content of Vitamin C six times higher (147 vs 23.5 mg/100 g of fresh product - FP), a four hundred times higher value of Vitamin E (24.1 vs 0.06 mg/100 g of FP) and a sixty times higher content of Vitamin K (2.4 vs 0.04 µg/g of FP) (Xiao *et al.,* 2012). Considering the daily intake levels recommended by the European Food Safety Authority (EFSA) for Vitamin C (60 mg), Vitamin E (13 mg) and Vitamin K (70 µg) for an adult of medium weight, the consumption of about 41 g of red cabbage microgreens would be enough to fulfill the recommended daily intake of Vitamin C, or 15 g of green radish microgreens would satisfy the daily intake of Vitamin E and just 17 g of garnet amaranth microgreens would be enough to fulfill the daily intake of Vitamin K. In addition to the high content of vitamins and anti-oxidant compounds, microgreens have a good content of minerals (Di Gioia *et al.,* 2015). Analyzing the content of the main minerals in few microgreens, it is possible to observe that microgreens represent a good source of potassium and calcium. In this perspective, the application of eco-sustainable production techniques and process innovations able to enhance the nutritive value of microgreens, can help to satisfy also consumers that have specific diet needs of fibers, proteins, carbohydrates, essential micro-elements and other phytonutrients. Undoubtedly, further studies are needed to examine these aspects more deeply and verify if microgreens can be considered 'super foods'. like vegetarians and vegans, that can diversify and enrich their diet by using the large variety of microgreens available.

The Health Benefits of Microgreens

Humans lack the necessary enzymes to synthesize the other essential vitamins, which therefore have to be obtained from food intake (Vitamin D Council).

- Plants are a great source of vitamins, and microgreens are an especially good source because their vitamin content is concentrated.
- Microgreens tend to provide more vitamins than their mature counterparts (Xiao *et al* 2012). highly nutritious and cleansing food source rich in vitamins, minerals, amino acids, antioxidants and enzymes. Other species such as flax, chia, broccoli and varieties of red brassica also have health compounds.
- Darkly colored purple/red varieties of radish microgreen which produce intensely-colored young leaves contain high levels of antioxidants linked to having anticancer properties.
- The variety of microgreens available not only provides different flavors, but also different vitamins. Even though microgreens are loaded with vitamins, their more mature counterparts tend to have more fiber, which makes digestion easier.
- Microgreens are a real superfood packed with antioxidants and other health-promoting nutrients. young lettuce seedlings, harvested 7 days after germination, had the highest antioxidant capacity as well as the highest concentrations of health-promoting phenolic compounds, compared with their more mature conterparts.
- Microgreen cotyledon leaves had considerably higher nutritional densities than their mature counterparts.
- Young edible seedlings are a superb source of vitamin C, an antioxidant that helps protect your body from the harmful effects of free radicals.
- Carotenoids, such as beta-carotene, are thought to reduce the risk of disease, particularly certain types of cancer and eye disease. Carrots are famous for being rich in beta-carotene, some microgreens appear to contain even more beta-carotene than carrots.
- Microgreens Are a Good Source of Vitamin E. The amount of alpha-tocopherol and gamma-tocopherol combined ranged from 7.9 to 126.8 milligrams per 100 grams in green daikon radish microgreens.
- It contain Vitamin K, Vitamin K also offers health benefits for humans by promoting normal blood clotting and preventing excessive bruising. Vitamin K also plays an important role in maintaining strong and healthy bones. microgreen found the highest levels of vitamin K in amaranth microgreens (Red Garnet variety).

Microgreens and Food Security

Predictive models indicate that by 2050 the world population could reach over 9 billion people. Today, in a world where about 795 million people (more than 14% of the world population) are malnourished (FAO, IFAD and WFP, 2015), the continuous population growth, especially in the developing countries, represents an important challenge for the achievement of food and nutritional security. Fulfilling the needs of the growing world population, by overcoming the lacks of food production, and by assuring that produced food is available to people in need, are the main challenges for the world agriculture (FAO, 2010). These challenges must be faced in a sustainable way in order to guarantee the availability of resources to the future generations. At the same time, agriculture has to face the effects of the climate change, the increasing competition for water resources, the loss of productive land and the competition for land; it also has to address the continuous migration of people from rural to urban areas, and the growing social concerns about the nature of the food production system (Kahane *et al.*, 2013). Given all these challenges to the food security, a greater diversification within the agricultural farming systems is increasingly recognized as an important pillar for a sustainable development (Kahane *et al.*, 2013). An approach to address these issues is to intensify the agricultural productions by increasing crop yields.

Microgreens and Agro-biodiversity

In their own small way, microgreens can contribute to preserve and valorize many local varieties that are at risk of genetic erosion or of extinction, offering an opportunity to recover and use such genetic material to produce this new category of vegetables. Preserve and valorize the plant biodiversity and agro-biodiversity, is one of the greatest challenges of our time. Although, the seeds of several ecotypes and varieties specifically selected for the production of microgreens are available on the market, the species and varieties potentially useful for the production of microgreens are numerous, and the vast heritage of agro-biodiversity of each geographical area may represent an extraordinary resource to be explored, especially for the production of highly nutritious microgreens. In the last decades, the selection of improved varieties of vegetables, according to characteristics such as high productivity, aesthetical quality and shelf life, has led to an undesired reduction of the flavor and to a decrease of the amount of the essential nutrients in several vegetables species (Davis *et al.*, 2004; Ebert, 2015). On the contrary, recent studies have shown that local varieties of traditional vegetables, as well as wild species, are often characterized by a higher nutrient density as compared to commercial improved varieties, widely grown at global level, and represent therefore, a good source of vitamins, essential micronutrients and other phytonutrients (Davis, 2009; Yang e Keding, 2009; Boari *et al.*, 2013). Thus, the production of microgreens from local varieties or populations and wild edible species, besides preserving and valorizing neglect plant resources at risk of genetic erosion, may provide a variety of novel, fresh and highly nutritious food (Ebert, 2014), which can satisfy the demand of innovation and novel products of the agri-food industry., as well as, the needs of the modern consumers, more and more health conscious and attentive to the quality and the nutraceutical properties of their food (Di Gioia *et al.*, 2015). Last but not least, it is important to highlight that the production of microgreens requires a great amount of seeds possibly characterized by high germinability and low cost, and the seeds of local varieties often have these characteristics.

Types of Microgreens

There are many types of microgreens to choose from (see Table 9.1). They can be divided into three groups: lettuce, herbs, and vegetables. From the lettuce group, the most common include red chard, mustard, cress, mizuna, pak choi, and brassicas. These tend to be the easiest to grow, and would probably be the best start for a beginner. The herbal group includes basils, chives, sorrel, stevia, and purslane. The vegetable group is composed of oriental and traditional offerings such as choy sum, Japanese parsley, amaranth, minutina, leeks, radish, and celery. germinate easily and grow quickly. These include cabbage, beet, kale, kohlrabi, mizuna, mustard, radish, swiss chard, and amaranth. Soaking some seeds prior to sowing, such as beets, helps facilitate germination. As many as 80-100 crops and crop varieties have reportedly been used as microgreens. Others that have been used include carrot, cress, arugula, basil, onion, chive, broccoli, fennel, lemongrass, popcorn, buckwheat, spinach, sweet pea, and celery.

Table 9.1: Different types of microgreens

Lettuce Microgreens	Herbal Microgreens	Vegetable Microgreens
Red Chard, Mustard, Cress, Mizuna, Pak Choi, Brassicas	Basils, Chives, Sorrel, Stevia, Purslane	Choy Sum, Japanese Parsley, Amaranth, Minutina, Leeks, Radish

Varieties of Microgreens

The seeds used to grow Microgreens are the same seeds that are used for full sized herbs, vegetables and greens. Microgreens are simply seedlings that are harvested before they develop into larger plants. Commonly grown varieties of microgreens include: Amaranth, Arugula, Beets, Basil, Cabbage, Celery, Chard, Chervil, Cilantro, Cress, Fennel, Kale, Mustard, Parsley, Radish, and Sorrel. Several varieties can be mixed together to create combinations of tastes, textures and colors.

Spinach

English spinach has a dark green leaf and very mild flavor. Spinach seed can have a low germination rate, particularly if conditions become overly warm. Optimum temperatures for germination are 16 to 22 degrees C. Under high temperatures, a large proportion of the seed may fail to germinate and this can then rot in the microgreen system and cause disease. Spinach is a cool season crop which benefits from summer shading and nutrient solution chilling.

Beet

Beet types such as Bulls Blood is primarily grown for its intense red color on even very young seedlings.

Tatsoi

Tatsoi has a rounded leaf and thick white petioles with a crisp texture and has a rapid germination and growth rate. This is a highly productive microgreen for hydroponic systems and has few problems.

Mitzuna

Mizuna has an attractive light green serrated leaf and is one of the fastest and most productive microgreens to grow. Germination is rapid and the crop usually has few disease problems. Mitzuna has a very mild mustard flavor and a wide range of uses.

Amaranth

Red amaranth is grown primarily for its deep color and attractive leaves, although green types with pink stems also exist.

Chard

Chard is available in a range of colors including yellow, pink, red and green and it has a mild spinach taste. Seed germinates readily although Chard is more of a cooler season crop with a slower growth rate than lettuce.

Kale

Microgreen kale produces succulent and tender leaves which are finely cut and almost blue-green in color. Another cooler season green, its color becomes paler under warm growing conditions.

Mache

Also called corn salad or lamb's lettuce, mache produces rounded leaves with a lettuce-like rowth. It's a common ingredient in baby leaf mixes and its microgreen version has many uses and can be harvested from the two to four leaf stage.

Lettuce

Lettuce microgreens are relatively easy to produce in most systems, however germination problems can occur once temperatures reach 26 degrees C or higher with seed going into secondary dormancy. Shading and chilling may be necessary in hot summer climates for high quality microgreen production of lettuce. This is just a selection of microgreen types being grown commercially using hydroponic methods, there are many other varieties of greens and the list continues to grow.

Chives

Baby chive leaves are highly decorative and often used to replace mature chopped chive leaves. Chives are slower to germinate than many other microgreens and production times are longer. They can be sown at a very high density and the clumps harvested by cutting at the base when they reach the required height.

Broccoli

Broccoli microgreens are rich in the compound sulforaphane, considered to have many health benefits due to its anti-cancer and anti-bacterial agents.

Cabbage

Red cabbage is used for its mild cabbage flavor and attractive color. Cabbage seed germinates rapidly in microgreen systems and is relatively easy to produce. There can be problems with caterpillars in greenhouses at certain times of the year and screens are required to prevent entry of egg laying butterflies.

Mustard and Cress

Mustard and cress are perhaps the oldest types of microgreens grown. Both have been produced as seedlings for use in sandwiches and salads for many years. Mustard and cress have a sharp, peppery flavor and are easy to grow as a microgreen crop.

Watercress

Watercress is a less common microgreen possibly because of its slow rate of growth from seed. Watercress has a peppery flavor and makes an attractive, bright green garnish. It also has proven health properties and contains good amounts of vitamin A, C, calcium ion and folate as well as isothiocyanates which are cancer-fighting compounds. Watercress grows extremely well in NFT and solution culture hydroponic systems and has considerable potential as a microgreen crop.

Parsley

Flat leaved parsley is one of the most popular microherbs and can be grown at a high density and harvested at the one or two true leaf stage depending on customer requirements. Its flavor is mild but distinctive and it contains none of the fibrous stems that older mature parsley can develop.

Fennel

With a mild aniseed flavor and attractive green feathery leaf, fennel microgreens have become popular with chefs. Fennel seed germinates readily, although this crop can be prone to aphid attack in spring.

Chrysanthemums

(Chinese Edible Chrysanthemum) Also called Shungiku, this is a herb used in oriental cooking and has become a popular microgreen due to its interesting flavor, which tastes similar to how chrysanthemums smell.

Cilantro

Cilantro microgreens are one of the most popular miniherbs and can develop a reasonably strong flavor under warm growing conditions. Cilantro is a warm season crop and needs at least 22 to 26 degrees C for germination — conditions similar to what's required by basil minigreens, making them ideal to be cropped together where heating is required.

French Sorrel

Sorrell has a very distinctive, sharp, acidic and slightly-bitter flavor and can be used as a salad spiker. Often mature sorrel becomes too intense or acidic, however the microgreen version is milder and less bitter, although can be slow growing and prefers cooler growing conditions.

Mint

Mint is a lesser grown miniherb, possibly because mint seed is tiny and slow to develop into a small plant. The flavor is mild, yet distinctive and the micro plants are highly attractive. Mint prefers cool growing conditions and performs well in NFT and other hydroponic systems where plenty of moisture is provided. Mint microgreens need to grown under shade in summer with the nutrient solution temperature monitored and chilled to prevent it from becoming too warm for good mint germination and production.

Dill

Dill microgreens have become popular in fish dishes, often replacing mature chopped dill. The flavor is very mild, but the foliage is similar to fennel in appearance — feathery and attractive, although very lightweight.

Shisho

Red/purple and green shisho (perilla) sometimes referred to as the Sushi herb used in Japanese cuisine has become more popular as a salad green. Perilla is an attractive and well-flavored microgreen with leaves resembling an ornamental coleus. It's a challenging microgreen to grow because the seed needs to be relatively fresh to germinate well and also benefits from stratification at 5 degrees C under moist conditions before sowing. Perilla seed also needs light to germinate and should be lightly sown into the top of the growing media or mats.

Tender Greens

While lettuce varieties often make up the bulk of mesclun or baby leaf salad mixes, the tender or succulent species used for microgreen production are quite diverse and includes a range of leaf sizes, shapes, colors and textures.

General Specifications of a Microgreen

Microgreen is a seedling having a a central stem which has been cut just above the soil line during harvesting. It has two fully developed cotyledon leaves, and usually one pair very small, partially developed true leaves. Differences in the size and leaf configuration are based upon the specific plant variety. For example, Micro Borage is a very large Microgreen. At 13 in height, it has a pair of very large cotyledon leaves and no true leaves. By comparison, Micro Mint has extremely tiny cotyledon leaves and will have 3-4 sets of true leaves at about 13 in height. More typical in size and leaf configuration for micro greens is Micro Basil at about 1-1 1/23 in height, and 1/23 to 13 in width across the top and includes the cotyledon leaves and one set of very small true leaves.

Production of Microgreens

Microgreens may be grown by individuals for home use. Growing small quantities at home is relatively easy; however, growing and marketing high-quality microgreens commercially is much more difficult. Having the right mix at the perfect stage for harvest is one of the most critical production strategies for success. The time from seeding to harvest varies greatly from crop to crop. When seeding a mixture of crops in a single planting flat, growers should select crops that have a similar growth rate so the entire flat can be harvested at once. Alternatively, growers can seed the various crops singularly and mix them after harvest. Microgreens can be grown in a standard, sterile, loose, soilless germinating media. Many mixes have been used successfully with peat, vermiculite, perlite, coconut fiber, and others. Partially fill a tray with the media of choice to a depth of 1/2 in. to 1 or 2 in., depending on irrigation programs. Overhead mist irrigation is generally used only through the germination stage in these media systems. After germination, trays should be subirrigated to avoid excess moisture in the plant canopy. An alternative production system uses one of several materials as a mat or lining to be placed in the bottom of a tray or longer trough. These materials are generally fiberlike and provide an excellent seeding bed. Materials may include burlap or a food-grade plastic specifically designed for microgreens such as those made by Sure to Grow (Beachwood, OH). These mat systems are often used in a commercially available production system using wide NFT-type troughs. The burlap mat may be sufficient alone for certain crops or may require a light topping with a media after seeding. Seeding may be done as a broadcast or in rows. Seeding density is difficult to recommend. Most growers indicate they want to seed as thickly as possible to maximize production, but not too thickly because crowding encourages elongated stems and increases the risk of disease. Most crops require little or no fertilizer, as the seed provides adequate nutrition for the young crop. Some longer-growing microgreen crops, such as micro carrot, dill, and celery, may benefit from a light fertilization applied to the tray bottom. Some of the faster-growing greens, such as mustard cress and chard, may also benefit from a light fertilization because they germinate quickly and exhaust their self-contained nutrient supply quickly. Light fertilization is best achieved by floating each tray of microgreens for 30 seconds in a prepared nutrient solution of approximately 80 ppm nitrogen. Microgreens are ready for harvest when they reach the first true leaf stage, usually at about 2 in. tall. Time from seeding to harvest can vary greatly by crop from 7 to 21 days. Production in small trays will likely require harvesting with scissors. This is a very time-consuming part of the production cycle and is often mentioned by growers as a major drawback. The seeding mat type of production system has gained popularity with many growers because it facilitates faster harvesting. The mats can be picked up by hand and held vertically while an electric knife or trimmer is used for harvesting, allowing cut microgreens to fall from the mat into a clean harvest container. Harvested microgreens are highly perishable and should be washed and cooled as quickly as possible. Some chefs are asking growers to deliver in the trays or mats and they will cut the microgreens as needed to improve quality. Wash the microgreens using good handling practices for food safety. Microgreens are usually packed in small, plastic clamshell packages and cooled to recommended temperatures for the crops in the mix. Growers should be aware that marketing agreements such as the National Leafy Green Marketing Agreement (NLGMA) have been proposed to reduce the risk of microbial contamination of mature and immature leafy greens.

Production site and Planting

The delicate nature of microgreens requires that they be protected from rainfall and other environmental stresses; thus, they need to be grown in a greenhouse, high tunnel, shade structure, or indoors. These crops may be grown in conventional bench-top production or hydroponically. Plastic flats with drainage holes at the bottom are generally used for microgreen production. The optimum seed density is one that maximizes production space while avoiding stands so thick that stems become elongated and/or disease issues develop. Depending on the crop and production system, a light layer of growing media may be spread over the seeds. It is best to seed only one type or cultivar per flat; however, if more than one species will be seeded in the same flat, the crops should have similar germination rates so the whole flat can be harvested at the same time. Irrigation with overhead mist or an ebb and flow bench system is common. Well or county water should be used for irrigation as surface water sources, such as ponds, pose a disease risk.

Crop Selection

A large number of vegetable, herb, and agronomic crops and crop varieties can be used for microgreen production. Lettuces may be too delicate, and are often not considered good candidates for microgreens. Crop selection is often based on seedling color, texture, flavor, and market demand. How quickly and easily the seed germinates should be another consideration for the producer. Growers may need to evaluate a number of crops before selecting the ones most suitable to their production system and market.

Selecting the Growing System

The commercial production of microgreens is usually performed under controlled environment, inside greenhouses or high tunnels provided either with simple or advanced technologies, depending on the size of the farm and the more or less favorable climatic conditions, and using soilless growing systems that can be essentially attributable to three types. One possibility is to grow microgreens in 'containers' constituted by plastic trays having different sizes, with height variable from 3 to 5 cm. Depending on the case, the bottom of the container holding the growing media can be intact, with no holes, or more often with holes, in order to enhance the drainage of the excess of water (or nutrient solution) and avoid water stagnation that can lead to the development of diseases and compromise the production and the quality of microgreens. Usually, the containers are placed on growing channels or benches, unmovable or movable, perfectly leveled and complete of a system for the drainage and recover of the excess water or nutrient solution. Irrigation water and nutrient solution can be delivered from the top by means of a nebulization system, activated manually or automatically, or from the bottom, through sub-irrigation. In the latter case, it is essential that containers have holes at the bottom. The cultivation in containers, generally allows the commercialization of the product along with the growing media, thus, avoiding the need to cut the product before it is shipped on the market. Such possibility prevents all the issue associated with the cut of a vegetable, with consequent advantages for the shelf life and the quality of the product, will be harvested by the consumer, just few minutes before actually using the product in the kitchen. In order to minimize the environmental impact possible to use biodegradable containers (polylactic acid PLA and others) rather than those made of plastic deriving from oil. A second possibility is to grow microgreens in 'channels' or in benches (made of plastic, aluminum, galvanized iron, wood) of different sizes, by placing the growing media right inside the channels or in the benches. In this case, channels and benches can be movable or unmovable and have to be perfectly leveled, to realize a slight slope in order to enhance the Állow of the water or the nutrient solution from one end of the channel or bench to the other, enabling also the recovery and recycling, if possible of the surplus water or nutrient solution. The cultivation of microgreens in regular greenhouses, in the last few years, with the availability of more efficient lamps, several companies have implemented very advanced and intensive indoor growing systems, in which trays, channels or benches can be placed on different levels, one on top of the other, in 'multi-layer' growing systems to produce microgreens even without natural light, by integrating or entirely replacing the sunlight with an artificial lighting system, using lamps with an emission spectrum adequate for the plant photosynthesis. It is important to highlight that, also microgreens, require an adequate level of radiation (at least 100 μmol m-2 s-1 of photosynthetically active photons for the less demanding species) to assure the achievement of a good commercial, hygienic-sanitary and nutritional quality of the product. In fact, in North Europe and North America, even in greenhouses, sometimes it is necessary to integrate the sunlight with supplemental lighting. When using supplemental radiation, the possibility to control the intensity and quality (wavelength) of the radiation can be exploited at commercial level even to modify and increase the nutritional value of microgreens (Kopsell and Sams, 2013; Samuolienë *et al.*, 2013).

Selecting the Cultivation Substrate

One of the most critical aspects involved in the production of microgreens is the selection of the growing media as it plays a fundamental role in determining the productivity and quality of microgreens, as well as the sustainability of the production process. In order to assure a good germination and an optimal growth of the seedlings, a good growing media should have in terms of physical properties a porosity over 85% of the total volume, an adequate ratio between macro and micro pores to guarantee at the same time a good water holding capacity (55-70% of the total volume) and a good level of aeration (20-30% of the total volume) of the root system (Abad *et al.*, 2001). As for the chemical properties, a good growing media for the production of microgreens should have a pH value ranging from 5.5 to 6.5 and an electrical conductivity below 500 μS/cm; yet, the substrate should not contain heavy metals or polluting compounds. Yet, it is of fundamental importance that the growing media is not microbiologically contaminated. Especially materials of organic origin can contain micro-organisms pathogenic to the human being, like Salmonella and Escherichia coli. To prevent hygienic-sanitary issues, it is important to choose substrates whose microbiological quality is guaranteed or materials that have undergone sterilization treatments (physical or chemical). Growing medias can be classified in organic and inorganic, the substrates are made of natural and biodegradable materials, like the peat for example, while the inorganic ones like the perlite, are usually inert. The growing substrates most commonly used for the production of microgreens, either at commercial or non professional level, are peat, perlite and vermiculite, which can be used individually or in mix. Mixing in adequate proportions substrates having different properties it is possible to obtain a growing media with optimal physical-chemical and, thus, agronomic properties or at least with better properties as compared to the single substrates. An organic material alternative to peat is the coconut coir, which has the advantage of being produced from a renewable source. Of course, when selecting the coconut coir, it is important to consider that, based on the size of the particles (Àber or pith), the properties of the substrate can remarkably change. In the case of the coconut coir or other organic substrates deriving from composting processes, it is important to verify that the content of salts is not too high, as it may limit the germinability of the seeds. Among the substrates that have been specifically developed for the production of microgreens, there are mats constituted by Àbrous materials, which can be natural (coconut coir, jute Àber, cotton Àber, algae Àber and paper pulp) or synthetic (produced by means of polyethylene terephthalate – PET). Usually, commercial mats have well defined and standardized physical, chemical and agronomic properties, and have a good balance between water holding capacity and air capacity and, not less important, have good hygienic-sanitary quality. Nevertheless, the high cost of commercial substrates has led many producers of microgreens to look for alternative materials, including discarded or recycled materials (possibly of natural origin and renewable) and to develop their own growing media, whose composition is often secret. For instance, many producers of microgreens buy discarded Àbrous materials deriving from industrial processes, such as the low cost cellulose pulp, cotton and jute Àbers, and they use these materials, usually characterized by limited water holding capacity after improving their agronomic properties.

The Quality of Seeds, Seeding and Germination

The production of microgreens requires high quantities of seeds. Therefore, the seed quality has a great influence on the speed and uniformity of germination and on the final outcome of the growing cycle. Seeds also represent one of the main cost items in the production process of microgreens; for this reason, when selecting the seed suppliers and the species/varieties to grow, the cost of this factor of production has to be taken into serious consideration. Seeds should be selected and calibrated, they should have a germinability over 95% and a good germinating power. Seeds for the production of microgreens should be not treated with chemicals. Moreover, to guarantee the consumers safety, it is important to assess the absolute absence of foreign bodies among the seeds that should have a good percentage of purity to avoid, the presence of infesting weeds that could be not edible. Considering that also the seeds, can be microbiologically contaminated, to prevent phytosanitary issues during the germination process and minimize the risks of microbiological contamination, especially for those species characterized by seeds with corrugated integuments, it is recommended to wash and disinfect the surface of the seeds by means of chemical treatments (sodium hypochlorite or calcium solutions, peroxide, ethanol, malic acid or lactic acid at different concentrations), physical treatments (heat, high pressure and radiation) combination of chemical and physical treatments (Ding *et al.*, 2013). Of course, it is important to preserve the quality of the seeds also during the storage, by keeping the seeds at low temperature and low humidity, in a controlled environment. After buying or producing a new lot of seeds, it is always advisable to make some germination tests before the seeding to verify the germination percentage and the germinating power. The germination percentage will be considered when calculating the amount of seeds to be used per unit area, in order to obtain the desired seedling density. While some species of microgreens germinate very easily, some others need more time and require the application of some expedients for a better germination. Especially in the case of commercial production it is important to have a fast, uniform and high germination, and the species that have more germination issues are usually subject to pre-germination treatments such as, for example, coldpriming, soaking, osmopriming, matrix priming and hydropriming, which have the common purpose of satisfying, under controlled conditions, the needs of the seed in terms of water, light and oxygen from the Àrst stages of the germination process until right before the emergence of the radicle. Accelerate the germination process is important also because, immediately after sowing, the environmental conditions can limit the germination process and seeds may be more exposed to parasitic attacks.The coldpriming is performed at low temperatures (5-10 °C), by placing the seeds in a moist substrate, so that they can absorb water and oxygen. Under such conditions, the germination process is activated, but the low temperatures do not allow the emergence of the radicle. The application of the coldpriming can enhance the speed and uniformity of the seed germination even under stress conditions. For example, on lettuce seeds the application of the coldpriming, for a maximum time of 48 hours, can reduce the occurrence of thermodormancy phenomena when temperatures are above 20 °C (Giulianini *et al.*, 1992). The soaking (or hardening) consists in a simple imbibition of the seeds before sowing; then, after the soaking treatment, the seeds can be dehydrated again. When seeds are subject to several hydration-dehydration cycles, the treatment is called presowing drought-hardening or simply hardening. The osmopriming technique, also known as osmotic conditioning, consists in soaking the seeds in an aerated water solution containing an osmotic agent capable of lowering the water potential (making the water less available), so that the seeds are hydrated just enough to start the germination process without completing it with the emergence of the radicle. In this way, since all the seeds reach the same physiological status, once they are placed under optimal conditions, the germination process will be very fast and uniform. The same principle is at the base of the matrix priming, which exploits the matrix potential by mixing the seeds, in adequate proportions, with a solid material characterized by very small particles, high surface area and high water holding capacity, such as vermiculite, and with water. At the end of the matrix priming treatment, the mix of seeds and vermiculate may be used directly for the sowing. The hydropriming is similar to the osmopriming and consists simply in a controlled imbibition of the seeds in aerated water, without the use of osmotic agents, before sowing. The seeds are directly immersed, for a certainperiod of time and at room temperature, in containers with aerated deionized water. Another fundamental aspect of the microgreens production, related to the seeds is the sowing density. At commercial level, most of the growers prefer to use high sowing densities to maximize the production. However, besides taking into account the cost of the seeds, it should be considered that increasing the sowing density the average weight of the single seedlings decreases and a high seedling density often promotes an undesired elongation of the stems, which being less exposed to the sunlight and growing in microclimatic conditions characterized by high humidity and scarce air circulations causing, will become more tender and can be easily susceptible to fungal diseases, with consequent reduction of the shelf life and quality of the microgreens. Approximately, the seeding density can range from 1 seed/cm^2 (for the bigger seeds like, for example, chickpea, corn, green pea, etc.) up to 4 seeds/cm^2 (for the smallest seeds like, for example, rappini, broccoli, cauliflower, chicory, etc.). Seed are usually broadcasted on the surface of the growing media by hand, while commercial farms often use precision seeding machines. The germination should take place in the dark, at the optimal temperature for the species (15-25 °C) and in presence of high relative humidity (80-90%). For the production of microgreens, the seed do not need to be placed deep in the growing media, also to avoid that during the germination the seedling gets dirty with the same growing media. However, the seeds must be kept wet to enable the complete germination. Therefore, especially in presence of sub-optimal climatic conditions, for two to three days after sowing, the growing trays, channels or benches, can be covered without touching the seeds, using for example a black plastic film, in order to increase the temperature and thus, speed up the germination, and maintain a high humidity level. Once the seeds germinate, the cover must be removed. Commercial farms often have germination chambers that can assure the complete control of the climatic conditions and the maintenance of optimal conditions for the germination of different species.

Irrigation and Fertilization

During the germination, seeds are usually watered using overhead mist systems. While, after the germination are preferred subirrigation systems that allow the irrigation of the young seedlings from the bottom, avoiding excesses of humidity, and thus, limiting the occurrence of phytosanitary issues (Treadwell *et al.*, 2010). Even though, microgreens are small seedlings with small cotyledon leaves and a hint of the first true leaves, fertilization is fundamental to achievea good production (Murphy *et al.*, 2010). Nutrients can be applied before sowing, by incorporating in adequate rate simple or complex mineral fertilizers in the growing media, or after germination is completed with a nutrient solution. Some slow-growing species as carrot, dill, celery and beet may benefit from the fertilization of the substrate in pre-sowing, while, other more fast-growing species, such as mustard, watercress, rappini, broccoli, radish and similar species, that germinate easily and deplete quickly the nutrient reserve provided by the seeds, can beneÀt more from the fertigation after the germination process. An example of nutrient solution that may be used for the commercial production of microgreens on mats or inert substrates is the one proposed by Hoagland (Hoagland and Arnon, 1950), but at half strength, using the following nutrient concentrations expressed in mg/L: N 105, P 15, K 117, Ca 100, Mg 24, B 0.25, Cu 0.01, Fe 2.5, Mn 0.25, Zn 0.025, Mo 0.005.

Pest and Disease Management

The microgreen high density cropping system provides the ideal environment for the development of seedling diseases. These young tender plants are particularly vulnerable to Pythium and Phytophthora damping-off; however, Sclerotinia and Rhizoctonia diseases may pose a problem on some hosts. Sanitation, proper plant spacing, and good cultural practices will be necessary to prevent these diseases from gaining a foothold. In addition, the use of a sterile soilless media, which is required for success, should reduce any potential disease problems. Potential insect problems include aphids and thrips. Prevention of fungal and bacterial outbreak is important and using sterilized growing media/mats, clean water, good hygiene and cleaning of growing surfaces after each crop - combined with humidity control and good air flow - all assist with prevention of disease attack.

Harvest, Hygienic-sanitary Quality and Post-harvest Storage

Depending on the cultivation system used, the weather conditions and the genotype, the microgreens growing cycle can last from 7 up to 21 days after the germination. Microgreens are ready to be harvested at the appearance of the Àrst true leaves, when the cotyledons are fully expanded and still turgid, and depending on the species have reached a height of 5-10 cm. The harvest can be performed cutting the seedling few millimeters above the growing media (Photo 14), either manually using a pair of scissors or a blade, or using an electric knife, avoiding to include particles of the growing media, and if possible, the integuments of the seeds that, in many species, cannot be easily excluded since they often remain attached to the cotyledons. Being highly perishable, microgreens should be washed and cooled (1-5 °C) immediately after the harvest, and of course they should be handled following all the good practices to preserve the hygienic-sanitary quality (cleaning harvesting tools, packing and storage room, using gloves, etc.) as for all the fresh cut vegetables. An alternative to the harvest of the microgreens by cut is to market the product directly into a tray or a package with the whole growing media, while the plants are still growing. In this case, although the producer must still ensure a good hygienic quality, the Ànal consumer will need to wash the product. The critical point in this case is to provide enough water to the seedlings in order to assure their survival and a good shelf life.

Marketing and Packaging

Most microgreens are sold either cut and packaged into various sized clamshells - two, four or eight ounce sizes or as a living product in cell packs or trays which can be cut just before serving. Shipment while still growing in trays or packs ensures maximum shelf life and the customer can decide at what size they want to harvest and use the different microgreen species. Many microgreen producers supply their markets with both individual species packs and mixtures of greens, ready to use. Examples of various microgreen mix products include 'spicy Asian' mixes and 'Mediterranean mixes', also rainbow colored and herb mixes are available with some growers creating customized micro green mixes for customers. Microgreens are young and tender and therefore have a high rate of respiration and potentially a short shelf life if not stored and handled correctly. Clamshell packaging helps retain moisture around the foliage and protect the delicate young tissue from bruising and damage. If stored under refrigeration, microgreens should have a shelf life of at least one week. However, basil microgreens need careful handling because basil is prone to chilling damage at temperatures below 40 degrees C with foliage discoloring and blackening resulting from cool storage. Basil microgreens need the same storage conditions as mature cut basil herb productions, at temperatures above 40 degrees F.

Case Studies

Dagmar *et al.* (2010). eeported that evaluation of buckwheat sprouts as microgreens from common and tartary buckwheat genotypes were evaluated for total flavonoid content (rutin, quercetineand kaempferol separately), bound phenolic acids content, carotenoids and α-tocopherol content and antioxidant activity. The results have shown that in common and tartary buckwheat microgreens antioxidant activity was found. High level of flavonoids, carotenoids, and α-tocopherol was detected as well. Higher amount of flavonoids was found out in tartary buckwheat microgreens.

Xiao *et al.* (2012) find that assessment of vitamin and carotenoid concentrations of emerging food products: edible microgreens. The present study was conducted to determine the concentrations of ascorbic acid, carotenoids, phylloquinone and tocopherols in 25 commercially available microgreens. Results showed that different microgreens provided extremely varying amounts of phytonutrients.

Ebert *et al.*, (2014) reported that amaranth sprouts and microgreens – a homestead vegetable production option to enhance food and nutrition security in the ruralurban continuum.The phytonutrient content was assessed different stages: (a) microgreens (b) fully grown plants. The comparison included landraces from the AVRDC Genebank and commercially available cultivars. This work may expand the use of genebank materials for specialty produce such as microgreens with great potential to improve food and nutrition security for people living in urban and peri-urban settings.

Pinto *et al.* (2015) revealed that mineral profile and nitrate content of microgreens and mature lettuces. Results showed that microgreens possess a higher content of most minerals (Ca, Mg, Fe, Mn, Zn, Se and Mo) and a lower NO3- content than mature lettuces. Therefore, microgreens can be considered as a good source of minerals in the human diet, and their consumption could be an important strategy to meet children's minerals dietary requirements without exposing them to harmful NO3-.

Xiao *et al.* (2016) analyzed that 30 varieties of microgreens, representing 10 species within 6 genera of the Brassicaceae family. Brassicaceae microgreens were assayed for concentrations of macroelements, including calcium (Ca), magnesium (Mg), phosphorous (P), sodium (Na), potassium (K), and of microelements, including copper (Cu), iron (Fe), manganese (Mn), and zinc (Zn). the results demonstrate that microgreens are good sources of both macroelements (K and Ca) and microelements (Fe and Zn.). Consumption of microgreens could be a health-promoting strategy to meet dietary reference intake requirements for essential elements beneficial to human health.

Lee *et al.* (2004) reveled that Seed treatments to advance the establishment of table beet or chard (*Beta vulgaris* L) for greenhouse microgreen production were examinied. While germination percentage was little affected, apprecial germination advancement in both crops was achieved usig all treatments of matric priming (-1MPa at 12 c for 6 d in fine varmiculite) or various soaks of (water 20 c for 48 hr;hydrogen peroxide, 0.3% at 20 c for 48 hr; hydrogen chloride 0.3M at 20 c for 2 hr or sodium hypochlorite, 4% at 20 c for 3hr).The most pronounceed seedling emergence advancement, however was gained by germinating seeds in fine grade vermiculite

Brazaityte *et al.* (2015) find that effects of UV-A irradiation on cultivation and quality of microgreens. Therefore, the goal of our study was to investigate the influence of 366, 390, and 402 nm UV-A LED wavelengths, supplemental for the basal solid-state lighting system at two UV-A irradiation levels on the growth and phytochemical contents of different microgreen plants. a significant increase in the investigated phytochemicals was found under 366 and 390 nm UV-A irradiation treatments resulted in increased leaf area and fresh weight, in higher 2,2–diphenyl–1–picrylhydrazyl free-radical scavenging activity, total phenols, anthocyanins, ascorbic acid, and α-tocopherol.

Viktorija and Akvile (2015) concluded that effect of industrially designed light-emitting diode (LED) lamp lighting on the nutritional quality of *Brassicaceae microgreens. Red pak choi (Brassica rapa var. chinensis 'Rubi F1'), tatsoi (Brassica rapa var. rosularis) and mustard (Brassica juncea L. 'Red Lion') were grown in a greenhouse (20±2/18±2* °C) during winter season. Microgreens treated with LED 150 and LED 250 were significantly (Pde0.05) shorter and formed smaller hypocotyls. The photooxidative changes were evoked by both lighting treatments and led to higher phytochemical (phenols, ascorbic acid, flavonols, anthocyanins) and mineral element (Ca, K, Mg, Na, P, Fe, Zn) contents, and the DPPH and ABTS free radicals scavenging activities in all microgreens.

Kou *et al.* (2014) investigated that effect of pre-harvest calcium application on the post-harvest quality and shelf-life of broccoli microgreens. Broccoli microgreen seedlings were sprayed daily with calcium chloride at concentrations of 1, 10 and 20 mM, or water (control) for 10 days. Results indicated that the 10 mM calcium chloride treatment increased the biomass by more than 50%, and tripled the calcium content as compared to the water-treated controls. Microgreens treated with 10 mM calcium chloride spray exhibited higher superoxide dismutase and peroxidase activities, lower tissue electrolyte leakage, improved overall visual quality.

Kou *et al.* (2013) investigated that Postharvest biology, quality and shelf life of buckwheat microgreens. Temperature significantly ($P < 0.0001$) affected package atmospheres and product quality. At the end of storage, microgreens stored at 1, 5 and 10 _C had smaller microbial populations and less tissue electrolyte leakage than those stored at 15, and 20 _C. Package film oxygen transmission rate (OTR) significantly ($P < 0.05$) affected package atmospheres. However, differences in quality and shelf life of microgreens packaged in different OTR films were slight and not evident until day 21 of storage. On day 21, buckwheat microgreens packaged in 16.6 pmol/(m^2

s Pa) oxygen transmission rate package films were observed to have the freshest appearance with lowest tissue electrolyte leakage. Chlorine (100 mg/L) wash significantly ($P < 0.05$) reduced microbial populations, initially; however, after 7 days of storage, all washed microgreens experienced accelerated microbial populations. Our findings suggest that buckwheat microgreens should be stored at 5 _C with moderately high O_2 (14.0e16.5 kPa) and moderately low CO_2 (1.0e1.5 kPa) content to maintain optimal quality and maximal shelf life.

Xiao *et al.* (2014) concluded that optimize postharvest handling conditions to reduce the quality loss and extend the shelf life of daikon radish (Raphanus sativus L. var. longipinnatus) microgreens. Storage temperature, packaging film, and wash treatment were investigated. Changes in headspace composition, quality index, chlorophyll concentration, tissue electrolyte leakage, and aerobic mesophilic bacteria (AMB) and yeast & mold (Y&M) counts were monitored periodically during storage. Results indicated that (1) storage temperature significantly ($P < 0.05$) affected package atmosphere, product quality and shelf life. One degree Celsius was the optimal temperature for storage of radish microgreens with no chilling injury observed; (2) film oxygen transmission rate (OTR) significantly ($P < 0.05$) affected O_2 and CO_2 composition, but OTR did not significantly affect quality attributes during 28 days of storage at 1 _C; (3) Chlorine wash treatment 100 mg/L) significantly reduced initial microbial populations by 0.5 log cfu g_1, including AMB and Y& M. However, microbial populations rebounded after day 7.

Chandra *et al.* (2012) reported that effects of different sanitizers on the quality and microbial populations of 'Tah Tasai' Chinese cabbage (*Brassica campestris* var. narinosa) microgreens were evaluated. Samples were washed in tap water (TW), 100 mL L -1 chlorinated water (Cl), 0.25% (w/v) each of citric and ascorbic acid mixed solution (CA + AS) as well as 0.5% (w/v) citric acid solution followed by 50% (v/v) ethanol spray (CA + E) and were packaged either in 35 µm polyethylene (PE) or polypropylene (PP) bag and stored at 5°C for up to 9 days. Off-odor scores were also higher in PP film packaged samples compared to that of PE. CA + E and CA + AS treatments showed lower off-odor scale in both films. However, CA + E treatment exhibited either the lowest aerobic counts our results suggest that CA + E treatment could be a useful replacement for Cl for the washing of microgreens and PE film would provide more benefits than PP for packaging microgreens.

Baenasa *et al.* (2017) concluded that microbiological status and phytochemical composition of broccoli and radish sprouts were evaluated at harvest (Day 0), and after seven and fourteen days of storage at 5 and 10^{C}. Pathogenic microorganisms were absent during shelf-life; nevertheless, the slight growth of Enterobacteriaceae organisms, aerobic mesophilic and psychotropic bacteria, molds and yeasts was assessed. The storage temperature influenced the quality and content of bioactives in the sprouts, and for practical applications, storage at 5^{C} is the most suitable option. Moreover, these fresh crucifers remain acceptable for consumers after 14 d storage period, being an interesting option for consuming fresh and naturally-functional foods.

Kopsell *et al.,* (2014) revealed that measure the impact of different percentages of blue light on the concentrations of nutritional quality parameters of sprouting broccoli microgreens and to compare incandescent fluorescent light with light-emitting diodes (LEDs). Microgreen seeds were cultured hydroponically on growing pads under light treatments of: (1) fluorescent/incandescent light; (2) 5% blue (442 to 452 nm)/95% red (622 to 632 nm); (3) 5% blue/85% red/10% green (525 to 535 nm); (4) 20% blue/80% red; and (5) 20% blue/70% red/10% green in controlled environments. Microgreens were grown at an air temperature of 24. 8C and a 16-hour photoperiod using a light intensity of 250 mmol_mL2_sL1 for all light treatments. Microgreens were harvested after 20 days under the light treatments and shoot tissues were processed and measured for nutritionally important shoot pigments, glucosinolates, and mineral nutrients. The highest concentrations of shoot tissue chlorophyll, b-carotene, lutein, total carotenoids, calcium (Ca), magnesium (Mg), phosphorus (P), sulfur (S), boron (B), copper (Cu), iron (Fe), manganese (Mn), molybdenum (Mo), zinc (Zn), glucoiberin, glucoraphanin, 4-methoxyglucobrassicin, and neoglucobrassicin were found in microgreens grown under the 20% blue/ 80% red light treatment.

Xiao *et al.,* (2012) investigated that assessment of Vitamin and Carotenoid Concentrations of Emerging Food Products: Edible Microgreens. Results showed that different microgreens provided extremely varying amounts of vitamins and carotenoids. Total ascorbic acid contents ranged from 20.4 to147.0 mg per 100 g fresh weight (FW), while β-carotene, lutein/ zeaxanthin, and violaxanthin concentrations ranged from 0.6 to 12.1, 1.3 to 10.1, and 0.9 to 7.7 mg/100 g FW, respectively. Phylloquinone level varied from 0.6 to 4.1 μg/g FW; meanwhile, α-tocopherol and γ- tocopherol ranged from 4.9 to 87.4 and 3.0 to 39.4 mg/100 g FW, respectively. Among the 25 microgreens assayed, red cabbage, cilantro, garnet amaranth, and green daikon radish had the highest concentrations of ascorbic acids, carotenoids, phylloquinone, and tocopherols, respectively. In comparison with nutritional concentrations in mature leaves (USDA National Nutrient Database), the microgreen cotyledon leaves possessed higher nutritional densities.

Xiao *et al.*(2014) reveled that optimize postharvest handling conditions to reduce the quality loss and extend the shelf life of daikon radish (Raphanus sativus L. var. longipinnatus) microgreens. Storage temperature, packaging film, and wash treatment were investigated. Changes in headspace composition, quality index, chlorophyll concentration, tissue electrolyte leakage, and aerobic mesophilic bacteria (AMB) and yeast & mold (Y&M) counts were monitored periodically during storage. Results indicated that (1) storage temperature significantly ($P < 0.05$) affected package atmosphere, product quality and shelf life. One degree Celsius was the optimal temperature for storage of radish microgreens with no chilling injury observed; (2) film oxygen transmission rate (OTR) significantly ($P < 0.05$) affected O2 and CO2 composition, but OTR did not significantly affect quality attributes during 28 days of storage at 1 _C; (3) Chlorine wash treatment (100 mg/L) significantly reduced initial microbial populations by 0.5 log cfu g_1, including AMB and Y& M. However, microbial populations rebounded after day 7.

Brazaitytė *et al.* (2016) evaluated that effect of 638 and 665 nm red lighting on growth and utritional quality parameters of *Brassicaceae* microgreens. Experiments were performed in closed-environment chambers (16 h photoperiod; 21/17°C). Mustard (*Brassica juncea* L., 'Red Lion'), red pak choi (*Brassica rapa* var. *chinensis*, 'Rubi F1') and tatsoi (*Brassica rapa* var. *rosularis*) were grown in peat substrate for 10 days. Solid-state lighting units, consisting of red 638 nm, 665 nm, blue 455 nm and far red 731 nm LEDs at total photosynthetic photon flux density (PPFD) of 200 µmol m-2 s-1 were used for microgreen illumination from sowing. Three days before harvest the total PPFD level was raised to 300 µmol m-2 s-1. In the control treatment, all four spectral components were raised proportionally. The red light treatment was illuminated with only 638 or 665 nm light at 300 µmol m-2 s-1. At harvest, growth parameters and phytochemical contents were determined. 638 and 665 nm light, applied before harvest, caused stem elongation, increased fresh weight and decreased leaf area, but this varied between species. Red light improved the nutritional quality of microgreens. Comparison of different red-wavelength effects showed that more antioxidants, especially ascorbic acid and β-carotene, were accumulated in microgreens exposed to 638 nm, than exposed to 665 nm light.

Brazaitytė *et al*, (2016) evaluated that differences in plant growth performance under LED light systems and traditional HPS lamps in growth chamber and greenhouse, leading to a broader understanding of plant response to the spectral components of light seeking to obtain products of high nutritional value. Short-term high PPFD red light exposure alters the action of protective antioxidant systems and thus enhances the accumulation of bioactive compounds. Such technological tool could be used for increasing nutritionally important phytochemical contents in microgreens. Irradiation with red 638 nm light was more efficient seeking to increase nutritional quality of *Brassicaceae* microgreens in comparison with red 665 nm light, due to more pronounced effect on free radical scavenging activity, ascorbic acid, α-tocopherol, lutein and β-carotene contents.

Weber (2017) examined that mineral concentration of broccoli microgreens produced using compost-based and hydroponic growing methods that are easily implemented in one's own home. The nutritional value of the resulting microgreens was quantitatively compared to published nutritional data for the mature vegetable. Nutritional data were also considered in the context of the resource demands (i.e., water, fertilizer, and energy) of producing microgreens in order to gain insights into the potential for local microgreen production to diversify food systems, particularly for urban areas, while minimizing the overall environmental impacts of broccoli farming. Regardless of how they were grown, microgreens had larger quantities of Mg, Mn, Cu, and Zn than the vegetable. However, compost-grown (C) microgreens had higher P, K, Mg, Mn, Zn, Fe, Ca, Na, and Cu concentrations than the vegetable. For eight nutritionally important minerals (P, K, Ca, Mg, Mn, Fe, Zn, and Na), the average C microgreen:vegetable nutrient ratio was 1.73. Extrapolation from experimental data presented here indicates that broccoli microgreens would require 158–236 times less water than it does to grow a nutritionally equivalent amount of mature vegetable in the fields of California's Central Valley in 93-95% less time and without the need for fertilizer, pesticides, or energy-demanding transport from farm to table. The results of this study suggest that broccoli microgreens have the potential to be a rich source of minerals that can be produced by individuals, even in urban settings, providing better access to adequate nutrition.

Gayathree *et al.* (2015) conducted to determine the germination potential, harvesting stage, antioxidant activity, total polyphenol content and consumer acceptance of species that have the potential to be introduced locally. Seeds were obtained from local retailers. Germination tests were carried for 10 species in light/dark (12/12 hours) and total darkness for 14 days in an incubator (at 25 °C and light intensity 16.4 µmol m-2 s-1). Harvesting stages were determined by growing in the same incubator in light/dark (12/12 hours). Consumer acceptance was determined by a 9-point hedonic scale with 50 panelists. Whole seed, sprouts without seed coat and microgreen shoots of green pea, millet and sesame were evaluated for antioxidant activity by 1, 1-diphenyl pycryl hydrazyl radical scavenging activity and total polyphenols by Folin Ciocalteu assay. Germination data were analyzed using independent t-test and total polyphenol content, antioxidant activity and consumer acceptance were analyzed using one way analysis of variance (ANOVA). The germination percentages were significantly higher ($P<0.05$) in light/dark for millet (*Eleusine coracana*), green peas (*Pisum sativum*), lettuce (*Lactuca sativa*), green radish (*Raphanus sativus*), fenugreek (*Trigonella foenum-graecum*) and sesame (*Sesamum indicum*) (35.3–100.0%) than those under total darkness (13.0-55.0%). Carrot (*Daucus carota*) germinated well under total darkness (56.0%). The germination percentages in red amaranth (*Amaranthus* sp.), mustard (*Brassica juncea*) and kale (*Brassica oleracea var. acephala*) were more or less similar under total darkness and under light/dark condition. Lettuce reached 75% germination in less than one day while sesame, fenugreek, kale, green radish and green peas within 1-3 days whereas millet, mustard, carrot and red amaranth took more than 14 days. Fenugreek and green radish reached the minimum height for microgreens (25 mm) within 4 days while carrot, green peas, millet, kale, mustard and sesame took 8 days and red amaranth and lettuce took 10-12 days. In millet, the seeds recorded the highest antioxidant activity (IC50 697 µg/ml) compared to its sprouts and microgreens. The antioxidant activity in microgreens was significantly higher in sesame (IC50 772 µg/mL) and green peas (IC50 1830 µg/mL) than their sprouts and seeds. The highest total polyphenol content was in sesame microgreens (4873 mg/ 100g dry weight (DW)). In sesame and green peas, microgreens showed a higher total polyphenol content than seeds and sprouts, while in millet, seeds showed a higher content (709 mg/100 DW) than sprouts and microgreens. The consumer acceptance rank was high for lettuce (2=like very much) and carrot (3=like moderately), and low for fenugreek and green radish (6=dislike slightly). Germination of some species seems to be affected by light condition. Increase in antioxidants and polyphenols suggest that these compounds are produced during germination and growth. Different choices of consumer may be due to taste, aroma and personal perceiving. These species can be harvested as microgreens within 14 days and the antioxidant and polyphenol content varies between the tested three species and also depends on their growth stage.

Xiao *et al.* (2015) reported that six species of microgreens, including Dijon mustard (Brassica juncea L. Czern.), opal basil (Ocimum basilicum L.), bull's blood beet (Beta vulgaris L.), red amaranth (Amaranthus tricolor L.), peppercress (Lepidium bonariense L.) and China rose radish (Raphanus sativus L.), were evaluated for their sensory attributes and chemical compositions. Results showed that bull's blood beet had the highest rating on acceptability of flavor and overall eating quality while peppercress the lowest. Chemical compositions also differed significantly among the six species. China rose radish had the highest titratable acidity and total sugars, while red amaranth had the highest pH value and lowest total sugars. Regarding the phytonutrient concentrations, the highest concentrations of total ascorbic acid, phylloquinone, carotenoids, tocopherols, and total phenolics were found in China rose radish, opal basil, red amaranth, China rose radish, and opal basil, respectively. The relationships between sensory–sensory attributes and sensory–chemical compositions were further studied. It was found that overall eating quality of microgreens was best correlated with flavor score and microgreen's pH value and total phenolic content were strongly correlated with flavor attributes, e.g., sourness, astringency, and bitterness. In general, despite the differences among individual microgreens, all of the microgreens evaluated in this study demonstrated "good" to "excellent" consumer acceptance and nutritional quality.

(Weber.C.F 2016) investigated that nutrient contents of lettuce and cabbage microgreens grown hydroponically (HP) and on vermicompost (C) were assessed and compared to each other as well as to the nutrient contents of store-bought cabbage and lettuce (mature vegetables). Of the 10 nutrients examined (P, K, S, Ca, Mg, Mn, Cu, Zn, Fe, Na), C cabbage microgreens had significantly larger quantities of all nutrients than HP cabbage microgreens (p-values <0.00321) with the exception of P; C lettuce microgreens had significantly larger quantities of all nutrients than HP lettuce microgreens (p-values <0.024) except for P, Mg and Cu. Compared to the mature vegetable, C or HP cabbage microgreens had significantly larger quantities of all nutrients examined (p-values <0.001) and C or HP lettuce microgreens had significantly larger quantities of all nutrients except for Ca and Na (p-values <0.0012). Results of this study indicate that microgreens grown on vermicompost have greater nutrient contents than those grown hydroponically. As microgreens can be grown easily in one's home using the methods used in this study, they may provide a means for consumer access to larger quantities of nutrients per gram plant biomass relative to store-bought mature vegetables, which had lower nutrient contents than microgreens with respect to most nutrients examined.

Brazaityt *et al.* (2016) investigated that antioxidant properties of *Brassica* microgreens grown in different types of organic substrates. however, significantly lower content of phenols in red pakchoi was determined. Contrary, compost and peat substrate had no influence for accumulation of anthocyanins in red pakchoi, and significantly reduced in tatsoi. The similar tendency was observed on flavonols in both microgreens species when significantly lower index was determined. Leafflavonol index significantly increased in tatsoi, which were grown in compost, and redpakchoi grown in coconut fibre's substrate. The highest DPPH radical scavenging activity was in both microgreens species grown in coconut substrate, and tatsoi in peat. However, the compost influenced reduced DPPH radical scavenging activity in both microgreens species. In summary, coconut fibre was the most appropriate substrate for enhanced antioxidant properties of microgreens, and less positive effects of compost and peat substrates were determined.

Dagmar *et al.* (2010). reported that microgreens from common and tartary buckwheat genotypes were evaluated for total flavonoid content (rutin, quercetine and kaempferol separately), bound phenolic acids content, carotenoids and α-tocopherol content and antioxidant activity. The results have shown that in common and tartary buckwheat microgreens antioxidant activity was found. High level of flavonoids, carotenoids, and α-tocopherol was detected as well. Higher amount of flavonoids was found out in tartary buckwheat microgreens. No significant differences were detected between common and tartary buckwheat microgreens in content of phenolic acids.

Samuolienë *et al.*(2010). reveled that effect of irradiance level produced by solid-state light-emitting diodes (LEDs) on the growth, nutritional quality and antioxidant properties of *Brassicaceae* family microgreens. Kohlrabi (*Brassica oleracea var. gongylodes*, 'Delicacy Purple') mustard (*Brassica juncea* L., 'Red Lion'), red pak choi (*Brassica rapa var. chinensis*, 'Rubi F1') and tatsoi (*Brassica rapa var. rosularis*) were grown using peat substrate in controlled-environment chambers until harvest time (10 days, 21/17°C, 16 h). A system of five lighting modules with 455, 638, 665 and 731 nm LEDs at a total photosynthetic photon flux densities (PPFD) of 545, 440, 330, 220 and 110 µmol m-2s-1 respectively were used. Insufficient levels of photosynthetically active photon flux (110 µmol m-2 s-1) suppressed normal growth and diminished the nutritional value of the *Brassica* microgreens studied. In general, the most suitable conditions for growth and nutritional quality of the microgreens was 330-440 µmol m-2 s-1 irradiation, which resulted in a larger leaf surface area, lower content of nitrates and higher total anthocyanins, total phenols and 2,2–diphenyl–1–picrylhydrazyl (DPPH) free-radical scavenging capacity.

Kou *et al.* (2014) investigated that microgreens consumption has been steadily increasing in recent years due to consumer awareness of their unique color, rich flavor, and concentrated bioactive compounds. However, industrial production and marketing is limited by their short shelf-life associated with rapid deterioration in product quality. This study investigated the effect of pre-harvest calcium application on the post-harvest quality and shelf-life of broccoli microgreens. Broccoli microgreen seedlings were sprayed daily with calcium chloride at concentrations of 1, 10 and 20 mM, or water (control) for 10 days. The fresh-cut microgreens were packaged in sealed polyethylene film bags. Package headspace atmospheric conditions, overall visual quality and tissue membrane integrity were evaluated on days 0, 7, 14, and 21, during 5 °C storage. Results indicated that the 10 mM calcium chloride treatment increased the biomass by more than 50%, and tripled the calcium content as compared to the water-treated controls. Microgreens treated with 10 mM calcium chloride spray exhibited higher superoxide dismutase and peroxidase activities, lower tissue electrolyte leakage, improved overall visual quality, and reduced microbial growth during storage. Furthermore, calcium treatment significantly affected expression of the senescence-associated genes BoSAG12, BoGPX6, BoCAT3 and BoSAG12. These results provide important information for commercial growers to enhance productivity and improve postharvest quality and shelf-life, potentially enabling a broadening of the retail marketing of broccoli microgreens.

(Viktorija and Akvilė, 2015) concluded that effect of industrially designed light-emitting diode (LED) lamp lighting on the nutritional quality of *Brassicaceae* microgreens. Red pak choi (*Brassica rapa* var. *chinensis* 'Rubi F1'), tatsoi (*Brassica rapa* var. *rosularis*) and mustard (*Brassica juncea* L. 'Red Lion') were grown in a greenhouse (20±2/18±2 °C) during winter season, and the solar daily integral (DLI) was ~3.46±1.16 mol m-2 d-1. The light spectra of lamp consist of 8 violet (420-430), 16 blue (460-470 nm), 8 orange (610-615 nm), 3 red (620-630 nm), 56 red (660-670 nm), 8 white (contain blue (400-500 nm), green (500-600 nm) and red (600-700 nm)) LEDs. The treatments of ~150 and ~250 μmol m-2 s-1 LED irradiance levels (LED 150 and LED 250) for 16 h d-1 in comparison with high pressure sodium (HPS) lamps (~150 μmol m-2 s-1) as a control were performed. Photophysiological response to the artificial light varied among *Brassicaceae* species. Microgreens treated with LED 150 and LED 250 were significantly (Pd"0.05) shorter and formed smaller hypocotyls. The photooxidative changes were evoked by both lighting treatments and led to higher phytochemical (phenols, ascorbic acid, flavonols, anthocyanins) and mineral element (Ca, K, Mg, Na, P, Fe, Zn) contents, and the DPPH and ABTS free radicals scavenging activities in all microgreens. Significantly lower content of nitrate was obtained with LED 150 treatment. Finally, LED lamps have the potential to be used as the main light source for growing high nutritional quality microgreens in greenhouses.

Marios *et al.* (2016) reported that microgreens garner immense potential for adapting leafy vegetable production to a micro-scale and for improving nutritional value in human diet. Scope and approach: Major preharvest factors of microgreens production, such as species selection, fertilization, biofortification, lighting and growth stage at harvest are addressed with respect to crop physiology and quality, as well as postharvest handling and applications, temperature, atmospheric composition, lighting and packaging technology which influence shelf-life and microbial safety. Key prospects for future research aiming to enhance quality and shelf-life of microgreens are highlighted.

Muchjajib *et al.*(2015). reported that growth media for microgreens were compared in the current study: sand, peat, coconut coir dust, sugarcane filter cake, vermicompost, coconut coir dust + peat 1:1, coconut coir dust + sugarcane filter cake 1:1, and coconut coir dust + vermicompost 1:1. The local organic bio-materials were found to be effective for the production of microgreens. The maximum microgreens yield of vine spinach (5.17 kg m-2) was obtained with coconut coir dust + peat 1:1. Coconut coir dust + sugarcane filter cake 1:1 produced maximum microgreens yields.

Viktorija *et al.* (2015) investigated that effects of blue light-emitting diode (LED) light dosages on the growth and antioxidant properties of red pak choi (*Brassica rapa* var. *chinensis* 'Rubi' F1), tatsoi (*Brassica rapa* var. rosularis) and basil (*Ocimum basilicum* L. 'Sweet Genovese') microgreens were determined. The plants were grown within a controlled-environment growth chamber (21/17 ± 2 °C day/night; 55 ± 5% relative air humidity) under five dosages (0%, 8%, 16%, 25%, 33%) of blue 447 nm in combination with red 638 nm, red 665 nm and far red 731 nm LEDs treatments (total PPFD ~ 302.5 μmol m-2 s-1; 16 h photoperiod). The influence of blue light dosage varied between microgreen species. The dosages of 16% and 33% led to significant lower hypocotyls and plant height of red pak choi, tatsoi and basil respectively. The highest concentration of ascorbic acid was determined in the tatsoi grown under 8% and in the red pak choi and basil under 16% blue light dosages. The tatsoi and basil showed the ability to accumulate more total phenols at 16-33% and the red pak choi at 8% blue light dosages.

Shabir *et al.* (2016). reveled that microgreens are emerging speciality food products which are gaining popularity and increased attention nowadays. They are young and tender cotyledonary leafy greens that are found in a pleasing palette of colors, textures and flavors. Microgreens are a new class of edible vegetables harvested when first leaves have fully expanded and before true leaves have emerged. They are gaining popularity as a new culinary ingredient. They are used to enhance salads or as edible garnishes to embellish a wide variety of other dishes. Common microgreens are grown mainly from mustard, cabbage, radish, buckwheat, lettuce, spinach etc. The consumption of microgreens has nowadays increased due to higher concentrations of bioactive components such as vitamins, minerals and antioxidants than mature greens, which are important for human health.

Conclusion

Nowadays microgreens are gaining popularity in the market due to change of life style pattern and health consciousness among consumers. Microgreens provides the high concentration of antioxidant, vitamins and minerals which are linked with the promotion of good human health. A thorough understanding of crop management of microgreens and their postharvest and storage characteristics is crucial for extending their shelf life and for expanding these products into larger markets. This review provides insight which will add to the knowledge base about the management and processing of this new specialty crop.

Future Research Prospective

There is a great potential for growing microgreens form variety of crops which will cater their demand in the market. Combined with the great advances from past years, the future development will contribute to deeper understating of microgreen production. Microgreen industry is the growing field and there is a good scope for future research in this area due to increase of consumer demand. The achievement of appropriate type of crop, harvesting and marketability will act as vehicle for this industry. Progress towards establishment of shelf life stable techniques will also likely to accelerate the demand of this crop in the coming years. The physiological and biochemical changes occurring during microgreen storage deserves more attention. Advancements of postharvest processing techniques and packaging technology will help to maintain the quality for longer periods of time and extend their shelf life. In addition to quality parameters, the functional information of microgreens will help to select the specific crop and harvest at appropriate stage of growth.

REFERENCES

Baenasa, N., Isabel, G.J., Morenoa,D.A., Cristina G.V., Periago, P.M. 2017. Broccoli and Radish Sprouts are Safe and Rich in Bioactive Phytochemicals. *Postharvest Biology and Technology*. 127: 60-67.

Brazaityt. R, Jankauskien. M, Sodininkyst. D and Pavelas. D. 2016. The Antioxidant Properties of Brassica Microgreens grown in Different Substrates.

Brazaityte A, Virsilë1 A., Jankauskienë J., Sakalauskienë S., Samuoliene G., Sirtautas R., Novickovas A., Dabacinskas L., Miliauskiene J., Vastakaitë V., Bagdonaviciene. A and Duchovskis. P. 2015. Effect of Supplemental UV-A Irradiation in Solid-state Lighting on the Growth and Phytochemical content of Microgreens. *Int. Agrophys.*, 29, 13-22.

Brazaityte. A, S. Sakalauskiene.S, Virsilë. A, Jankauskiene. J, Samuoliene. G, Sirtautas. R, Vastakaitë. V, Miliauskienë. J, Duchovskis.P, Novickovas. A and Dabasinskas. L. 2016. The Effect of Short-term Red Lighting on *Brassicaceae* Microgreens Grown Indoors. *Acta horticulturae* · vol(2): 181-184.

Brazaitytë. S, Virsilë. A, Samuolienë. G, Jankauskienë. J, Sakalauskienë. S, Sirtautas. R, Novickovas. A, L. Dabasinskas. L, Vastakaitë. V, Miliauskienë. J and Duchovskis. P. 2016. Light Quality: Growth and Nutritional Value of Microgreens under Indoors and Greenhouse Conditions. *Lithuanian Research Centre for Agriculture and Forestry*. Vol 9 (7): 98-106.

Chandra. D, Kim, J and Yong Phil Kim.Y.P Changes in Microbial Population and Quality of Microgreens Treated with Different Sanitizers and Packaging Films. *Hort. Environ. Biotechnol.* 53(1): 32-40. 2012.

Cheryl Kaiser and Matt Ernst 2012 Microgreens *Reviewed by Tim Coolong, Extension Specialist (Issued 2012)*

Dagmar. J, Lenka. S, and Zdenek S. 2010 Evaluation of Buckwheat Sprouts as Microgreens. *Acta Agriculturae Slovenica,* 5(2): 157-162.

Dorband, Wayne. 2012. "What are the Water Needs of These Fodder Systems October 12. http://sustainablelivestocknutrition.com/what-are-the-water-needs-of-these-fodder-systems.

Ebert, A.W. Wu, T.H. and Yang, R.Y. 2014. Amaranth Sprouts and Microgreens - A Homestead Vegetable Production Option to Enhance Food and Nutrition Security in the Rural Urban Continuum. SEAVEG: Families, Farms, Food Sustaining Small-Scale Vegetable Production and Marketing Systems for Food and Nutrition Security. Vol. 1(3) 233-244.

Gayathree I. S, Gama-Arachchige. N.S, Anjani.B and Karunaratne. M 2015. Preliminary Investigations on Microgreens: An Emerging Health Food. *Plant Sciences and Forestry* Vol. 19(6): 103-108.

Gioia.F.D, Mininni. C and Santamaria.P. 2015. How to Grow Microgreens. https://www.researchgate.net/publication/288798806

Kopsell, D.A, Sams, C.E, and Barickman, T.C. 2014 Sprouting Broccoli Accumulate Higher Concentrations of Nutritionally Important Metabolites under Narrow-band Light-emitting Diode Lighting. *J. AMER. SOC. HORT. SCI. 139(4):469-477.*

Kou. L, Luo Y, Yang T, Xiao. Z, Turner E.R., Lester.G.E, Wang Q and Camp M.J. 2013. Postharvest Biology, Quality and Shelf Life of Buckwheat Microgreens. *Food Science and Technology*. 51: 73-78.

Kou. L, Yang.T, Luo.Y and Eton. C. 2014. Pre-harvest Calcium Application Increases Biomass and Delays Senescence of Broccoli Microgreens. *Postharvest Biology and Technology* 87: 70-78.

Kou. L, Yang.T, Luo. Y and Codling. E 2014. Pre-harvest Calcium Application Increases Biomass and Delays Senescence of Broccoli Microgreens. *Postharvest Biology and Technology* 87: 70-78.

Lee, J.S., Kim, J.G., Park, S., 2009. Effects of Chlorine Wash on the Quality and Microbial Population of 'Tah Tasai' Chinese Cabbage (*Brassica campestris* var. *narinosa*) Microgreen. *Korean J. Hortic. Sci. Tech.* 27, 625-630.

Lee. J.S, Pill W.G., Cobb. B.B and Olszewski. 2004 Seed Treatment to Advance Greenhouse Establishment of Beet and Chard Microgreens *Journal of Horticultural Science and Biology*. 79(4) 564-570.

Marios. C.K, Rouphael. Y, Gioia. F.D, Angelos. K Serio.F, Renna .M, Pascale. S.D, Santamaria. P. 2016. Micro-scale Vegetable Production and the Rise of Microgreens *Trends in Food Science & Technology*. 57: 103-115.

Microgreens: A New Specialty Crop (University of Florida, 2010) http://edis.ifas.ufl.edu/hs1164

Muchjajib.U, Muchjaji.S, Suknikom.S and Butsai. S. 2015 Evaluation of Organic Media Alternatives for the Production of Microgreens in Thailand. *Acta Hortic*. 19 (1): 157-162.

Gioia. F,D and Santamaria. P. 2015 Microgreens, *Agrobiodiversity and Food Security.*

Murphy, C.J., Pill, W.G., 2010. Cultural Practices to Speed the Growth of Microgreen Arugula (Roquette; *Eruca vesicaria* subsp *sativa*) *J. Hortic. Sci. Biotech.* 85, 171-176.

Pill W.G., Collins C.M., Gregory N. and Evans T.A. 2011. Application method and Rate of Trichoderma Species as a Biological Control Against Pythium Aphanidermatum (Edson) Fitzp. in the Production of Microgreen Table beets (*Beta vulgaris* L.). *Scientia Horticulturae*. 129: 914-918.

Pinto.E, Almeida.A, Aguiar. A and Ferreira. I 2015. Comparison between the Mineral Profile and Nitrate Content of Microgreens and Mature Lettuces. *Journal of Food Composition and Analysis*. 37(4): 57-61.

Samuolienë. G, Brazaitytë. A, Jankauskienë. J, Akvilë. V, Sirtautas.R, Algirdas. N, Sandra.S, Jurga. S, Pavelas D. 2013. LED Irradiance Level Affects Growth and Nutritional Quality of Brassica Microgreens. *Cent. Eur. J. Biol.* 8(12) 1241-1249.

Shabir. A.M, Manzoor A.S, and Mohammad M.M. 2016. Microgreens: Production, shelf Life and Bioactive Components Critical Reviews in Food Science and Nutrition ISSN: 1040-8398 *(Print) (Online) Journal*. 1549-7852.

Treadwell, D., Hochmuth, R., Landrum, L., Laughlin, W., 2010. Microgreens: A New Specialty Crop. University of Florida IFAS Extension. HS 1164.

Viktorija V, and akvilë V. 2015. Light - Emitting diodes (leds) for Higher Nutritional Quality of *brassicaceae* Microgreens. *lithuanian Research Centre for Agriculture and Forestry Research for Rural Development*, Vol. 1: 111-117. v.vastakaite@lsdi.lt

Viktorija. V, Akvilë. V, Ausra.B, Giedre. S, Jule. J, Ramûnas. S, Algirdas. N, Laurynas. D, Sandra. S, and Jurga. M 2015 The Effect of Blue Light Dosage on Growth and Antioxidant Properties of Microgreens. Scientific Works of the Institute of Horticulture, Lithuanian Research Centre for Agriculture and Forestry and aleksandras stulginskis university. Sodininkystë ir darÞininkystë. 34(1-2).

Viktorija.V and Akvilë.V 2015. Light - emitting diodes (leds) for Higher Nutritional Quality of *rassicaceae* Microgreens. *Research for Rural development*. Vol 1(7): 144-149.

Weber.C.F 2016. Nutrient Content of Cabbage and Lettuce Microgreens Grown on Vermicompost and Hydroponic Growing Pads, *J Hortic*, 3(4): 76-83.

Weber.C.F. 2017. Broccoli Microgreens: A Mineral-Rich Crop That Can Diversify Food Systems *Plant Nutrition, a section of the journal Frontiers in Nutrition*. Vol. 4 (7): 213-216.

Xiao, Z., Lester, G.E., Luo, Y., Wang, Q., 2012. Assessment of Vitamin and Carotenoid Concentrations of Emerging Food Products: Edible Microgreens. J. Agr. Food Chem. 60, 7644-7651.

Xiao, Z., Lester,G.E., Luo,Y, and Wang,Q 2012 Assessment of Vitamin and Carotenoid Concentrations of Emerging Food Products: Edible Microgreens. *J. Agric. Food Chem.* 60(3), 7644-7651.

Xiao. Z, Luo.Y, LesterG.E, Kou.L, Yang T, Wang. Q. 2014. Postharvest Quality and Shelf Life of Radish Microgreens as Impacted by Storage Temperature, Packaging Film, and Chlorine Wash Treatment. *Food Science and Technology* 55: 551-558.

Xiao. Z, Codling E.E., Luo. Y, Nou. X, Lester G.E. and Wang. Q. 2016. Microgreens of Brassicaceae: Mineral Composition and Content of 30 Varieties. *Journal of Food Composition and Analysis*. 49: 87-93.

Xiao. Z, Lestera. G.E, Parka. E, Robert. A, Saftnera, Luoa. S.Y and Wang.Q 2015 Evaluation and Correlation of Sensory Attributes and Chemical Compositions of Emerging Fresh Produce: Microgreens. *Postharvest Biology and Technology*. 110 (15): 140-148.

Xiao. Z., Luo. Y, Lester G.E, Kou.L, Yang.T and Wang.Q. 2014 Storage Temperature, Packaging Film, and Chlorine Wash Treatment of daikon Radish (*Raphanus sativus* L. var. longipinnatus) Microgreens. *Food Science and Technology*. 55 (4) 551-558.

Pages: 157-180

Food Technology and Research Advancement

Edited by: Dr. Avnish Chauhan and Dr. Pawan Kumar 'Bharti'

ISBN: 978-93-86841-49-0

Edition: 2018

Published by: Discovery Publishing House Pvt. Ltd., New Delhi (India)

10 Case Studies on Achievement of Makhana Farmers and Two Fishermen Cooperative Societies on Prawn and Fish Production

Subrato Ghosh and Himadri Chandra[1]

ABSTRACT

Descriptive accounts on the farming and management procedure of vocations like edible aquatic crop Makhana production in Karandighi Block of Uttar Dinajpur district, fish production in ponds by using treated domestic sewage by a successfully functioning FCS in Bhangore-II Block of South 24 Parganas district, giant prawn farming in modified extensive method in Canning-I Block of same district and the art of prawn and shrimp seed collection from inundated agricultural lands on bank of river Rupnarayan in Sahid Matangini Block of Purba Medinipur district during monsoon have been presented in this article. Authors have made on-site communication with the fish farmers and prawn seed collectors in afore-mentioned districts of West Bengal intimately, studied and noted their farming processes which are definitely means of livelihood support to them. Text matter supported by photographs of our own will make the case studies and article more lively and give a clear understanding to readers.

Chachcharia Fishermen Cooperative Society

Fishermen Cooperative Society (FCS) is a form of business organization, wherein professional fishermen or fish farmers voluntarily associate together as human beings on a basis of equality for promotion of economic interest of themselves on honest means. It was formed under the Cooperative Societies Act 1925. In a developing country like India, small-scale and medium-scale fish farmers have opted for establishment of *fishermen's co-operative societies for all-round fisheries and aquaculture development*. Development

Formerly Guest Lecturer, MSc Fisheries and Aquaculture Department, Utkal University, Bhubaneswar - 751 004 (Odisha) (India)

[1] Vill. Amarshi, PS Potashpur, Dist. Purba Medinipur, Pin - 721 454 (West Bengal) (India)

of fishery cooperative is now recognized as one of the major step for improving the socio-economic condition of fishermen and professional fish farmers.

The fishery cooperative movement in India began in 1913, and the first fishermen society was organized under the name 'Karla Machimar (Fishermen) Cooperative Society' in Maharashtra. Primary FCS is formed at village level, comprising fishermen or fish farmers of a village or group of villages. About 10% of the total number of PFCSs in India is in West Bengal. The sewage-fed freshwater fish ponds in West Bengal are within the jurisdiction of Bhangore-I, Bhangore-II, Tiljala, Salt Lake and Sonarpur Police Stations in North and South 24 Parganas districts. There is a small cluster of cooperative sewage-fed fish ponds in the region. Unlike experience of cooperatives elsewhere, these ponds are run fairly capably. As an actively and successfully functioning Primary FCS, Chachcharia Fishermen Cooperative Society is very well-known to elderly fish farmers in these two districts.

Fish Culture Scenario beyond East Kolkata

Daily domestic sewage and storm (rain) water from Kolkata city are mostly carried through combined sewers, separately termed as Dry Weather Flow (DWF) channel and Storm Water Flow (SWF) channel; the latter is four times wider than former and both constructed almost parallel to one another. In 1935, it was decided to discharge the sewage and storm water of the city eastwards into river Kulti at Ghusighata (32km from Topsia Pumping Station in east Kolkata) by these two channels. The wastewater or sewage-fed aquaculture system in regions beyond eastern boundary of Kolkata has been developed over the past 85 years by fish farmers, who have gained experience in regulating the intake of raw sewage of DWF channel into fish ponds. There are many pumping stations at certain locations in Kolkata, plan-wise built, to drain out such wastewater into DWF channel. It was constructed on the northern side of SWF channel, fishery owners on all regions got full benefit of feeding their fisheries' ponds with sewage water. The DWF Channel runs at a high level and its level is adjusted by means of a regulator to ensure uninterrupted feeding/ supply in ponds, *jheels*, *beels*, *bheris* and wetlands.

In 1930, a Zamindar in East Kolkata Wetlands in Salt Lake attempted to culture Indian major carps in vast water-logged areas by letting in sewage in small doses. Result obtained was very encouraging and within a short period, the whole of this area was converted into fish farming region for culturing freshwater fishes. When the ponds are 20-25 hectare or more, the wastewater inflow is almost continuous.

Significance

It is a zero-cost treatment of the city's wastewater or organic sewage by means of fish culture and production of marketable-sized economically-important fishes. The Kolkata sanitary sewage that is conveyed through DWF channel is being utilized by local poor- to medium-scale fish farmers through feeding in fisheries' ponds or fish farming wetlands. In this process, most of dry weather flow of the city gets treated through fish culture. The SWF channel was constructed in 1940, which facilitated draining of the fish culture ponds and sewage was fed into the fisheries' ponds as and when required. Clarified effluent from fish ponds, which is acceptable and will not have any adverse impact upon environment and ecology of river Kulti and river Bidyadhari, was carried by these two channels further eastwards towards Kulti (Bhowmick and Ayyappan, 2001). During the dry weather, *i.e.*, in non-monsoon months, there is a great demand from the fishery pond owners for Kolkata sewage and without it, culture of Indian major carps and exotic carps, Pangas catfish, Tilapia in this area would not have been either possible or profitable. Sewage contains chemical constituents, like nitrogen and phosphorus, which possess fertilizing value. It enhances the productivity of fish ponds, facilitating growth of fishes under culture. It is a low-cost but effective and viable technology (Ghosh, 1988).

At 6.5km from Topsia, the outfall channels were connected with two large sedimentation tanks at Bantala. These tanks were constructed in 1943. At Bantala, away from human habitations, the DWF channels from the city and Manicktala were led into the sedimentation tanks through a common carrier channel. About 90 minutes retention was considered necessary to get a good settlement of sludge, 85% of settleable sewage solids were deposited by this period. Inside diameter of each of two such settling tanks was 260 feet and average depth 13 feet. Clear effluent properly settled in the tanks was then led by gravitation into the head end of DWF channel. For the purpose of fish culture, sewage or effluent from sedimentation tanks was distributed amongst the fisheries' ponds through controlled channels. This primary treatment facility is not working for more than 45 years and presently has become totally defunct.

Chachcharia FCS and Chachcharia Feeder Channel

There are 296 hectare and 506 hectare of sewage-fed fish farming regions at two places Hatgachha and Hadia respectively, located in Bhangore-II Community Development Block. Bamanghata village is located 8.6km from Science City and 3km from Bantala, beyond the eastern fringes of Kolkata in Bhangore-II CD Block of South 24 Parganas district. Here lies the office and fish farm of Chachcharia Fishermen Cooperative Society, a Government of WB registered society. Its complete address is: Vill. Uttar Bamanghata, P.O. Hadia, PS Kolkata Leather Complex, Bamanghata Gram Panchayat under Bhangore-II CD Block and PS, Dist. South 24 Parganas. This society functioned as Fish Production Group during 1989 to 1999 and had its Registration as FCS at Office of the Assistant Director of Fisheries,

South 24 Parganas on 25th November 1999. Presently this FCS is having 127 male and 19 female members. Chachcharia FCS has 45 hectare of water area under its possession, that includes eight ponds (obtained on lease) and 10 hectare of land area, that includes a large single-storied dormitory for FCS members, office room, four night sheds, store house, vegetable garden and embankment of ponds. There are four nursery ponds, two rearing ponds and two stocking-cum-grow out ponds, each of about 180 bigha in area (3 bigha = 1 acre). Ownership of these water bodies lies with Department of Land and Land Reforms, Government of WB.

Till 2010, Chachcharia FCS had to pay annual revenue amounting to Rs. 41,200/- for its 55 hectare area. This FCS obtained lease for its fish ponds for a continuous period of ten years till 2010. Domestic wastewater is let into fish ponds in a planned manner, preferably at 15 days interval (as and when felt necessary) from the main DWF channel at three positions. A sub-channel 3.5-4.0 mt wide (sluice gate connects it with DWF channel) runs within the farm area and supplies wastewater to nurseries and rearing ponds *via* narrow inlets, separate ones provided in each pond. Main channel runs along the south-western boundary of fish farm, outside its territory, and wastewater/sewage is let into farm at two locations 600mts apart, *via* a large pump machine and large motor. These two points supply wastewater to two large grow-out ponds or bheris; where sewage is let in more frequently in comparison to nurseries and rearing ponds. In post-monsoon months and when renovation needs to be done, sewage supply in DWF channel is stopped. Daily sanitary sewage of Kolkata is let out directly *via* SWF channel in periods of heavy rain and thereafter. In conditions when sewage supply is halted, DWF channel measure 4.0-4.2 metre in width and in conditions of normal sewage supply, it measure 6.2-6.5 metre.

Fish Farming Practices

Members of Chachcharia FCS purchase spawn of major carps of pure variety from reliable fish seed traders of Dimghata fish seed market, Sealdah. These best quality spawn are supplied from Bankura district, which have been produced under controlled conditions judiciously by means of 'Bundh-breeding' technology. One spawn measuring cup-full spawn costs Rs. 800/-. Those are stocked in pre-prepared nursery ponds 33 decimal (1 bigha) in area, and within few days are transferred to 80-100 decimal ponds. About 15000-20000 pieces weigh 1kg. Those are reared for next fifteen days till they attain fry stage (1500-2000 pieces weigh 1kg). Fry are stocked in 900-1000 decimal ponds (30 bigha) and within next 45-50 days of culture, they attain fingerling stage (90-100 pieces weigh 1kg). These are subsequently stocked in two grow-out ponds and at the end of next three months, fishes attain 250gm and more in weight (4 pieces weigh 1kg), which are periodically harvested and marketed. Everyday such fishes, along with bigger ones are harvested in between 4.00-5.00am, landed near FCS office, loaded over three-wheeler cycle vans and supplied to Bamanghata wholesale fish market at 5.30am, which is 800-900mts away from this fish farm.

Indian major carps of 250gm size are sold at Rs. 65-70/-/kg, *Labeo rohita* and *Hypophthalmichthys molitrix* of size 800-1000gm at Rs. 120/-/kg, *Labeo bata* at Rs. 105/-/kg, *Cyprinus carpio* at Rs. 80/-/kg. Marketable-sized *Pangasianodon hypophthalmus* and *Oreochromis niloticus* are also produced and sold. Liming is done in fish ponds every month during culture using solution of agricultural limestone. Cowdung is used if felt necessary, but chemical fertilizers (Urea, SSP) are never used. As farm property, Chachcharia FCS has three big pump machines, two big motors, three small motors, twelve boats for harvesting fishes, eight small nets and one large seine net (360 feet length). Mustard oil cake is first composted for 15-20 hours in big aluminium Hundis or in rectangular cement cisterns, then the semi-solid semi-compost material (further diluted) is spread over water surface in nursery and rearing ponds, upon which the growing spawn and fry feed. Members of Chachcharia FCS have obtained experience in using Mohua oil cake as feed to growing fry and fingerlings, after a sufficient time of composting. It has good protein content, become feed for developing fingerlings as its toxicity is diminished.

In the two large grow-out ponds, sewage is let in more frequently which leads to sufficient production of planktonic organisms. Fingerlings feed upon those. In addition to it, traditional bag feeding system is employed. Two full sacks of mustard oil cake (45-50kg) are kept in immersed condition by tying to erect poles at two points in each of the two big water bodies and perforations are made (drilled) on the jute sacks. The quantity of leftover feed in sack is estimated and subsequent feed rations are adjusted accordingly. Mass of semi-moist duckweed *Lemna minor* is collected from small ponds, packed in jute sacks and thrown over surface of grow-out ponds in fresh condition, taking out handful amount from bags. This tiny free-floating aquatic plant is readily accepted by growing fingerlings as food. For every three quintal fishes, 40-45kg *Lemna minor* is used once in every 24 hours.

Input Support and Recognitions

In the financial year 2016-2017, Chachcharia FCS has received five aluminium Hundis of 18 inch diameter, two fish harvesting nets, two solar lights, 400kg fingerlings of Indian major carps, 9000kg floating pelleted fish feed (180 sacks) from Office of the Assistant Director of Fisheries, South 24 Parganas district. Similarly in the preceding years also, this FCS has been considered as beneficiary by ADF, South 24 Parganas in one of different schemes of Directorate of Fisheries, GoWB and received input support in the form of goats (for integrated fish farming), fish fingerlings, ducklings and other materials. Under Social Fishery scheme 2015-2016, Chachcharia FCS pond was selected as Demonstration Centre for production of big fishes (IMC) of above 2kg weight.

Chachcharia FCS has always strived hard for betterment and development, members are always keen to learn new technologies, give importance to every step of fish pond management practices. Chachcharia FCS has received 'Krishak Samman' Award from Hon'ble Chief Minister of WB for best performance on *Maati Utsav* on 15th January, 2015; received 'Best Performer of the Year' Award on the occasion of Bengal Fish Fest from Minister of Fisheries, GoWB on 18th December, 2015; received 'Best Fish Farmer Group Award' from ICAR-CIFE Kolkata Centre on 10th July, 2011; received 'Productivity Award' from National Productivity Council of India, New Delhi as best performer in Inland and Marine Fish Production in Cooperative Sector on 24th September, 2009; received 'Best Performer Award in District' for year 2008-2009 from South 24 Parganas District Cooperative Union; received award on Silver Jubilee Year celebration of BENFISH from Former Minister of Fisheries, GoWB on 6th February, 2006; received State-level 'Fish Productivity Award' for achieving second maximum production per acre water area on 10th July, 2004; received 'Dr Hiralal Chaudhuri Productivity Award' for year 1999-2000 for achieving first position in fish production in WB; obtained first position amongst Fishermen Cooperative Societies in WB and 'Best Performer' Award for year 2001-2002 from West Bengal State Cooperative Bank Limited on 14th November, 2002.

Epilogue

Chachcharia FCS ensures that its accounts are audited annually and audit report is presented for consideration in its annual general body meeting. In every year, on the day of this meeting, clothes are distributed generously to poor and under-developed people in Bamanghata village. Night guards take every measure to repel away hundreds of water fowls which arrive during morning hours in the vicinity of the two large grow-out ponds. Thick growth of water hyacinth is maintained at a stretch all along the sides of fish ponds at water-pond slope interface, it protects the bank from erosion and prevents retreat or receding of pond banks.

The objective in fertilizing an aquaculture pond with wastewater is to produce live and minute natural food for fish, *i.e.*, plankton. Wastewater is used in fish ponds of Chachcharia FCS in a controlled manner. Likewise, for many other elderly and professional fish farmers in surrounding regions, sewage is the source of livelihood; pond water becomes enriched with essential nutrients without the use of commercially-available inorganic fertilizers. Series of coconut trees on pond embankments in nearby and far sight, Chinese hibiscus flower garden, small organic farm and vegetable garden, well-maintained fish ponds, clean pond banks and clean water, two big wetlands/bheris, indigenous boats on water bodies, cordial reception of elderly fish farmers, truly disciplined life style and their wealth of Indigenous Technological Knowledge – all together constitute a sacred and serene environment which prevails within the 55 hectare fish farm complex of Chachcharia Fishermen Cooperative Society Limited.

Entrance gate of Chachcharia FCS Ltd.

A big pump machine

A big motor machine and DWF channel

Rearing pond in Chachcharia FCS fish farm

The DC pond to produce 2kg fish

Duckweed *Lemna minor* applied in pond

A sewage inlet in grow-out pond 180 bigha

Sewage channel within Chachcharia farm

Larger fingerlings of major carps (100gm)

Fingerlings of major carps (40-50gm)

Sewage channel towards grow-out pond

Fish farmer with *Lemna minor* as fish feed

Sewage inlet channel in small pond

Close view of sewage inlet in large pond

One grow-out pond at Chachcharia farm

DWF channel beside Chachcharia fish farm

Makhana Farmers at Karandighi, Uttar Dinajpur

The lotus *Nelumbo* sp., water lily *Nymphaea* sp., water spinach *Ipomoea aquatica*, water chestnut or 'Paanifol' *Trapa bispinosa* and fox-nut or 'Makhana' *Euryale ferox* are the commercially-important aquatic crops of plant origin. The highly remunerative Makhana is extensively grown in northern and eastern districts of Bihar, contributing 85-90% of India's total production. About 8-12 small, marble-sized, black to blackish-brown, membrane-covered seeds are found in interior of Makhana fruit. This membrane covers the soft white edible portion or the starchy cotyledon, which is eaten. Starchy, white pea-sized edible seeds (having 9.7% of easily digestible protein, 0.01% fat and zero cholesterol) of high demand, produced by the hydrophytic Makhana plant, are exported to consumers' markets at Delhi, Kanpur, Varanasi and some districts in Punjab. Makhana puffs and Makhana powder are used as snacks and in preparation of many costly sweet dishes and porridge. Makhana stem is rhizomatous; the large elliptical to disc-shaped closely-placed green floating leaves with purple bottom are the main characteristic feature. It is cultivated in old, perennial, stagnant and shallow ponds having organic load (33-100 decimal, waist-height depth). A profit of Rs. 4000/- may be achieved from 33 decimal plot (Pustey, 2001).

Makhana farming is the main source of livelihood for resource-poor marginal farmers (downtrodden fishermen community), and is established in districts of Kishanganj, Katihar and Purnia in Bihar (amongst other districts), adjacent to Uttar Dinajpur in West Bengal. Karandighi Community Development Block in Uttar Dinajpur is adjacent to Bihar State Border; which is surrounded by Purnia and Katihar on its western and south-western sides respectively. Encouraged by the success of Makhana farmers of neighbouring districts, 90 farmers of four GPs of Karandighi Block, namely Bazargaon-I GP, Lahutara-I GP, Karandighi-I and Karandighi-II have adopted Makhana farming seriously. It begun in Karandighi in 1998, success could be achieved steadily.

Farming Practices

Sri Abdul Khalil, aged 56, is an experienced Makhana farmer of Andhoria village, Bazargaon-I GP, Karandighi Block. Since 2009-2010, he is producing Makhana in 4 acre (12 bigha) water area, comprising three perennial ponds. Culture duration is 5-6 months. He sows *Euryale ferox* saplings during 15th March - 15th April in plots having 2.5-3.0 feet depth, bottom soil is loamy to clayey-loam and hygienic. Makhana pond is fertilized using a mixture of 80kg Di-ammonium phosphate, 15kg Potassium/Potash and 40kg mustard oil cake/acre area 8-10 days prior to sowing of saplings. He brought saplings 1.0-1.5 feet in height (3 months old) from Bhagalpur, costing 50 paisa. To prevent occurrence of 'Dhosa rog' disease in growing Makhana plants, in every acre plot, Sri Khalil applies 5ml insecticide and 10gm disease-preventive medicine Carbendazim mixed in 16lits water; it is done a week before sowing. Symptoms of 'Dhosa rog' are black spots/ patches formed over Makhana leaves in younger stage of plant, making plants unhealthy. About 2000 Makhana saplings are sown/33 dec plot, maintaining a space of 2.5-3.0 feet on all sides in between two saplings. Leaves of healthy saplings float on water surface. On 4th day, a mixture of 5ml insecticide, 10gm Carbendazim medicine and 15ml Vitamin is used/ acre area, which is repeated three more times in next 22 days.

Intact marble-sized Makhana seeds are harvested during August-September. Coat of fruits rupture after maturation, resulting in spread over of seeds on pond bottom which are collected manually. Makhana fruit takes 7-10 days to mature. A quintal of fruits produces about 35kg seeds. Makhana plants are cut with sickle 'Kasti' and subsequently, split-bamboo built structure 'Ganja' is used as Makhana collecting device, of length 50cm and open end diameter 35cm. Seeds are cautiously collected as the whole plant bears thorn except on upper surface of leaf. Skilled labourers from Bihar are employed for harvest, who sieve Makhana seeds from a mass of bottom mud, it is continued several times. Bottom muck and mud is washed away during its sieving in Ganja, leaving the intact seeds. Hundred seeds weigh 80-100gm.

From every 33 dec plot or more, Sri Khalil harvests marketable-sized Makhana seeds in three phases at fortnight interval; 200kg in first phase, 70-80kg in second and 50kg in third. Complete harvest is quite impossible. Rate of production is 300kg/33 dec (av.), which increases to 350kg in ideal weather conditions. Professional labourers engaged by Sri Khalil for harvesting are paid Rs. 2000/- per quintal Makhana seeds in first phase, Rs. 3500/- per quintal in second and Rs. 5000/- per quintal in third. Harvesting becomes progressively difficult in successive phases as amount of seeds collected is maximum in first phase, labourers have to work harder in rest two phases. Some people of Pichhla village of Karandighi-I GP are proficient in harvesting Makhana. At farm site, cleaned marble-sized seeds are sun-dried to 30% moisture content, stored in jute sacks (35-40kg). Sometimes Sri Khalil directly markets freshly-harvested wet Makhana seeds from farm site. Makhana seeds which could not be harvested at the end of first crop remain in pond; those germinate into seedlings/saplings in next season.

Sri Khalil sells his farm produce at Harda wholesale market in Purnia, 45km from Andhoria village. Approximately 3500 tonnes of Makhana is traded annually in Purnia. For Sri Khalil, investment cost amounts to Rs. 10,000/- in 33 dec pond; expenses incurred on cost of Makhana saplings and plantation (Rs. 2000/-), maintenance and cost of medicine, insecticide (total Rs. 2000/-) and wages to labourers for harvesting (Rs. 6000/-). By selling Makhana seeds, he earns Rs. 27,000/-/33 dec area (@ Rs. 9000/-/ quintal according to present market rate; it depends on international market conditions). He makes profit of Rs. 17,000/- from every 33 dec plot. Price of harvested Makhana varies between Rs. 80-200/-/kg; most of it is exported to Pakistan, Sri Khalil stated. Ponds are seeded or saplings sown in first year only; in subsequent years, the left-over seeds germinate automatically and plants produced.

Cultivation of Makhana is a lucrative proposition in rain-fed lowlands, unutilized shallow perennial ponds and left-fallow wetlands, max^{m} water depth 4 feet. Generally 12-20 quintals of Makhana seeds may be harvested/ hectare plot. During 2000-'01, in Bihar and Uttar Pradesh, freshly harvested Makhana seeds were sold @ Rs. 2200/- quintal. During 2014, this farm gate price increased to Rs. 55/-/kg. Sundried, packed and stored Makhana are sold @ Rs. 65-130/- kg. About 55-60kg white edible Makhana is obtainable from 100kg seeds. Nutritious Makhana powder having neutral taste is incorporated as ingredient in powdered protein drink and other health drinks. Sri Khalil opined that Makhana powder helps in weight loss without compromising normal strength.

Puffed Makhana Production

Sri Santosh Saha and Seben Saha are another two professional Makhana farmers in Picchla village, who own 15 acre and 8.3 acre plots respectively. Their average production is 250kg/33 decimal. Predominant monsoon temperature during late evening and night and warmer daytime favour Makhana production. Freshly-harvested Makhana seeds may be kept in good condition in water for 12-14 days, seeds germinate and quality impair when kept for more time. Pipeline water is sprinkled for 4-5 days over those packed in sacks in storehouses. Since last four years, puffed Makhana is produced in four processing centres each at Picchla and Dalkhola villages in Uttar Dinajpur, from where Makhana puffs are sold to markets at Delhi, Kanpur, Lucknow and Gwalior *via* two Makhana traders of Dalkhola. About

45 families, native of Darbhanga district, are involved in Makhana processing. Makhana farmers of Karandighi Block sale their produce here, instead of marketing at distant markets in Purnia. Sun-dried Makhana seeds are first separated according to size in sieves (earthen furnace temperature vary to produce puffs from different sized seeds separately). Intact black seeds are heated in black iron cauldron in presence or absence of sand on glowing earthen furnace fire, then hit hard by wide wooden hammer over wooden slab to get puffed Makhana. In the process, hard shells of hot seeds are broken and the kernel puffs up in expanded form. The puffs have low fat content and are good for human health. Almost-round Makhana puffs are packaged in 44 × 27 inch bags, 7-8kg in each and sold to traders within 4 months. Makhana is a sustainable source of income for both producers and processors at Karandighi.

Makhana farmers in Karandighi Block

Makhana seed harvesting device Ganja

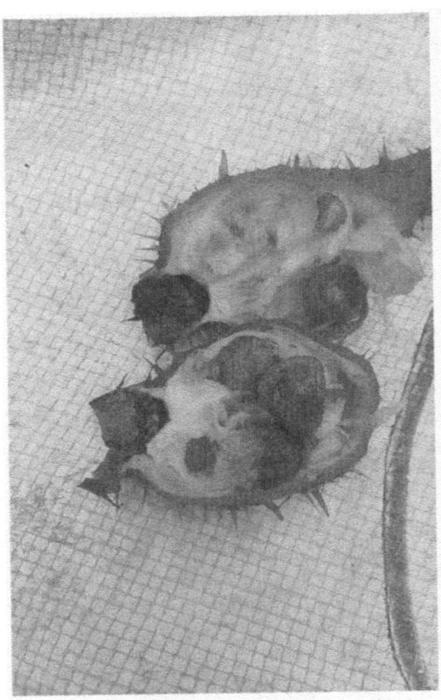

Black seeds inside Makhana fruit

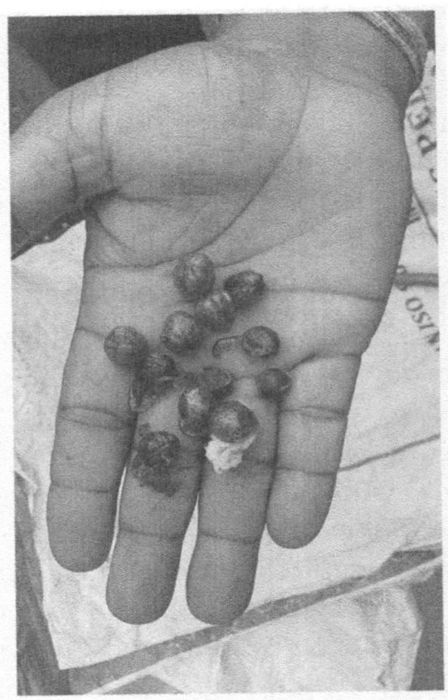

Marble-sized intact Makhana seeds

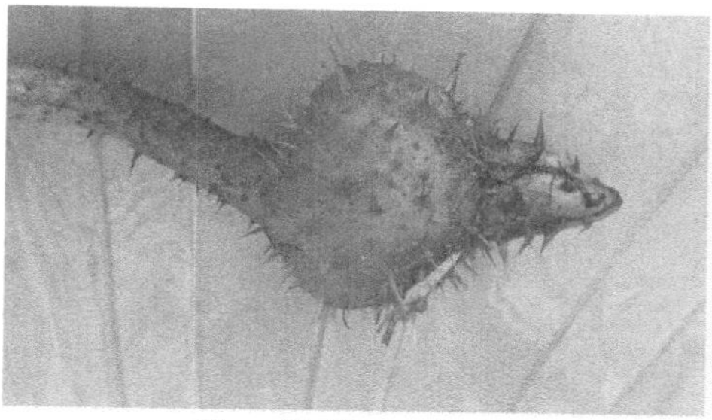

Ripe Makhana fruit

The Ganja

Sri Abdul Khalil

The Kasti or Makhana plant-cutter

Leaf and stem of Makhana plant

Sprinkling water over harvested Makhana

Different sieves for grading Makhana

Processing and puffed Makhana production

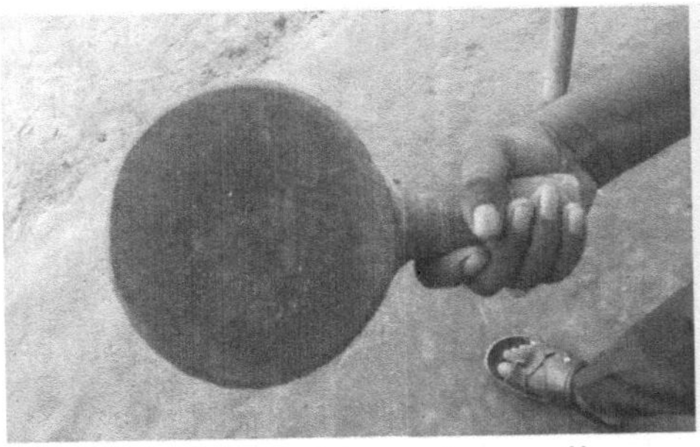

Hammer used to produce puffs

Puffed Makhana production (another view)

Shell of Makhana used to produce fuel

Makhana puffs produced at Karandighi

Scampi Farming by Cooperative Society at South 24 Parganas, West Bengal

Scampi farmers in West Bengal have evolved innovative culture strategies based on their experiences. They produce high value product at low to medium investment and low risk. Sri Ganesh Mondol, aged 67, President/Chairman, *Gangadevi Samudrik Matsyajibi Samabaay Society Limited* (Gangadevi Fishermen Co-operative Society Ltd) is one of such farmers, elderly and experienced in profession. This co-operative society is based at Vill. Uttar Taldi under Taldi Gram Panchayat, under Canning-I Community Development Block in South 24 Parganas district of WB. It had its registration at Office of the Asst. Director of Fisheries, South 24 Parganas on 6/8/2010 with 25 member farmers, presently which has increased to 46nos. Sri Mondol and associate farmers are practicing Scampi farming in a 247 decimal pond (800 feet x 135 feet) with 4.5 feet water depth, which they have gained possession in December 2013 from Taldi GP; it was a three year term lease agreement valued Rs. 93,000/-, with extension of one year. The water body was constructed during May-June 2013 under the initiative of Taldi GP in 2013; construction cost amounting to Rs. 3,00,000/-. It is not a traditional endogenously-managed farming system, but a more extensive and commercial venture.

M. rosenbergii Seed Stocking and Harvesting

In June 2015, Sri Mondol had stocked 7500nos. of naturally-occurring *M. rosenbergii* seeds of 7-8mm size. It was bought (Rs. 1000/- per 1000 pieces) from prawn seed collectors in brackishwater region of Diamond Harbour in South 24 Parganas, which is a low saline zone (≤2ppt). In January 2016, 120kg of marketable-size Scampi was harvested (partial harvesting), those were found to attain 90-125gm in weight. It was sold locally @ Rs. 500-550/- per kg. In October 2016, those attained 200-250gm with giant blue claws and sold @ 700-750/- per kg. Sri Mondol opined that Scampi will grow to 250-300gm in 18 months with adequate supply of quality feed and in ponds with predominantly sandy bottom.

In April 2017, Sri Mondol stocked 1000nos. of *M. rosenbergii* juveniles, 1.5-2.0 in size, riverine, Rs. 3.00/- per piece. It was captured at Amjhara village, located on opposite side of Canning river under Basanti Block in South 24 Parganas. It attained 4 inches as on 8th July, 2017 and will be harvested at the end of six months from stocking. Additionally 2900nos. of hair-like post-larvae, lengthing 8-10mm were stocked in 1st week of June 2017, which were captured from river Roydighi in Mathurapur-II Block of this district, bought in oxygen-packed condition @ Rs. 850/- per 1000nos. It has attained 1.5-2.0 inches in one month. It will grow to 75-120gm at the end of ten months, Sri Mondol stated. He uses 'Magic Fish Feed' brand supplementary prawn feed (2-3mm dia pellets, 1cm long, 18-20% protein content, price: Rs 900/- per 50kg sack), marketed by Glup Aqua Farm, Kolkata. It is used in between 7.30-8.00pm, once in 24 hours, 12kg every time, broadcasted on all four sides of pond from embankment. The pellets become soft like rice and are accepted by growing Scampi of all size.

In addition to prawn, presently there is about 400kg of Indian major carps in this pond, of 350-400gm and upto 1250gm in size. With input support from Office of the Assistant Director of Fisheries, South 24 Parganas, carp fingerlings (80-100gm) were stocked in this pond in October 2015. Most of the marketable-sized fishes were harvested in end of May 2017 and left with this amount. For IMC and *Puntius javanicus*, 50kg Magic Fish Feed is applied on every alternate day, suspended in perforated polyethylene bags or mosquito nets (having larger drilled pores) on bamboo pole fixed at one location.

Pond Management

Dr. A.K. Das, Senior Scientist and Head, Training and Extension Cell, ICAR-Central Inland Fisheries Research Institute, Barrackpore had once visited this site and appreciated Sri Mondol's efforts. He is using the commercial dust-form aquaculture product 'Reegain' (Rs. 350/- per kg), 8kg everytime in 247 decimal pond, once or twice in a month when felt necessary. It maintains the optimum dissolved oxygen level, good condition of pond water and soil, and favours growth of both Scampi and major carps. Lime and inorganic fertilizers need not be applied if Reegain is used, Sri Mondol stated. He is using another product 'AFP Forte', a prawn feed supplement (Price: Rs. 1900/- per 5kg pack). During April, water table in pond recedes to 2 feet, which is increased by drawing out groundwater and filling using a 2 HP pump bought by the society, costing Rs. 12,000/-. Use of pelleted feeds of renowned manufacturers and high cost aquaculture products will not be possible for a large number of small-scale and resource-poor farmers. For *Gangadevi Samudrik Matsyajibi Samabaay Society Limited*, Scampi farming has proved to be a good profit-generating small scale business idea.

Importance of Giant Prawn Farming

In West Bengal (WB), India, freshwater pond aquaculture and capture-based fishery activities are mainly rural-based and operated by small- to medium-scale farmers. Farming of the giant freshwater prawn *Macrobrachium rosenbergii* or Scampi in monoculture or polyculture systems in ponds is lucrative because of its fast growth rate, easy acceptability of both plant- and animal-based diets, ability to withstand wide fluctuation in salinity, resistance to diseases, high demand and market price. It is getting popular owing to increased availability of post-larvae (10-12mm) and juveniles (30mm) both from wild waters and those produced in hatcheries. Scampi farming can be conducted by unskilled rural people on small establishments in modified-extensive type of management. It is predominantly a cooperative venture and does not necessitate specialized training but needs proper management and monitoring. Prawn farming yields higher net profits than most other occupations and vocations and farmers rarely subsidize their income with other activities (Sahu, 2014). Scampi culture is considered to have the potential to raise income among impoverished farmers; an increase in cultured *M. rosenbergii* will likely improve livelihoods (Banu and Christianus, 2016). The species grows well even with 15% protein feeds in ponds with sufficient natural food. Unlike *Penaeus monodon*, Scampi are grown on low protein and relatively inexpensive diets (Mitra *et al.*, 2005).

Uttar Taldi was originally an unirrigated village beside a creek of the Bidyadhari, a tidal river. The creek ceased to exist since 1963 when bundh was constructed across it and Canning-I Block and Bhangore-II Block (or Jibontala) were connected on roadway *via* Uttar Taldi. Canning town is 7km ahead from Uttar Taldi, and is the gateway to Sundarbans, which is a huge mangrove forest on the coast of Ganges delta by the Bay of Bengal. The rivers, numerous creeks, tidal inlets, marshes and estuaries of Sundarbans form a network and constitute its low saline brackish water body. Scampi or *M. rosenbergii* has wider potentiality for culture in many brackish water areas of Indian Sundarban delta (Chand *et al.*, 2015). Low saline water culture at 5ppt and upto 7ppt has been found to be conducive for Scampi farming, which gives better production and survival (Rao, 2010). According to Sri Mondol, the 247 decimal pond is low saline in nature, bottom soil is having the characteristics of that of a river, sandy-loam/sandy-clay in texture, favouring growth of Scampi.

Scampi and fish feed used by Sri Mondol

Water body of Gangadevi FCS Ltd.

M. rosenbergii at harvest (90-125gm)

Marketable-sized *M. rosenbergii*

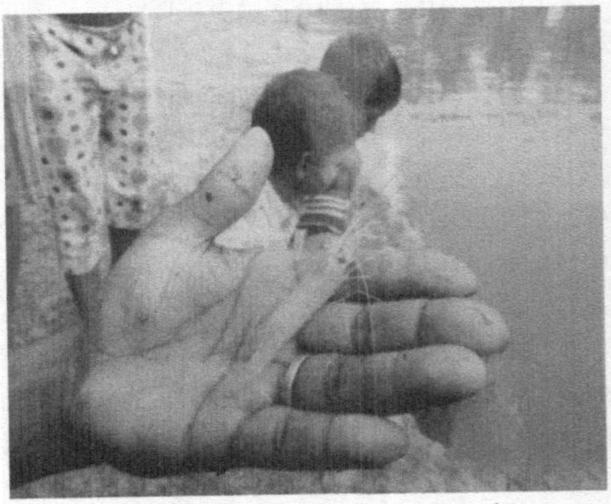

Juvenile of *M. rosenbergii* at stocking

Another view of the 247 decimal pond

Sri Mondal applying cast net in pond

Simple means of aeration in pond

Lime application in pond

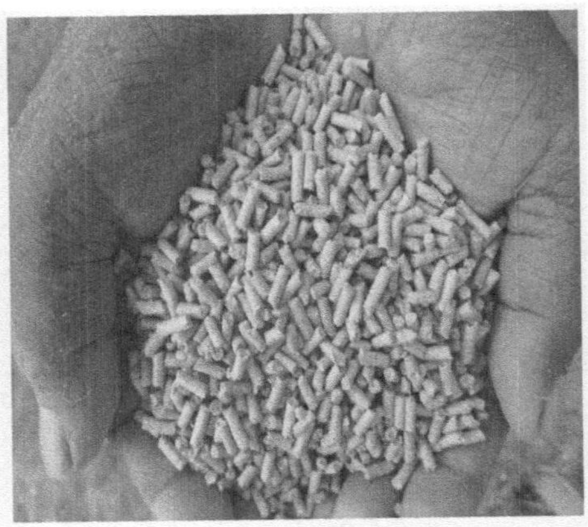

Pelleted prawn feed used

Commercial aquaculture product Reegain

Few members of Gangadevi FCS, Uttar Taldi

Sri Ganesh Mondol

Makhana seed collector with Ganja

Prawn and Shrimp Seed Collection from inundated Land on Bank of River Rupnarayan

Rupnarayan river system is a major river network of eastern India which is a major source of water for irrigation, agriculture, and industrial purposes of the people living in the river bank. Conventional practice of prawn and shrimp seed collection on western bank of Rupnarayan river at Kharui, Gujarkharui and Jamitta villages in Sahid Matangini Block of Purba Medinipur district in WB is a supplementary source of income for local agro-based people. From month of Aashar (June-July) to Bhadro (August-September) every year, river water inflates during spring tide supported by monsoon downpour and the extended open tract of unsown paddy plots (2.5-3.0km on Kolaghat-Tamluk road and 400-700mts across towards river) on its western bank gets inundated at times of full moon and new moon. It remains stagnant for 3-4 consecutive days twice a month at 1.5-3.5 feet depth.

During this period, innumerable numbers of riverine giant prawn *M. rosenbergii* post larvae and juveniles 0.75-3.00 inch size and also that of penaeid shrimp enter into these tracts, which offer an opportunity for local farmers and elderly men and women to exploit them. During Aaashar and mid of Shravan (July end), 3-5 persons in each of the plots 8-25 decimal in area enthusiastically capture these young stages of prawns and shrimps with indigenous triangular bamboo-built nets 2.5-3.0mt in length dragged along water column several times and circular nets 3 feet in diameter. As water table recedes, these get confined within embankments 1.5 feet high in each plot and caught in stationary triangular-shaped split bamboo and nylon net made traps 'Mugri' (Rs. 80/- each, 2.0-2.5 feet length) placed at specific positions in embankments. Prawn seeds amounting to 2.0-2.2kg are collected/hour/person on first 1-2 days of spring tide when these abundantly occur. This amount reduces later on. Live ones are sold to prawn farmers at Rs. 250-300/- per kg for stocking in ponds and fresh dead ones sold at Kolaghat, Kaktia and Tamluk markets at Rs. 150-200/- per kg. Those are used for household consumption also locally as delicious recipes. Prawn and shrimp seeds are kept alive in Hundi or shallow hapa cloth enclosures constructed at one end of the flooded agricultural tracts.

A Mugri seen in submerged condition

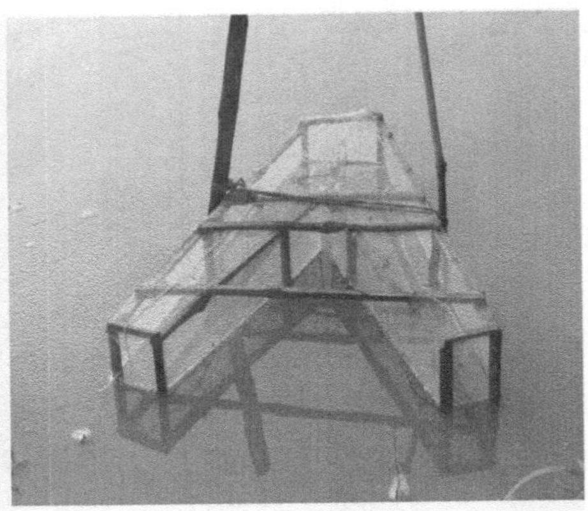

Close view of indigenous fishing trap Mugri

Women involved in prawn seed collection

Women involved – another view

Another woman collecting prawn seeds

Another view of Mugri

Old farmer collecting prawn seeds

Old man with triangular net - another view

Prawn seed keeping in Hundi

Prawn seed collection for supply to farms

Inundated Rupnarayan river bank

Prawn seed collection for livelihood

Another view of prawn seed collection

A husband and wife collecting prawn seeds

Another villager collecting prawn seeds

Cloth container for storing live prawn seeds

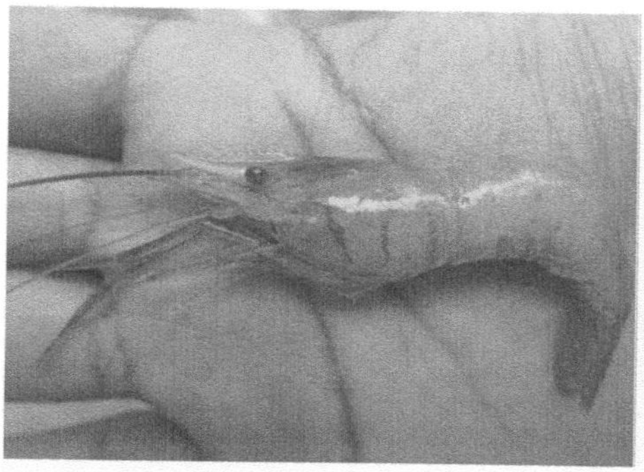

A riverine prawn juvenile caught

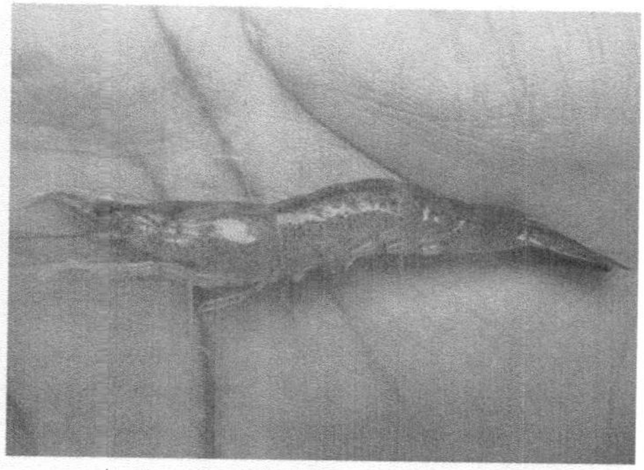

A riverine shrimp seed caught

Mass of prawn and shrimp seeds caught

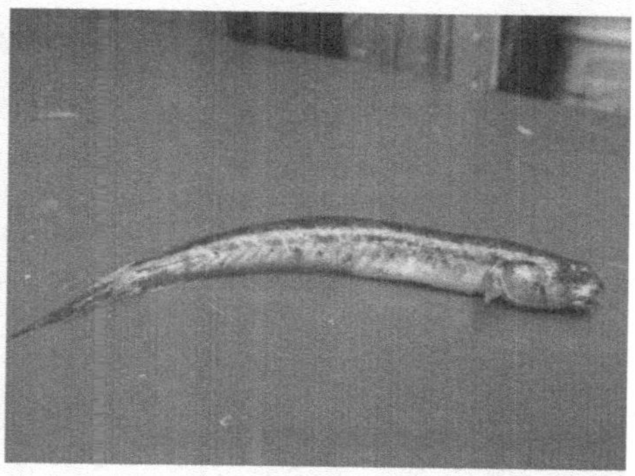

A finfish species caught from flooded field

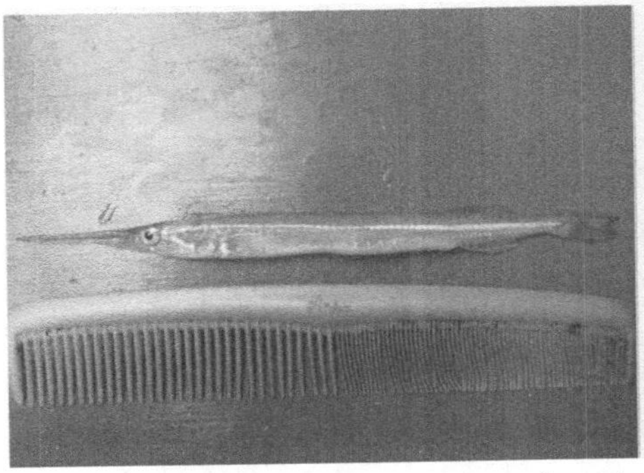

Xenentodon cancila amidst prawn seed catch

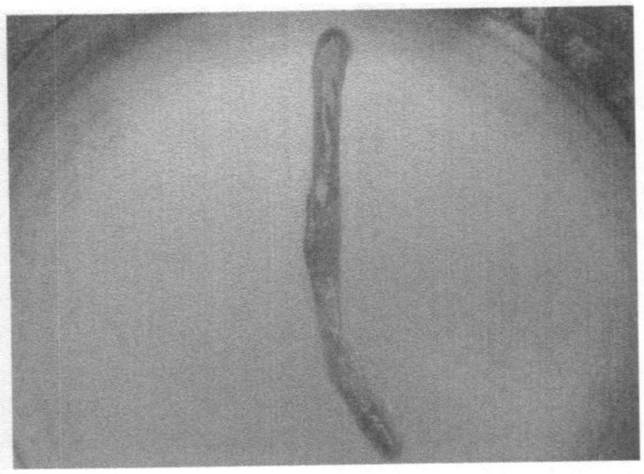

Alimentary tract of *X. cancila*

Another view of shrimp seeds caught

Small crabs amidst prawn and shrimp seeds

REFERENCES

Bhowmick, M.L. and Ayyappan, S. (2001): Sewage-fed Aquaculture in Kolkata – A Critical Review, *In. Souvenir Int. Symposium. Fish for Nutritional Security in 21st Century. ICAR-CIFE Publication, Mumbai*: 115-120.

Ghosh, D. (1988): Wastewater-Fed Aquaculture in the Wetlands of Calcutta - An Overview, *In. Proceedings of International Seminar on Wastewater Reclamation and Reuse for Aquaculture, Kolkata. GoWB Publication*.

Pustey, A. (2001): Cultivation of Makhana and Water Chestnut in Lowland Wetlands (in Bengali), *Salmoli Publications, Kolkata*: 1-36.

Banu, R. and Christianus, A. (2016): Giant Freshwater Prawn *Macrobrachium rosenbergii* Farming: A Review on its Current Status and Prospective in Malaysia, *J. Aquac. Res. Development*, 7: 423.

Chand, B.K., Trivedi, R.K., Dubey, S.K., Rout, S.K., Beg, M.M. and Das, U.K. (2015): Effect of Salinity on Survival and Growth of Giant Freshwater Prawn *Macrobrachium Rosenbergii* (de Man), *Aquaculture Reports*, 2: 26-33.

Mitra, G., Mukhopadhyay, P.K. and Chattopadhyay, D.N. (2005): Nutrition and Feeding in Freshwater Prawn Farming, *Aqua Feeds: Formulation and Beyond*, 2(1): 17-19.

Rao, K.J. (2010): Grow-out Technology of *Macrobrachium rosenbergii*, *In. Compendium of Training on Freshwater Prawn Breeding and Culture, ICAR-CIFA, Bhubaneswar publication*: 19-24.

Sahu, S. (2014): Economic Analysis of Scampi (*Macrobrachium rosenbergii*) Polyculture in Selected Ponds at Contai Subdivision in Purba Medinipur District, West Bengal, *IJIRSET*, 4(10): 9760-9767.

Pages: 181-189

Food Technology and Research Advancement

Edited by: Dr. Avnish Chauhan and Dr. Pawan Kumar 'Bharti'

ISBN: 978-93-86841-49-0

Edition: 2018

Published by: Discovery Publishing House Pvt. Ltd., New Delhi (India)

11 Incidence of Zoonotic Parasites in Egyptian Raw Vegetable Salads

Sylvia O. Ahmad[1]; El Fadaly H.A.[2]; Mona S.Zaki[3] and Barakat A.M.A.[2]

ABSTRACT

Feeding on Vegetables which probably contaminated order to pre or post-harvesting activities through soil, animals or wastage water contacts, consider as non-neglected source for several zoonotic parasites. So, this study describes the possible parasites contamination in raw vegetables salads, directly reflect public health hazard. A total of 527 salad samples of seven varied types as; 94 sample of Onion, 93 Cucumbers, 88 dill & Parsley, 87 Tomatoes, 73 Lettuce, 51 cabbages and 41 carrots were collected from different types of restaurants within two Egyptian governorates (Mnia and Assiut). Samples were directly washed each byTris-buffer-saline (TBS), followed by concentration of the extract by centrifugation, staining of the different stages by modified Zeihl–Neelsen stain centrifuged and the sediments were fast microscopic examined for parasites. The overall incidence of parasite contamination in each type of vegetable were; 7.4% in *Onion*, 22.6% in *Cucumbers*, 19.3% in *Dill & Parsley*, 13.8% in *Tomatoes*, 8.2% in *Lettuce*, 15.7% in *Cabbages* and 34.5% in *Carrots*. Also, five types of parasites were detected by 16.1% in the total examined samples. Also, the overall incidence of each parasite reference to total vegetable samples were; *Ascarislumbricoides* (3.2%), *Cryptosporidium parvum* (1.7%), *Entamoeba spp. cysts* (3.4%), *Giardia lamblia* (2.8%), and *Toxoplasma gondii* (4.9%). The study validates some zoonotic parasites of public health worry in vegetables salad. The results alarm must be connected to the Egyptian health authorities for

Department of animal Hygiene and zoonosis, Faculty of Veterinary Medicine, Assiut University Egypt.

Zoonotic Diseases Department, National Research Center, Giza, Egypt.

Prof. of Clinical Pathology, Hydrobiology Department, National Research Centre, Dokki, 12622, Giza, Egypt.

fast adjustment the public health educational progressions, and modified sterilization or radiation techniques for raw vegetable.

Key words: Zoonotic parasites, Vegetable Salads, Egypt.

Introduction

Vegetables containing fiber, vitamins and mineralsare essential source for health fitness. But, it's an important mode of parasites diffusion and has been shown to be an important source for food borne outbreaks in both developed and wealthy countries. (Pires, *et al*. 2012). The higher request for vegetables is the motive of increased reports of zoonotic parasitosis in recent years (Vazquez *et al*. 1997). Humans can be infected via vegetables which polluted pre or post-harvesting, connect harmfully effects on people's health especially in non-industrialized countries. However, extra changing of vegetables eating habits, production systems, increased awareness and better diagnostic tools are some of the main drivers affecting the emergence or re-emergence of these parasitic diseases (Northrop-Clewes & Shaw; 2000). Vegetables possibly contaminated through pets contact and other people. Also, thru rodents, insects and improper treated waste water associates (Simoes M, *et al*. 2001 and MahviAH & Kia EB. 2006).

The immune-compromised individuals cannot repel parasite infection, and they involving digestive disturbances such as dysentery, diarrhea, obstruction and anemia (Srikanth R & Naik D. 2004). Also, some parasites could be invade internal organs, discharging toxins and tissue-destroying enzymes, probable stimulate abortion, arthritis, asthma, degenerative muscle diseases, ovarian cysts, cutaneous ulcers, dermatitis, and more (Robertson & Gjerde, 2001).

The purpose of the current study was to judge the pollution degreeand the public health hazards of zoonotic parasites in consumed vegetables salad from Egyptian restaurant.

Methodology

Sample Collection

A total of 527 raw and ready to eat vegetable samples were collected once weekly of seven varied types as; (*n*=94) Onion, (*n*=93) Cucumbers, (*n*=88) dill & Parsley, (*n*=87) Tomatoes, (*n*=73) Lettuce, (*n*=51) cabbages and (*n*=41) carrots. All vegetable samples were picked randomly from the commercial different types of Egyptian restaurants within two Egyptian governorates (Mnia and Assiut). It were transported in sterile plastic bags to lab. (Zoonotic Disease Department-National Research Center, Egypt). The study covered a period from 11/2014 to 1/2016.

Sample Preparation and Parasites Recognition

According to Opara KN & Udoidung NI (2002), we were recycled TBS for the extraction. Each vegetable sample wasvisible to Tris-buffer-saline (TBS) (20 mMtris base, 0.5 mM sodium chloride, 0.2% tween 20 and double-distilled water), were usedas washing solutions. Portions of about 100 gm of each vegetable sample were assorted together and were soaked in 150 ml of the extraction solution, with the aid of a mechanical shaker; the beaker was shaken at 150 rpm for 30 minutes. The washing solution (TBS), was poured via a sterile gauze into a sedimentation flask and left to residue for 60 minutes. The supernatant was decanted and the sediment was relocated into a 15 ml conical centrifuge, and centrifuged at 1500 rpm for 5 minutes. The supernatant was decanted, a few drops of 10% formal-saline (10ml formal in in 90 ml of 9% normal saline), was added and the mixture was spread on at least 3 slides and inspected for parasites. A drop of the sediment was put on the slide. A clean cover slip was gently placed to avoid air bubbles., a drop of the sediment was mixed with a drop of Lugol's Iodine solution and examined as before, Simple and iodine smears were used for detection of parasitic eggs, cysts and larva. The process was analytically recurrent until the end of the mixture in each test tube. Eggs, cysts and oocysts of parasites found under the light microscope were identified. Staining of sediment smear was performed by Modified Zeihl–Neelsen14 and modified trichrome15 to detect protozoal parasitic (oo)cysts. The preparation was tested under a light microscope using × 10 and × 100 objectives (Garcia LS. 2007). Infective stages of parasites were recognized according to Downesand Ito (2001).

Results

The results are summarized in (Table 11.1). The incidence of the total parasite contamination reference to each type of vegetable were; 7.4% in *Onion,* 22.6% in *Cucumbers,* 19.3% in *Dill & Parsley,* 13.8% in *Tomatoes,* 8.2% in *Lettuce,* 15.7% in *Cabbages* and 34.5% in *Carrots* (Table 11.1). The overall percent of parasites detected were 16.1% in the total examined samples (Table 11.1). Also, the results encountered five types of parasites during the study; and the total isolation of each parasite reference to total vegetables were; *Ascarislumbricoides* (3.2%), *Cryptosporidium parvum* (1.7%), *Entamoeba spp. Cysts* (3.4%), *Giardia lamblia* (2.8%), and *Toxoplasma gondii* (4.9%) (Table 11.1). Carrots and Cucumbers were detected the most parasites contaminated vegetables (34.5 & 22.6) respectively. While sporulatedoocysts of *Toxoplasma gondii* and cysts of *Endameba histolytica* were the most prevalent isolated parasites (Table 11.1).

Discussion

The present study is on target zoonosis, evaluates the public health hazards via direct Egyptian consuming vegetable salad through the detected of overall 16.1% of contaminated vegetable samples with varied pollution percentages sequence to the different examined vegetable types.

Table 11.1: The numbers and percentages of the isolated parasite stages in relation to various vegetable types

Parasite Types	The Examined Vegetables NO/(%)							
	Onion	**Cucumbers**	**Dill and Parsley**	**Tomatoes**	**Lettuce**	**Cabbages**	**Carrots**	**Total**
No. of samples	94	93	88	87	73	51	41	527
Ascarislumbricoides eggs.	2(2.1)	6(6.5)	4(4.5)	2(2.3)	1(1.4)	0	2(4.9)	17(3.2)
Cryptosporidium spp. oocysts.	1(1.5)	3(3.2)	3(3.4)	1(1.1)	0	0	1(2.4)	9(1.7)
Entamoebaspp. cysts	1(1.5)	4(4.3)	5(5.7)	3(3.4)	0	2(3.9)	3(7.3)	18(3.4)
Giardia lamblia cysts.	1(1.5)	5(5.4)	0	2(2.3)	2(2.7)	2(3.9)	3(7.3)	15(2.8)
Toxoplasma gondii oocysts.	2(2.1)	3(3.2)	5(5.7)	4(4.6)	3(41)	4(7.8)	5(12.2)	26(4.9)
Total/(%)	7(7.4)	21(22.6)	17(19.3)	12(13.8)	6(8.2)	8(15.7)	14(34.5)	85(16.1)

The isolation of parasite infective stages from vegetable salad that are fully prepared and ready to eat is a good indicator of sapro-zoonotic hazards via improper washing. This authorize that tap water doesn't completely eliminate parasites. Ali *et al.*, (2006) were settling our impression, and practical that 7.8% of parasites still after the use of tap water. Also, we observed that washed *Carrots, Cucumbers and Dill & Parsley were* recorded higher parasitic contamination than the other vegetable types. This may be due to it cultivated in soil contact than others. Also, other factors are stimulating vegetables contamination, where leafy vegetables likely exposed to parasites via dust than the roots ones. Also, irregular uneven surface facilitate parasite connection and survival. *Carrot, Cucumbers* and leafy vegetables as *lettuce* and *parsley* have uneven surfaces and makes parasitic eggs, cysts and oocysts more tight attached (Kniel. *et al.*, 2002). This concept approve the pre-harvesting soil pollution, order to inadequate treated water used for irrigation.

In the present study the values of contaminated percentages were lower than the former recorded by Doaa, (2012); presented a significant higher level of vegetables pollution (31.7%) in Alexandria-Egypt. Probably attributed to unwashed vegetables used in his study. Also, several factors may contribute to such differences include, geographical location, type and number of examined samples, methods used for parasites isolation and the post-harvesting handling and transmission methods. So, varied level of parasites contamination were detected in many studies; one in Ghana the overall parasitic contamination of the vegetables as 36% (Amoah *et al.* 2006). In Nigeria was also 36% (Damen. *et al.*, 2007). Ettehad *et al.*, (2008) reported, slightly lower level of contamination of consumed native garden vegetables with intestinal parasites (29%) in Ardabil city, Iran. Higher rate of contamination of vegetables was detected in wholesale and retail markets in Tripoli, Libya, the study done by Abougraina. *et al.*, 2010. This study identified 58% positive samples for intestinal parasites (Abougraina. *et al.*, 2010). Inspection of vegetable samples in Kenya by Nyarango RM. *et al.*, (2008) also publicized higher rate of contamination (75.9%). In contrasts, other study in Saudi Arabia in 2006 shown that the highest number of contaminated samples was found in green onions (28%) and the lowest contamination was in leek (13%). The prevalence of parasites in other vegetables in the same study was 17% in each of lettuce and water cress (Al-Binali. *et al.*, 2006).

The sporulated oocysts of *Toxoplasma gondii* and the cysts of *Endameba spp* were the most prevalent isolated parasitic stages (4.9 & 3.4%) respectively. The isolation of *T.gondii oocysts* confirm habitat of stray shedder kittens in the vegetables cultivated zone, the oocysts were sporulated in soil and pollutes vegetables via dusting during pre-or post-harvesting dynamics. Also, possibly indirectly maximize human infection through meat tissue cysts of herbivores animals (Hassanain *et al.*, 2011).The opportunistic *T. gondii*protozoan signifies varies complicated pregnancy induces abortion, fetus malformation and latent brain cyst (Sibley *et al.*, 2009). The dormant bradyzoites persist viable for the rest of the host survives and probable reverted to acute infection sequence to pregnancy estradiol hormonal sift (Elfadaly *et al.*, 2012) or in diabetic personals (Hassanain *et al.*, 2014). In addition to anti-inflammatory corticosteroids therapy (Elfadaly *et al.*, 2015). *Entamoeba spp* cysts could be survive outside hosts in water, soils, and on vegetables, especially under moist conditions. Its isolation (Table 11.1) approves fecal contamination through farms used insufficient treated waste water or unutilized human or animal fertilizers (Srikanth R & Naik D. 2004).

Ascarislumbricoides is the largest and the most common human round worm, it grow to a length of up to 35 cm, responsible for human ascariasis (Harhay *et al.*, 2010). The fertilized egg become infectious and resistsome chemicals (Murray *et al.*, 2005). So, the egg can persist in soil for 10 years or more (Piper R, 2007). Ascaris ova are sticky and can tight adhere to vegetables (Kagei, 1983). In the present study *A. lumbricoides* was frequently encountered in different vegetable types (Table 11.1). The results were agree with some reports who found *A. lumbricoides* as the most common parasite in vegetables (Mesquita *et al*, 1999 and Simoes M, *et al.* 2001), in contrast to Robertson & Gjerde, 2001, who did not encounter Ascaris at all. The varied human and environmental factors might explain this difference.

Ingestion of *Cryptosporidium* sporulated oocysts is a water-borne zoonosis, responsible for the prolonged diarrhea in both immune-competent and immune-compromised hosts, It is resistant to all practical levels of chlorination, surviving for 24hrs at 1000 mg/L free chlorine (Deng *et al*, 2004). Oocyst of Cryptosporidium is not often looked in routine microbiology laboratories. Its presence in our study is a call for increased vigilance by microbiologists and clinicians in our region. Its isolation (Table 11.1), confirm human or animal fecal contamination.

Giardia lamblia is a flagellated protozoan parasite, the infection can occur through ingestion of dormant microbial cysts in contaminated water and vegetables. The *Giardia* cysts found within surface water, it of great sapro-zoonotic concern, suggested that dogs, cats, cattle, sheep and humans are reservoirs (Robertson LJ, Gjerde B; 2000).

The wide variation in reported frequencies of parasitic contamination in vegetables doesn't relates to the level of environmental contamination only, but also to the accurate diagnostic methods (Akujobi, *et al*; 2005). However, Robertson and Gjerde (2000) found that the use of immune-magnetic separation and identification by immuno fluorescence, appreciably improved the yield for *Giardia* and *Cryptosporidium*. Similarly, Knieland

Jenkins (2005) found that the use of polyclonal sera specific to the recombinant viral capsid protein (rCPV40) in a dot blotted hybridization assay to detect *Cryptosporidium oocysts* from green onions and was superior to other methods. Also, the wide variation of results in developing countries was related to the nonexistent systems for routine diagnosis and monitoring or reporting for many of the food-borne pathogens.

Conclusion

Raw vegetable salads are connecting zoonotic parasites of public health impact, different chemical or radiation methods for vegetables disinfection or sterilization should be developed. Further researches and inspections should be done concerning viability bio-assays of parasite stages in raw vegetable.

REFERENCES

Abougraina AK, Nahaisi MH, Madia NS, Saied MM, Chengheshc KS. (2010); Parasitological Contamination in Salad Vegetables inTripoli – Libya. Iran Food Control; 21: 760-2.

Akujobi CN, Ogunsola FT, Iregbu KC, Odugbemi TO. (2005); Comparative Evaluation of Direct Stool Smear and for mol ether Concentration methods in the Identification of Cryptosporidium Species. Nigerian Journal of Health and Biomedical Sciences; 4: 5-7.

Al-Binali AM, Bello CS, El-Shewy K, Abdulla SE. (2006); The Prevalence of Parasites in Commonly used Leafy Vegetables in South Western, Saudi Arabia.Saudi Med J; Vol. 27 (5): 613-616.

Amoah P, Drechsel P, Abaidoo RC, Ntow WJ. (2006); Pesticide and Pathogen Contamination of Vegetables in Ghana's Urban Markets. Arch Environ Con Tox; 50(1): 1-6.

Damen JG, Banwat EB, Egah DZ, Allanana JA. (2007); Parasitic Contamination of Vegetables in Jos. Nigeria Ann Afr Med; 6: 115-8.

de Oliveira CA, Germano PM. (1992); Presence of Intestinal Parasites in Vegetables sold in the Metropolitan Region of Sao Paulo, SP, Brazil. -search of Helminthes. Rev Saude Publica; 26: 283-289.

Deng, M.; Lancto, C.A.; Abrahamsen, M.S. (2004)."Cryptosporidium parvum Regulation of Human Epithelial Cell Gene Expression". International Journal for Parasitology 34(1): 73 82. doi:10.1016/j.ijpara.2003.10.001.PMID 14711592.

Doaa El Said Said (2012); Detection of Parasites in Commonly Consumed Raw Vegetables.

Downes FP, Ito K. (2001); Compendium of methods for the Microbiological Examination of Foods. 4th ed. Washington, DC: American Public Health Association.

Elfadaly HA, Hassanain MA, Shaapan RM, Barakat AM, Toaleb NI (2012). Serological and Hormonal Assays of Murine Materno-Fetal *Toxoplasma gondii* Infection with Emphasis on Virulent Strains. World J. Med. Sci., 7 (4): 248-254.

Elfadaly HA, Hassanain MA, Shaapan RM, Hassanain NA, Barakat AM (2015). Corticosteroids Opportunist Higher T.gondii Brain Cysts in Latent Infected Mice. International Journal of Zoological Research.

Ettehad GH, Sharif M, Ghorbani L, Ziaei H. (2008); Prevalence of Intestinal Parasites in Vegetables Consumed in Ardabil. Iran Food Control; 19: 790-4.

Garcia LS. (2007); Macroscopic and Microscopic Examination of Fecal Specimens. In: Garcia LS, Editor. Diagnostic Medical Parasitology. 5th ed. Washington, DC: American Society of Microbiology (ASM); p. 782-830.

Harhay, Michael O; Horton, John; Olliaro, Piero L (2010). "Epidemiology and Control of Human Gastrointestinal Parasites in Children". Expert Review of Anti-infective Therapy 8(2): 219-34.doi:10.1586/eri.09.119.

Hassanain MA, Elfadaly HA, Shaapan RM, Hassanain NA, Barakat AM (2011). Biological Assay of Toxoplasma gondii Egyptian Mutton Isolates. Int. J. Zoo. Res.; 7 (4): 330-337.

Hassanain MA, El Fadaly HA, Hassanain NA (2014). *Toxoplasma gondii* Parasite Load Elevation in Diabetic Rats as Latent Opportunistic Character. Annals of Tropical Medicine and Public Health 7 (2): 110-115.

Kagei, N. (1983) Techniques for the Measurement of Environmental Pollution by Infective Stages of Soil-transmitted Helminths. In *Collected Papers on the Control of Soil-Transmitted Helminthiases* (ed. M. Yokogawa, S. Hayashi, A. Kobayashi, N. Kagei, N. Suzuki, and C. Kunii), Vol. 2, pp. 27-46, Asian Parasite Control Organization, Tokyo.

Kniel KE, Jenkins MC. (2005); Detection of Cryptosporidium Parvum Oocysts on Fresh Vegetables and 1 Herbs using Antibodies Specific for a Cryptosporidium parvum viral antigen. J Food Prot; 68: 1093-1096.

Kniel KE, Lindsay DS, Sumner SS, Hackney CR, Pierson MD, Dubey JP. (2002); Examination of Attachment and Survival of Toxoplasma gondiioocysts on raspberries and blueberries. J Parasitol; 88: 790-3.

Mahvi AH, Kia EB. (2006); Helminthes Eggs in Raw and Treated Wastewater in the Islamic Republic of Iran. East Mediterr Health J; 12(1-2): 137-43.

Mesquita VC, Serra CM, Bastos OM, Uchoa CM. (1999); The Enteroparasitic Contamination of Commercial Vegetables in the Cities of Niteroi and Rio de Janeiro, Brazil. Rev Soc Bras Med Trop; 32: 363-366.

Murray, Patrick R.; Rosenthal, Ken S.; Pfaller, Michael A. (2005); Medical Microbiology, Fifth Edition. United States: Elsevier Mosby.

Northrop-Clewes CA, Shaw C. Parasites. (2000); Br Med Bull; 56: 193-208.

Nyarango RM, Aloo PA, Kabiru EW, Nyanchong BO. (2008) The Risk of Pathogenic Intestinal Parasite Infections in Kisii Municipality, Kenya.BMC Public Health; 14(8): 237.

Odeman WA (1996). "Intestinal Protozoa: Amebas". *Baron's Medical Microbiology* (Baron S *et al.*, eds.) (4th ed.). Univ of Texas Medical Branch. ISBN 0-9631172-1-1.

Opara KN, Udoidung NI. (2002); Parasite Contamination of Leafy Vegetables: A Function of the Leaf Area Index (LAI). Global Journal of Pure and Applied Sciences; 9: 25-30.

Piper R (2007). Extraordinary Animals: An Encyclopedia of Curious and Unusual Animals, Greenwood Press.

Pires SM, Vieira AR, Perez E, Lo Fo, Wong D, Hald T. (2012); Attributing Human Foodborne Illness to Food Sources and Water in Latin America and the Caribbean using Data from Outbreak Investigations. Int J Food Microbiol; 152(3): 129-38.

Robertson LJ, Gjerde B (2000); Isolation and Enumeration of Giardia Cysts, Cryptosporidium oocysts and Ascaris Eggs from Fruits and Vegetables. J Food Prot; 63: 775-778.

Robertson LJ, Gjerde B. (2000); Isolation and Enumeration of Giardia Cysts, Cryptosporidium Oocysts, and Ascaris Eggs from Fruits and Vegetables. J Food Prot; 63: 775-778.

Robertson LJ, Gjerde B. (2001); Occurrence of Parasites on Fruits and Vegetables in Norway. J Food Prot; 64: 1793-1798.

Sibley L D, Khan A, Ajioka J W, Rosenthal B M (2009). Genetic Diversity of *Toxoplasma gondii* in Animals and Humans. Philos. Trans. R. Soc. Lond. B. Biol. Sci.; 364 (1530): 2749-2761.

Simoes M, Pisani B, Margues EGL, Prandi MAG, Martini MH, Chiarini PFT, *et al*. (2001); Hygienic-sanitary Conditions of Vegetables and Irrigation Water from Kitchen Gardens in the Municipality of Campinas, SP. Braz J Microbiol; 32: 331-333.

Srikanth R, Naik D. (2004); Health Effects of Waste Water reuse for Agriculture in the Suburbs of Asmara City, Eritrea. Int J Occup Environ Health; 10: 284-288.

Vazquez Tsuji O, Martnez Barbabosa I, Tay Zavala J, Ruiz Hernandez A, Perez Torres A. (1997);Vegetables for Human Consumption as Probable Source of Toxocara spp. Infection in man. BolChilParasitol; 52: 47-50.

Index

A

Ahmad, Sylvia O., 181

ALA, 85

Amaranth, 72

Amaranthus spp., 72

ANOVA, 113, 116

Apitherapy, 48

Arif, Mohd., 89

Atta spp., 47

Australian Dung Beetle Project, 41

B

Barakat, A.M.A., 181

Beels, 158

Ber, 106

Bheris, 158

Bio technology revolution, 4

Blue revolution, 4

Bombyx mori, 47

C

Catla (*catla catla*), 51

Central Advisory Committee (CAC), 14

Chandra, Himadri, 157

Chenopodium genus, 76

Cirrhinus mrigala, 51

Clarius batrachus, 51

Codex Alimentarius Commission, 14, 21

Coleopteran, 41

Commercial fish farming in West Bengal, 50-71

Consumer Protection Act, 32

Controlled Ecological Life Support System (CELSS), 85

Cooperative Societies Act 1925, 157

Cowpea, 89

Ctenopharyngodon idella, 51

Cyprinus carpio, 161

D

Dadan (imprest money), 56

Developmental biology of *Pseudodiaptomus serricaudatus* (crustacean: copepod), 110-123

  introduction, 111

  materials and methods, 111-112

  results, 112-120

  discussion, 120-121

DHA, 43, 44

Dhutmal, R.R., 89

DNA, 11

Dry Weather Flow (DWF), 158

E

El Fadaly, H.A., 181

ELISA, 31

Evergreen revolution, 4

F

FAO/WHO Codex guidelines, 12

FDA, 7

Food allergy, 20-36

  additives causing allergic reactions, 32-34

  avoiding food allergens when dining out, 31-32

  difference between allergies and asthma, 28

food allergens in non-food items, 23
Food Safety and Security (FSS) Act, 14
Food Safety and Standards Authority (FSSA), 14
how food regulation safe guard against food allergens, 30-31
how to identify or diagnose food allergies, 25-26
how to prevent food allergies, 28-29
introduction of food allergens, 20-21
major reasons for food allergens, 22
personal contact and food allergies, 26-28
treatment, 29-30
types of food allergies, 23-25
cross-reactivity and oral allergy syndrome, 24
allergic protocolitis, 25
eosinophilic esophagitis, 25
food protein-induced enterocolitis syndrome, 25

G

GDP, 4
GHGs, 39
Ghosh, Subrato, 50, 157
Giardia lamblia, 186
Global Positioning System (GPS), 4
Glossogobius giuris, 60
GM crops, 11, 12
Government of India, 7
Government of West Bengal, 59
Grass carp, 51
Green revolution, 4
Guar, 89
Gupta, Priti, 6

H

H. binata, 107
HACCP program, 30
HDL, 84
Homoptera, 41

I

ICT, 17
Insects, 37-49
beneficial role of insects for humans, 40-41
entomophagy around the world, 41
insects as delicacy: an album, 44-45
introduction, 38-39
major groups of edible insects, 41
medicinal use of insects, 45
nutritional quality, 42
fatty acid composition and concentration, 43-44
proximate composition, 42-43
various insects and their parts used in medicine, 45-48
why eat insects, 39-40
International Year of Quinoa, 72
Introduction, 1-5
research and development, 3-4
scope of food technology, 2-3

J

Jheels, 158

K

Kadam, S.S., 89
Koteswararao, G., 124
Kranthikumar, T., 124
Kumar, Ashok, 89

L

LDL, 43
Lemna minor, 161

M

Macrobrachium rosenbergii, 52
Mahajans, 56
Makhana farmers and two fishermen cooperative societies on prawn and fish production, 157-180
Chachcharia FCS and chachcharia feeder channel, 159-160

Chachcharia fishermen cooperative society, 157-158
epilogue, 162-165
farming practices, 166-167
fish cultural scenario beyond east Kolkata, 158
fish farming practices, 160-161
importance of giant prawn farming, 172-175
input support and recognitions, 161-162
M. rosenbergii seed stocking and harvesting, 171-172
Makhana farmers at Karandighi, Uttar Dinajpur, 165
pond management, 172
prawn and shrimp seed collection from inundated land on bank of river rupnarayan, 175-180
puffed makhana production, 167-170
scampi farming by cooperative socity at south 24 parganas, west Bengal, 170-171
significance, 158-159

Melanoplus sp., 45

Microgreens, 124-156
amaranth, 131
beet, 131
broccoli, 132
cabbage, 132
chard, 131
chives, 131-132
chrysanthemums, 132
cilantro, 133
crop selection, 135-136
definition of microgreens, 125
dill, 133
fennel, 132
French sorrel, 133
general specifications of a microgreen, 133-134
harvest, hygienic-sanitary quality and post-harvest storage, 141-142
health benefits of microgreens, 127-128
introduction, 125
irrigation and fertilization, 141
kale, 131
lettuce, 131
mache, 131
marketing and packaging, 142
microgreens and agro-biodiversity, 129-130
microgreens and food security, 128-129
mint, 133
mitzuna, 131
mustard and cress, 132
nutritional properties of microgreens, 127
parsley, 132
pest and disease management, 141
production of microgreens, 134-135
production site and planning, 135
quality of seeds, seeding and germination, 138-140
reasons to grow microgreens, 126
selecting the cultivation substrate, 137-138
selecting the growing system, 136-137
shisho, 133
spinach, 130
tatsoi, 131
tender greens, 133
types of microgreens, 130
varieties of microgreens, 130
watercress, 132
what are microgreens, 126

Mishra, V.K., 37

Mitigation strategies for fodder scarcity, 89-109
adoption of improved methods of fodder production, 99
advantages of hydroponics technology, 100

agro forestry approach, 95-96
alternate source of fodders during acute shortage, 102
common agro forestry fodder production models, 96-97
controlled grazing systems, 97
converting wasteland into grassland, 98
fodder requirement and planning for one year, 91-96
fodder requirement and planning for one year: preservation of fodder, 92-94
horti-pasture, 106-107
hydroponics fodder production, 99-100
introduction, 89-90
massive cultivation of fodder trees, 97-98
present scenario of fodders, 90-91
promotion of technique for treatment of crop residues, 99
review of research work, 102-106
silvi-pasture, 107-108
strengthening extension activities, 102

Moth, 89
Mrigal, 51
MUFA, 43
Myurmecosistus spp., 47

N

Nagaraju, M.M., 124
NFT, 133
NLGMA, 135
NPD Group Health Track, 15

O

OECD, 21

P

Padmavati, G., 110
Polybia sp., 42
Pond farming of *Chitala chitala*, 50-71
Pseudodiaptomus serricaudatus, 110-123
PUFAs, 43

Q

QOL (quality of life), 17
Quinoa, 72-88
description of the plant, 73
distribution, 73
financial analysis, 74-75
health benefits, 82-84
history, 72
individual concerns, 81
introduction, 72
nutritional quality of quinoa, 76-80
preparation and cooking of quinoa, 81
processing/manufacturing, 73-74
saponins and oxalic acid, 75-76
selection and storage of quinoa, 80
what new about quinoa, 84-85

R

Radio Allergo Sorbent Testing (RAST), 27
Ranganna, G., 124
River Rupnarayan, 175-180
Rohu (*Labeo rohita*), 51

S

Sharma, Anubhuti, 6
Shukla, Priyanka, 20, 72
Silver carp (*Hypopthalmichthys*), 51
Singh, Satyapriya, 37
Siva, M., 124
Sphenarium spp., 45
Storm Water Flow (SWF), 158
Stylosanthes hamata, 102
Surendrababu, M., 124

T

Taenipoda sp., 45
Tecomena undulate, 108
Thomson, T., 124
Trend and opportunities for functional and genetic food in Indian market, 6-19
future food, 9

food regulation in India, 13-14
food safety and standard authority of India (FSSAI), 14
nutrition labeling and education act (NLEA), 14
benefits of regulation, 14-16
future challenges to food industry based on trends in life science, 16-17
introduction, 6-7
can we predict the future food production, 7-9
nutraceutical/functional food, 9-11
genetically modified food, 11-13

U

Unique approach to commercial fish farming in West Bengal, 50-71
business terms made by pisciculturists with fish feed dealers and fish auctioneers, 56-57
characteristics of paddy fields-turned-fish farming regions, 51-53
end note, 58-59
introduction, 51
morphology of alimentary tracts of small freshwater fishes, 66-70
other salient features, 57-58
particulars of fish farming system, 53
activity of Sri Debtosh Moni, 54-55
activity of Sri Dibakar Mal, 55-56
activity of Sri Dipankar Barman, 53-54
pond farming of freshwater food fish chitala chitala, 59-66
C. chitala as policefish, 61
farming in ponds of FPG and SHG, 64
freshwater prawn as food, 64-66
growth in ponds, 61-63
many species combined farming, 64
pond management, 60-61
riverine seeds in Bangladesh, 63
seeds of river Brahmaputra, 60
stocking density, 63-64

V

Vashney, Anurag, 6
VOCs, 26

W

White revolution, 4
World Health Organisation (WHO), 12

Y

Yellow revolution, 4

Z

Zaki, Mona S., 181
Zizyphus spp, 106
Zoonotic parasites in Egyptian raw vegetable salads, 181-189
discussion, 183-187
introduction, 182
methodology, 182
results, 183
sample preparation and parasites recognition, 182-183

❑ ❑ ❑ ❑ ❑